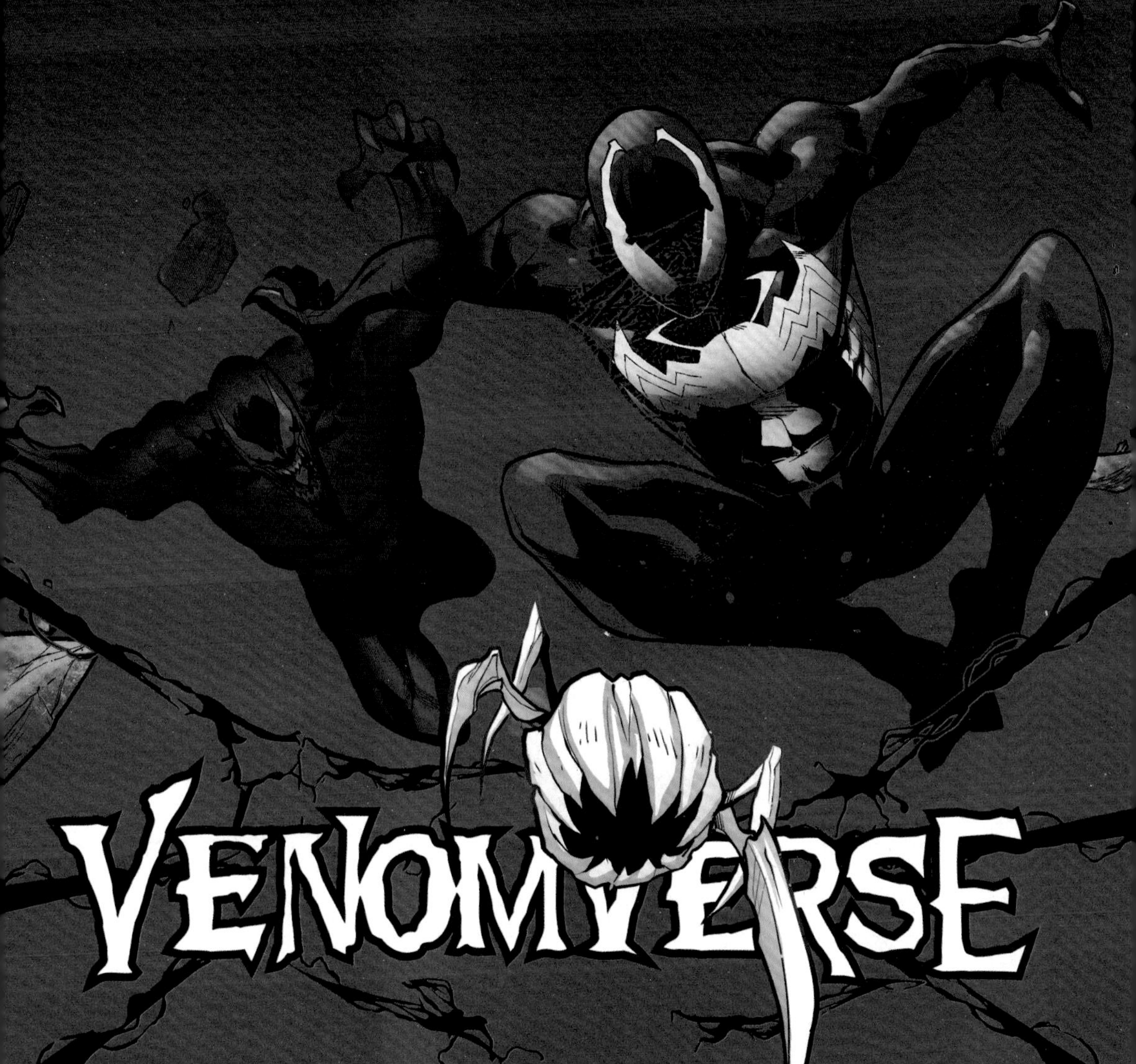
VENOMVERSE

VENOM

AFTER ONE OF HIS STORIES WAS DISCREDITED BY SPIDER-MAN, REPORTER EDDIE BROCK LOST EVERYTHING. READY TO END IT ALL, HE SOUGHT FORGIVENESS AT HIS LOCAL CHURCH – THE VERY SAME CHURCH WHERE SPIDER-MAN WAS REJECTING AN AGGRESSIVE AND SENTIENT ALIEN CALLED A SYMBIOTE.

SENSING BROCK'S ANGER, SORROW AND HATRED TOWARD SPIDER-MAN, THE SYMBIOTE BONDED WITH HIM, AND THE TWO BECAME THAT MOST WICKED OF WEB-SLINGERS – VENOM!

BUT THE SLIGHTEST ALTERATION TO THE EVENTS THAT BIRTHED VENOM WOULD HAVE RESULTED IN A DIFFERENT CREATURE ALTOGETHER. JUST BEYOND EDDIE'S VIEW LAY INNUMERABLE POSSIBILITIES, A MULTIVERSE OF POTENTIAL, A...VENOMVERSE!

VERSE

CULLEN BUNN
WRITER

IBAN COELLO
ARTIST

MATT YACKEY
COLOR ARTIST

VC's JOE CARAMAGNA (#1-2, #4-5) & JOE SABINO (#3)
LETTERER

NICK BRADSHAW & EDGAR DELGADO
COVER ART

ALLISON STOCK
ASSISTANT EDITOR

DEVIN LEWIS
EDITOR

NICK LOWE
EXECUTIVE EDITOR

COLLECTION EDITOR JENNIFER GRÜNWALD
ASSISTANT EDITOR CAITLIN O'CONNELL
ASSOCIATE MANAGING EDITOR KATERI WOODY
EDITOR, SPECIAL PROJECTS MARK D. BEAZLEY

VP PRODUCTION & SPECIAL PROJECTS
JEFF YOUNGQUIST
SVP PRINT, SALES & MARKETING
DAVID GABRIEL
BOOK DESIGN
JAY BOWEN WITH ADAM DEL RE

EDITOR IN CHIEF AXEL ALONSO
CHIEF CREATIVE OFFICER JOE QUESADA
PRESIDENT DAN BUCKLEY
EXECUTIVE PRODUCER ALAN FINE

1

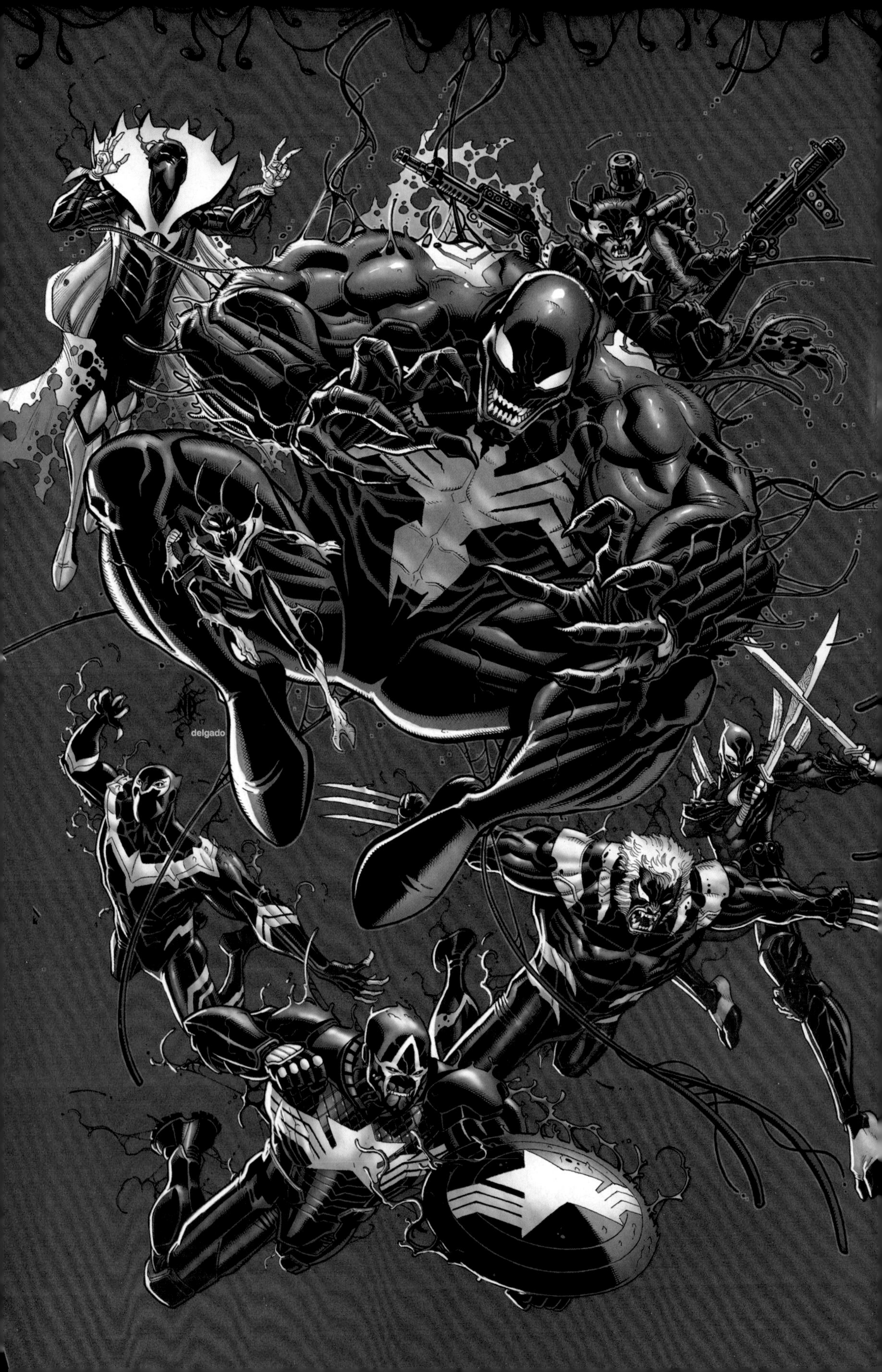
delgado

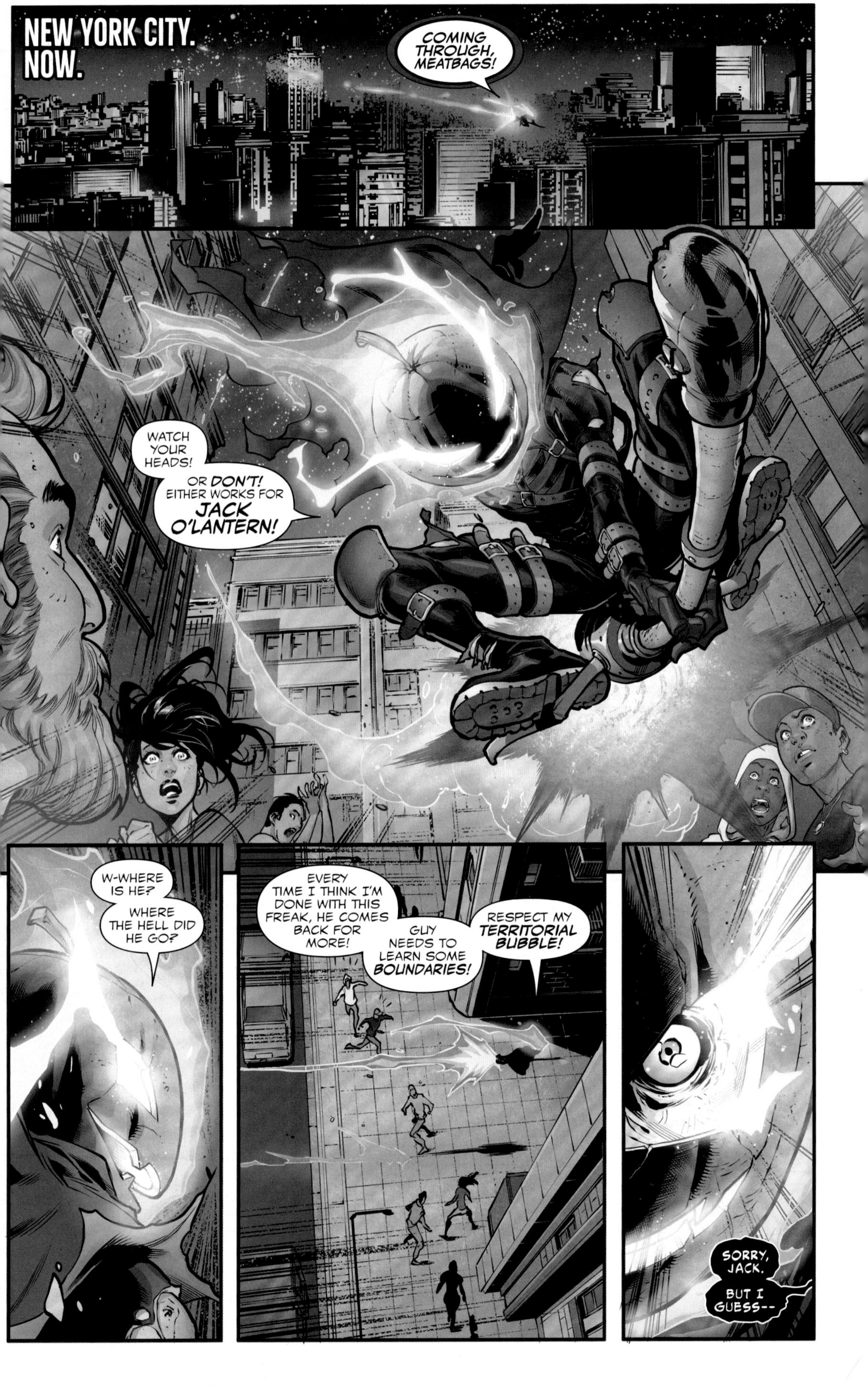

NEW YORK CITY. NOW.
COMING THROUGH, MEATBAGS!
WATCH YOUR HEADS!
OR DON'T! EITHER WORKS FOR JACK O'LANTERN!
W-WHERE IS HE?
WHERE THE HELL DID HE GO?
EVERY TIME I THINK I'M DONE WITH THIS FREAK, HE COMES BACK FOR MORE!
GUY NEEDS TO LEARN SOME BOUNDARIES!
RESPECT MY TERRITORIAL BUBBLE!
SORRY, JACK.
BUT I GUESS--

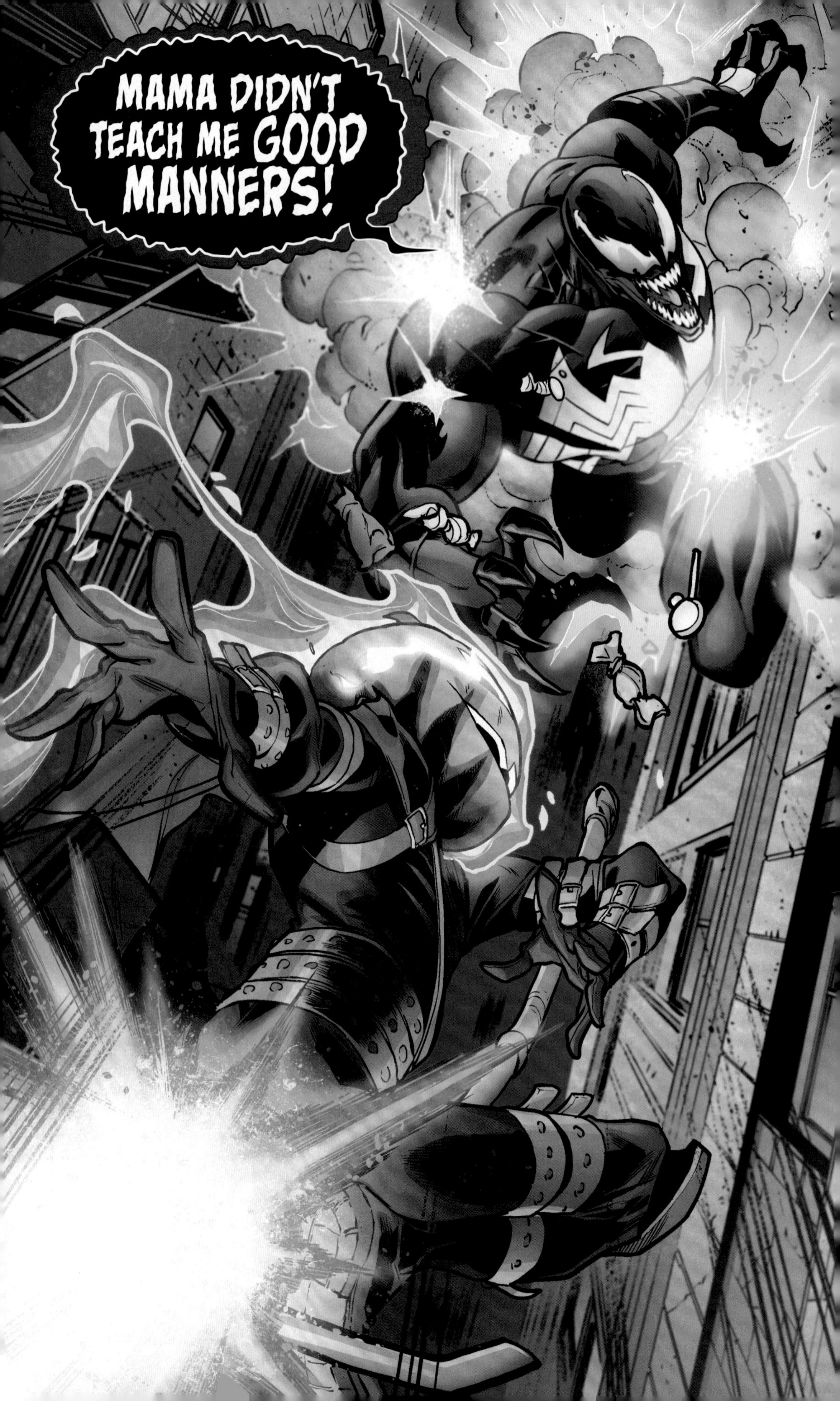
MAMA DIDN'T TEACH ME GOOD MANNERS!

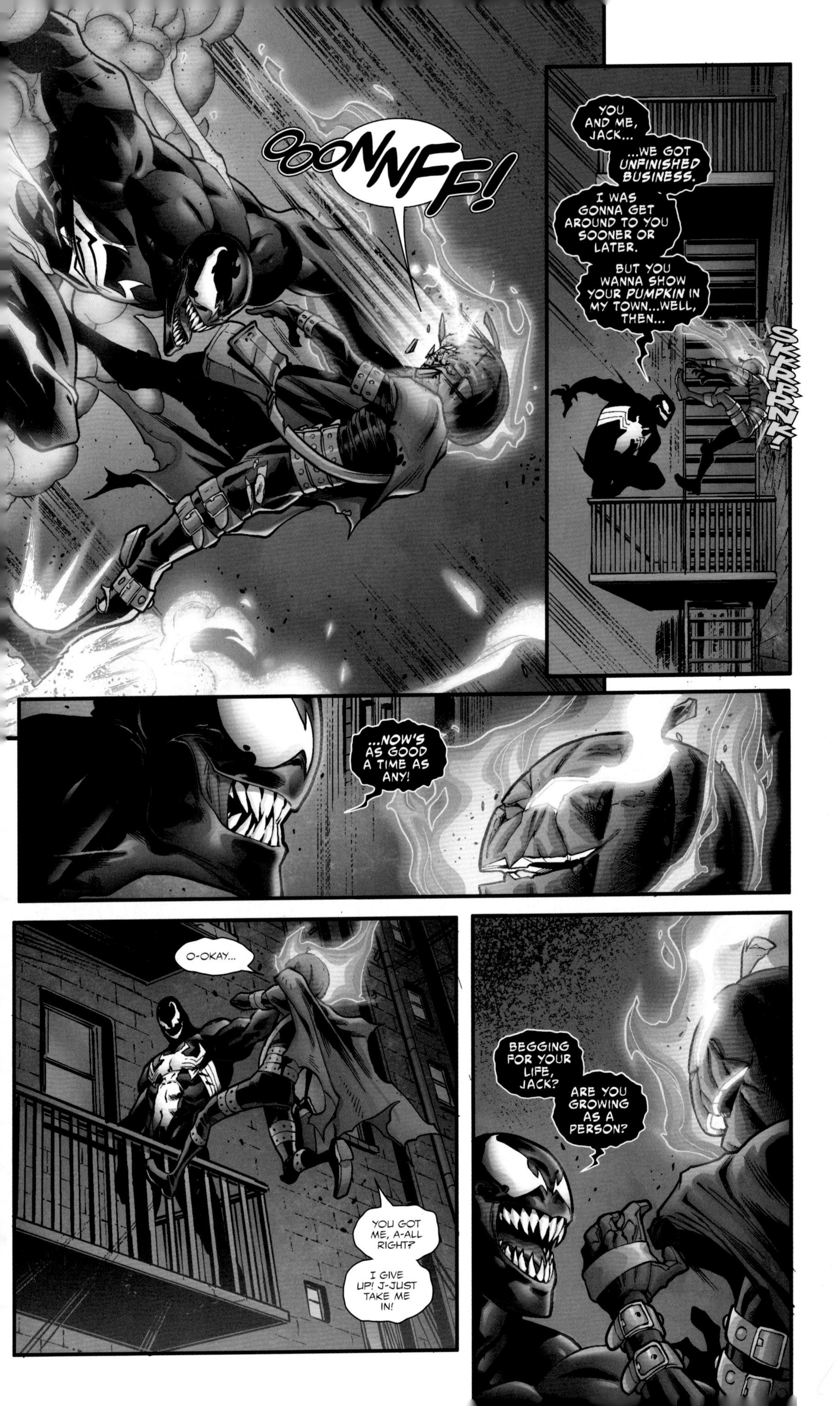

OOONNFF!
YOU AND ME, JACK...
...WE GOT UNFINISHED BUSINESS.
I WAS GONNA GET AROUND TO YOU SOONER OR LATER.
BUT YOU WANNA SHOW YOUR PUMPKIN IN MY TOWN...WELL, THEN...
SKRRRNK!
...NOW'S AS GOOD A TIME AS ANY!
O-OKAY...
YOU GOT ME, A-ALL RIGHT?
I GIVE UP! J-JUST TAKE ME IN!
BEGGING FOR YOUR LIFE, JACK?
ARE YOU GROWING AS A PERSON?

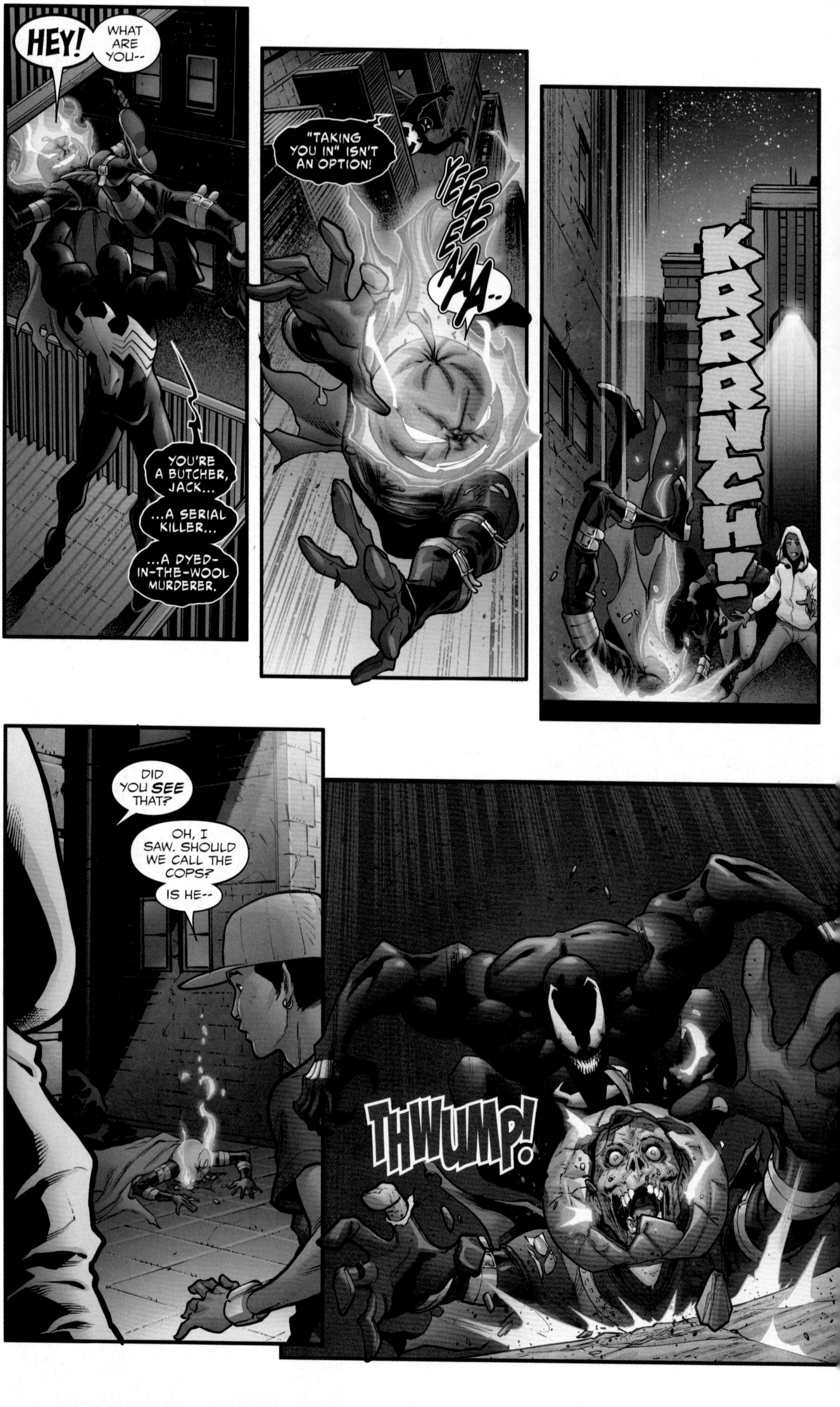
HEY!
WHAT ARE YOU--
YOU'RE A BUTCHER, JACK...
...A SERIAL KILLER...
...A DYED-IN-THE-WOOL MURDERER.
"TAKING YOU IN" ISN'T AN OPTION!
YEEEEAAA..
KRRRANCH!
DID YOU SEE THAT?
OH, I SAW. SHOULD WE CALL THE COPS?
IS HE--
THWUMP!

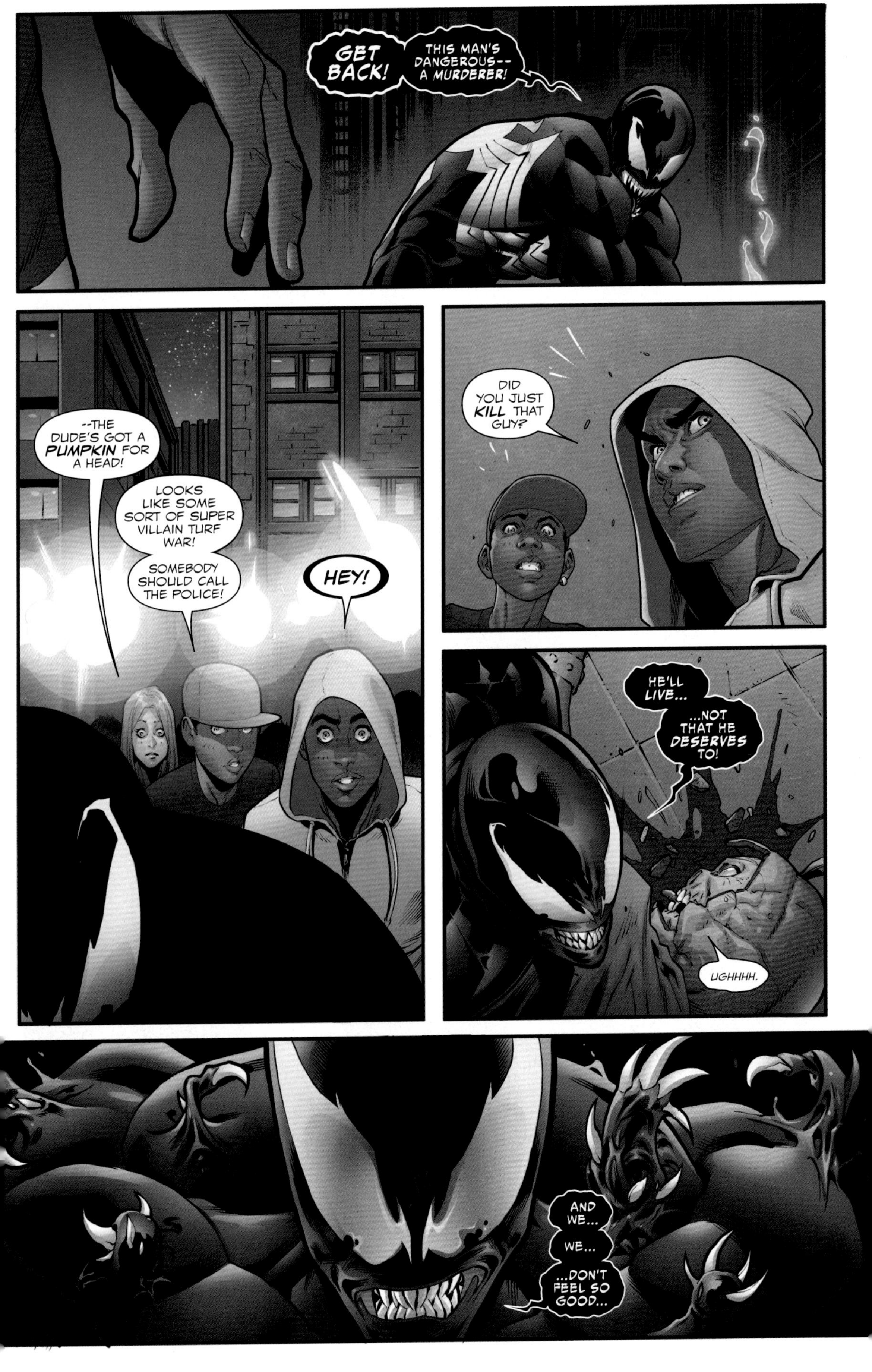
GET BACK!
THIS MAN'S DANGEROUS-- A MURDERER!
--THE DUDE'S GOT A PUMPKIN FOR A HEAD!
LOOKS LIKE SOME SORT OF SUPER VILLAIN TURF WAR!
SOMEBODY SHOULD CALL THE POLICE!
HEY!
DID YOU JUST KILL THAT GUY?
HE'LL LIVE...
...NOT THAT HE DESERVES TO!
UGHHHH.
AND WE...
WE...
...DON'T FEEL SO GOOD...

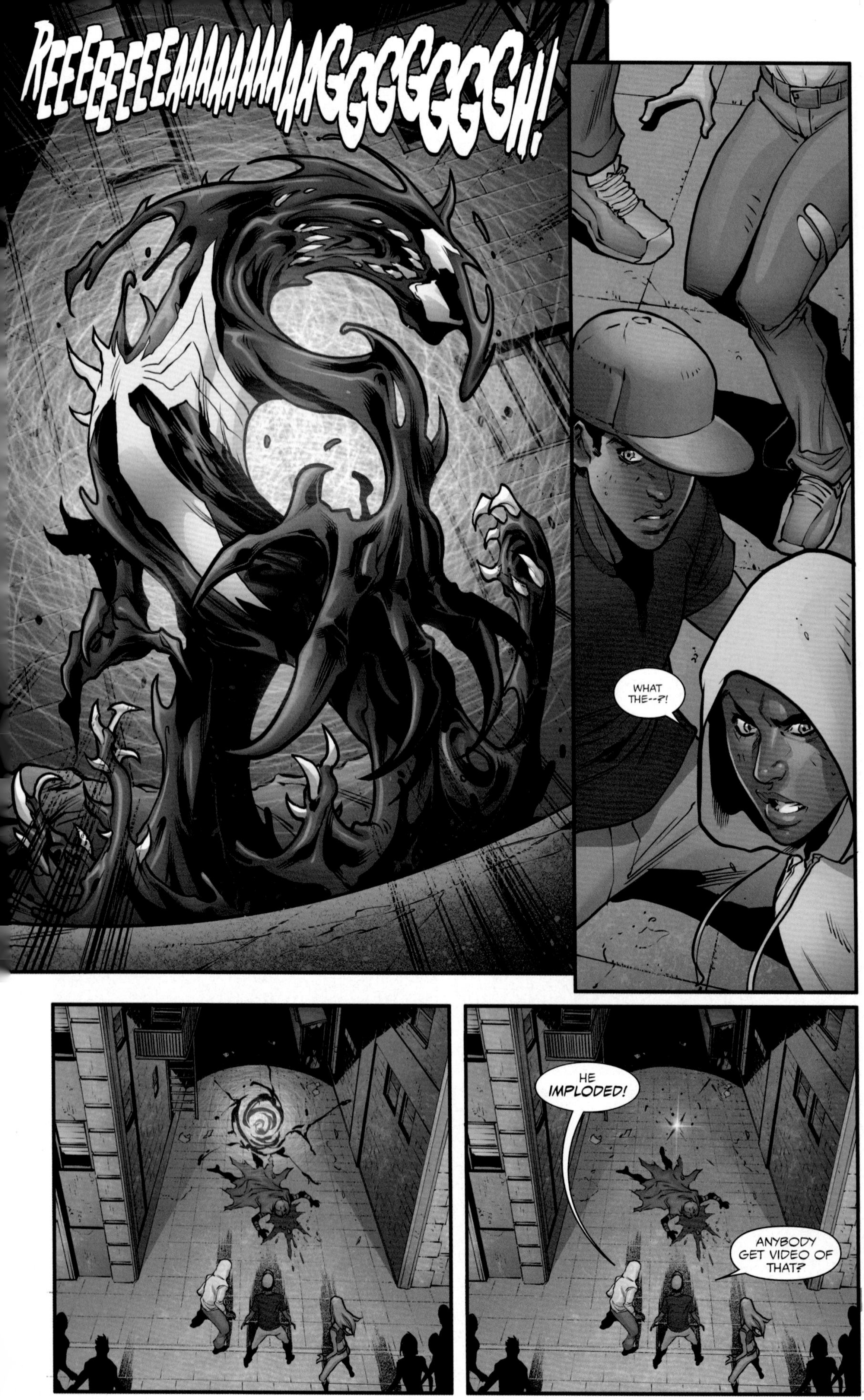
REEEEEEEEAAAAAAAAAAGGGGGGH!
WHAT THE--?!
HE IMPLODED!
ANYBODY GET VIDEO OF THAT?

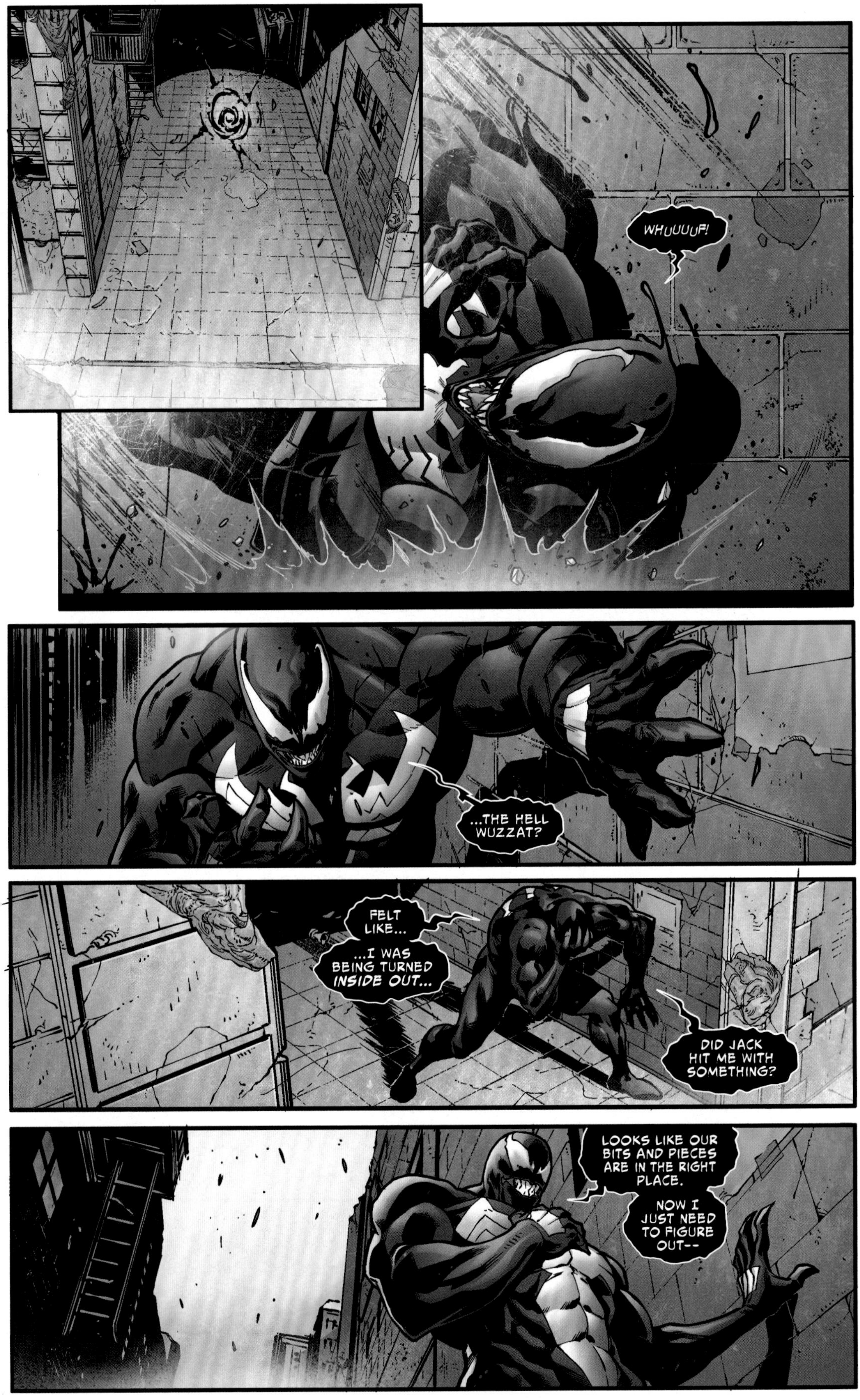
WHUUUUF!
...THE HELL WUZZAT?
FELT LIKE...
...I WAS BEING TURNED INSIDE OUT...
DID JACK HIT ME WITH SOMETHING?
LOOKS LIKE OUR BITS AND PIECES ARE IN THE RIGHT PLACE.
NOW I JUST NEED TO FIGURE OUT--

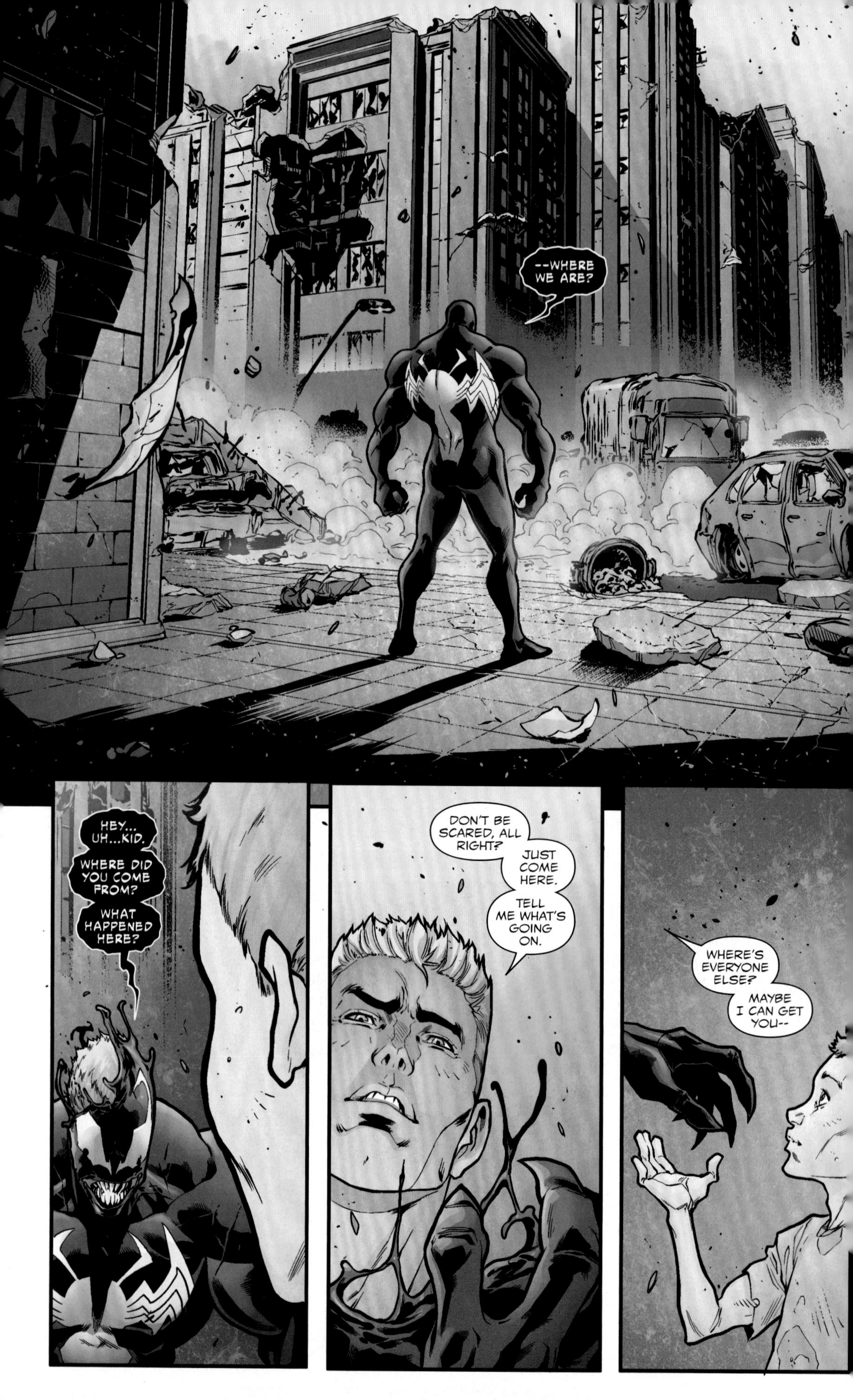
--WHERE WE ARE?
HEY... UH...KID.
WHERE DID YOU COME FROM?
WHAT HAPPENED HERE?
DON'T BE SCARED, ALL RIGHT?
JUST COME HERE.
TELL ME WHAT'S GOING ON.
WHERE'S EVERYONE ELSE?
MAYBE I CAN GET YOU--

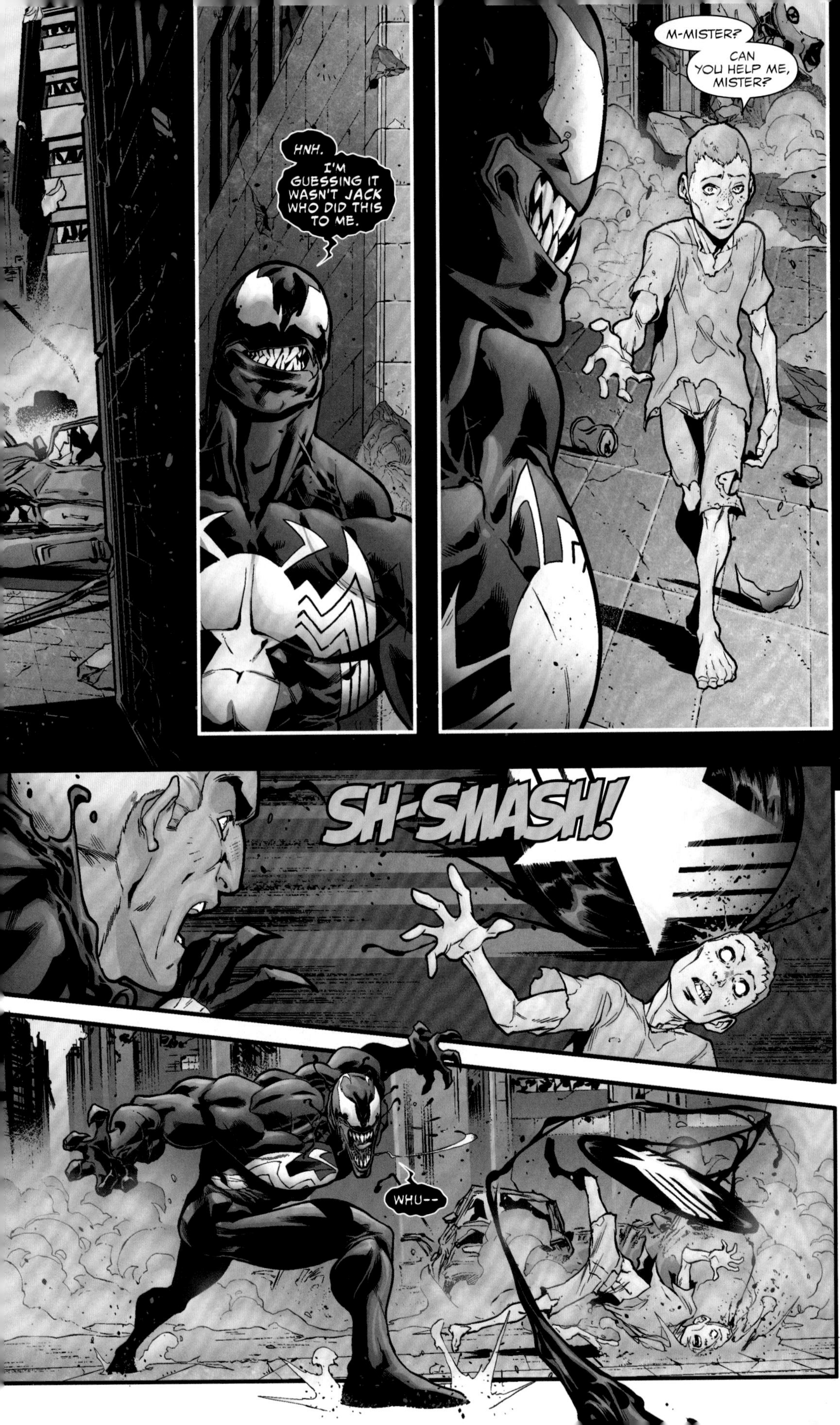
HNH.
I'M GUESSING IT WASN'T JACK WHO DID THIS TO ME.
M-MISTER?
CAN YOU HELP ME, MISTER?
SH-SMASH!
WHU--

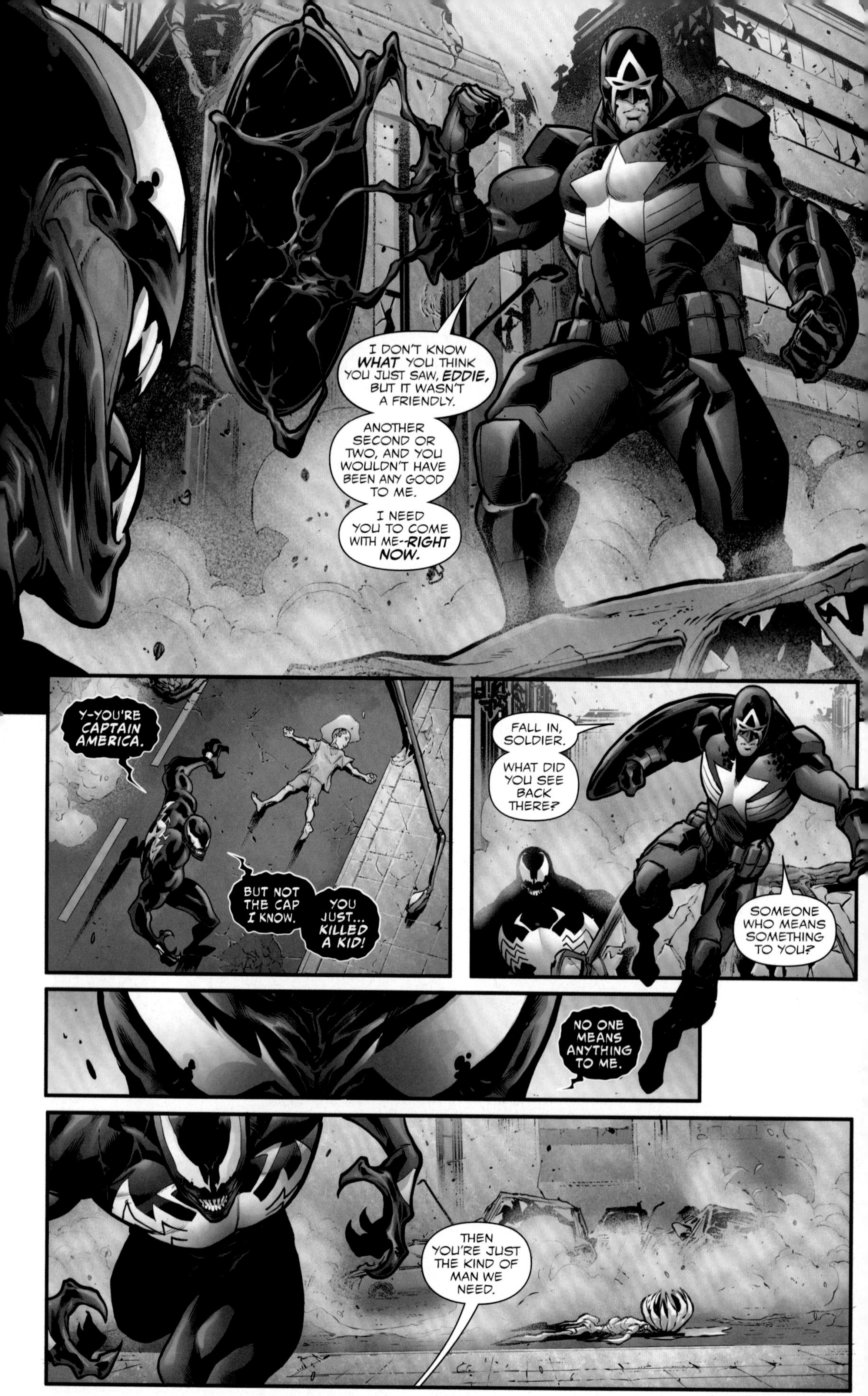
I DON'T KNOW WHAT YOU THINK YOU JUST SAW, EDDIE, BUT IT WASN'T A FRIENDLY.
ANOTHER SECOND OR TWO, AND YOU WOULDN'T HAVE BEEN ANY GOOD TO ME.
I NEED YOU TO COME WITH ME--RIGHT NOW.
Y-YOU'RE CAPTAIN AMERICA.
BUT NOT THE CAP I KNOW.
YOU JUST... KILLED A KID!
FALL IN, SOLDIER.
WHAT DID YOU SEE BACK THERE?
SOMEONE WHO MEANS SOMETHING TO YOU?
NO ONE MEANS ANYTHING TO ME.
THEN YOU'RE JUST THE KIND OF MAN WE NEED.

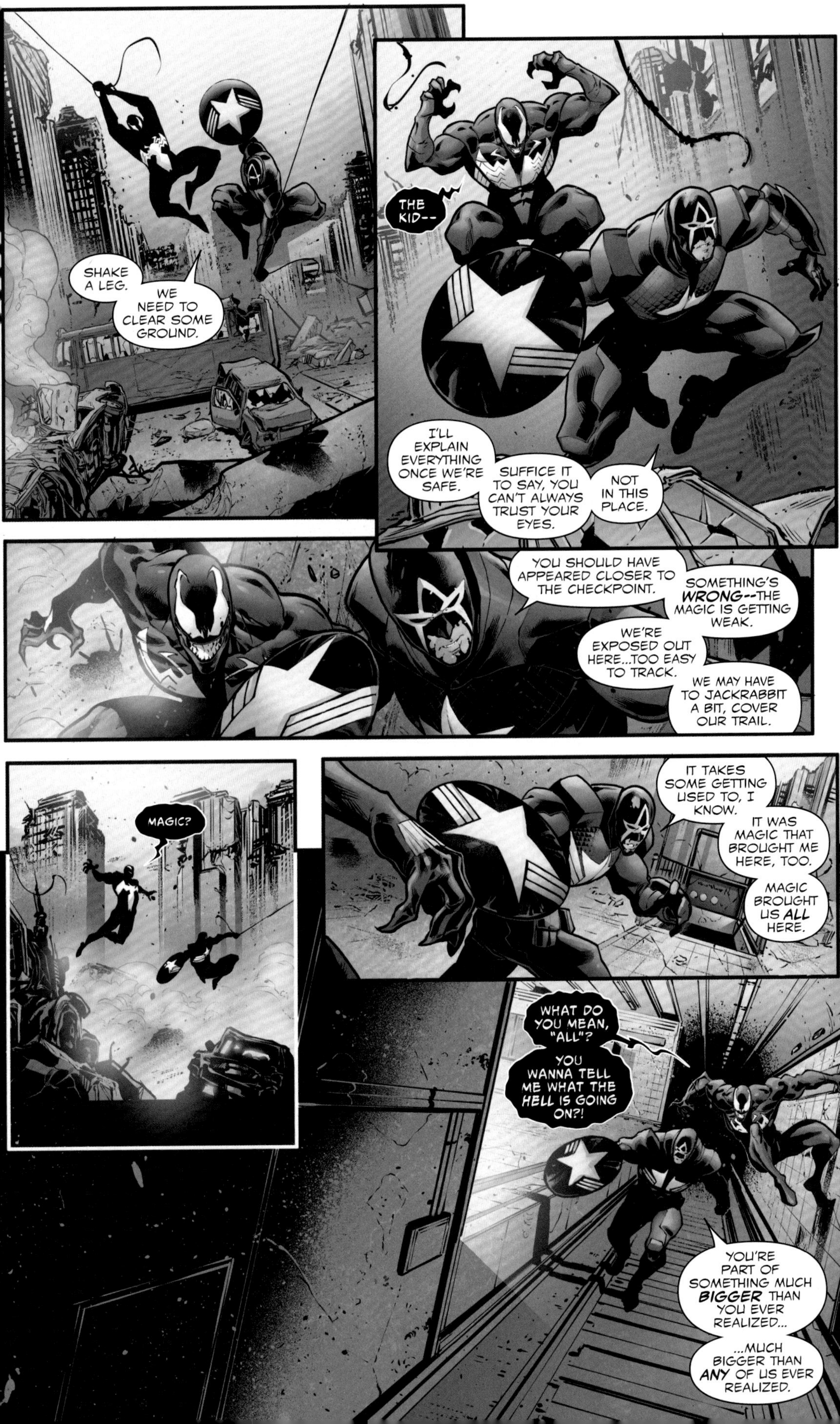
SHAKE A LEG.
WE NEED TO CLEAR SOME GROUND.
THE KID--
I'LL EXPLAIN EVERYTHING ONCE WE'RE SAFE.
SUFFICE IT TO SAY, YOU CAN'T ALWAYS TRUST YOUR EYES.
NOT IN THIS PLACE.
YOU SHOULD HAVE APPEARED CLOSER TO THE CHECKPOINT.
SOMETHING'S WRONG--THE MAGIC IS GETTING WEAK.
WE'RE EXPOSED OUT HERE...TOO EASY TO TRACK.
WE MAY HAVE TO JACKRABBIT A BIT, COVER OUR TRAIL.
MAGIC?
IT TAKES SOME GETTING USED TO, I KNOW.
IT WAS MAGIC THAT BROUGHT ME HERE, TOO.
MAGIC BROUGHT US ALL HERE.
WHAT DO YOU MEAN, "ALL"?
YOU WANNA TELL ME WHAT THE HELL IS GOING ON?!
YOU'RE PART OF SOMETHING MUCH BIGGER THAN YOU EVER REALIZED...
...MUCH BIGGER THAN ANY OF US EVER REALIZED.

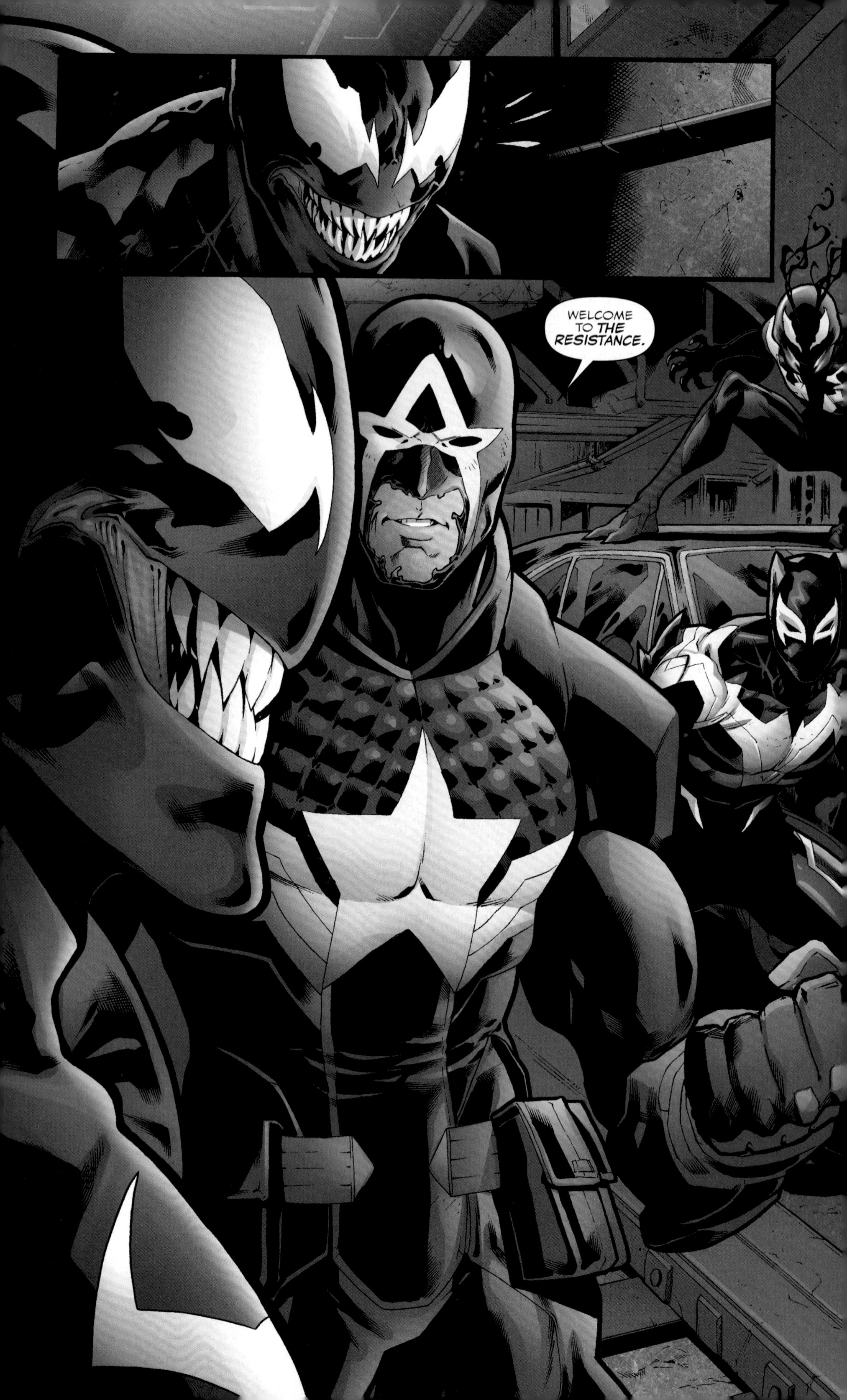
WELCOME TO THE RESISTANCE.

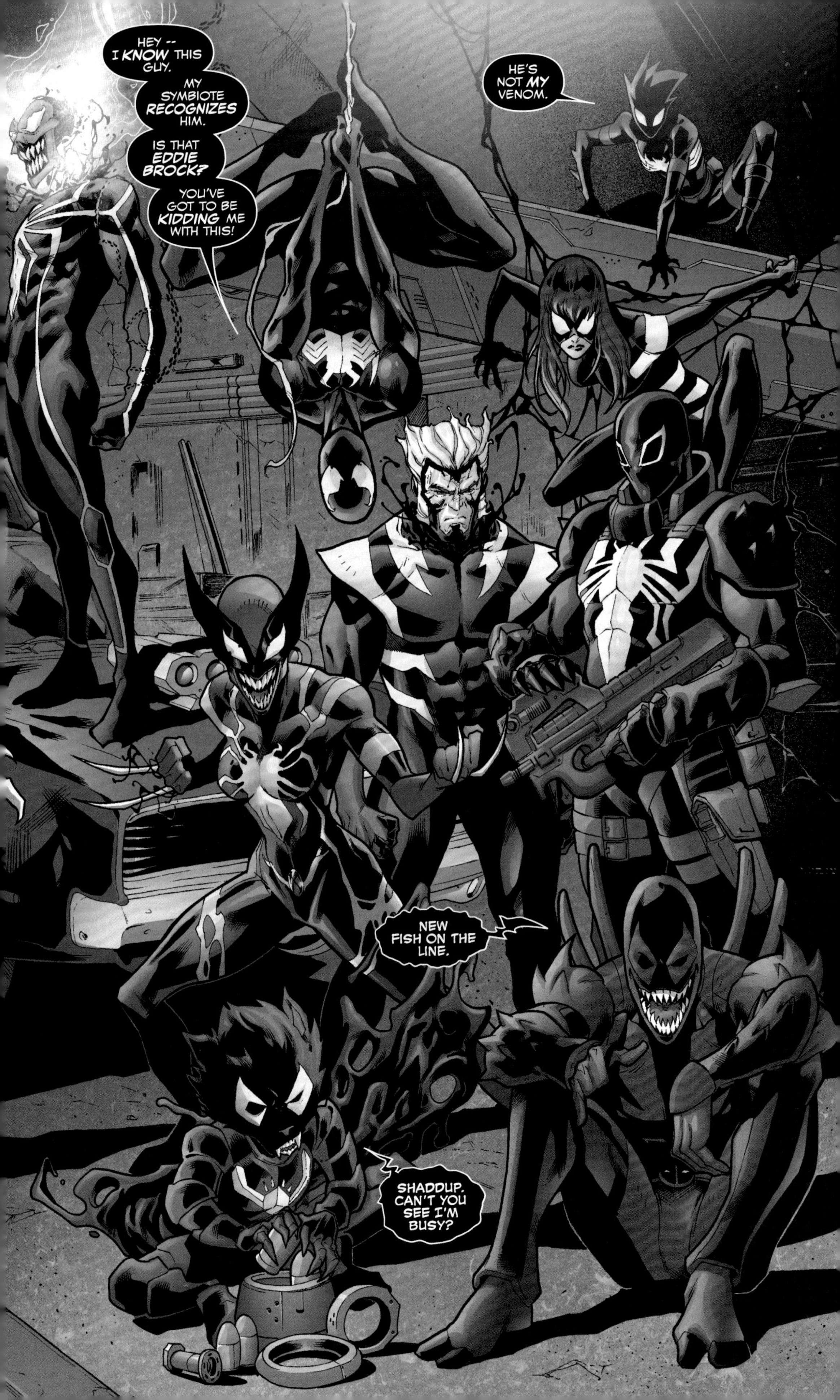
HEY -- I KNOW THIS GUY.
MY SYMBIOTE RECOGNIZES HIM.
IS THAT EDDIE BROCK?
YOU'VE GOT TO BE KIDDING ME WITH THIS!
HE'S NOT MY VENOM.
NEW FISH ON THE LINE.
SHADDUP. CAN'T YOU SEE I'M BUSY?

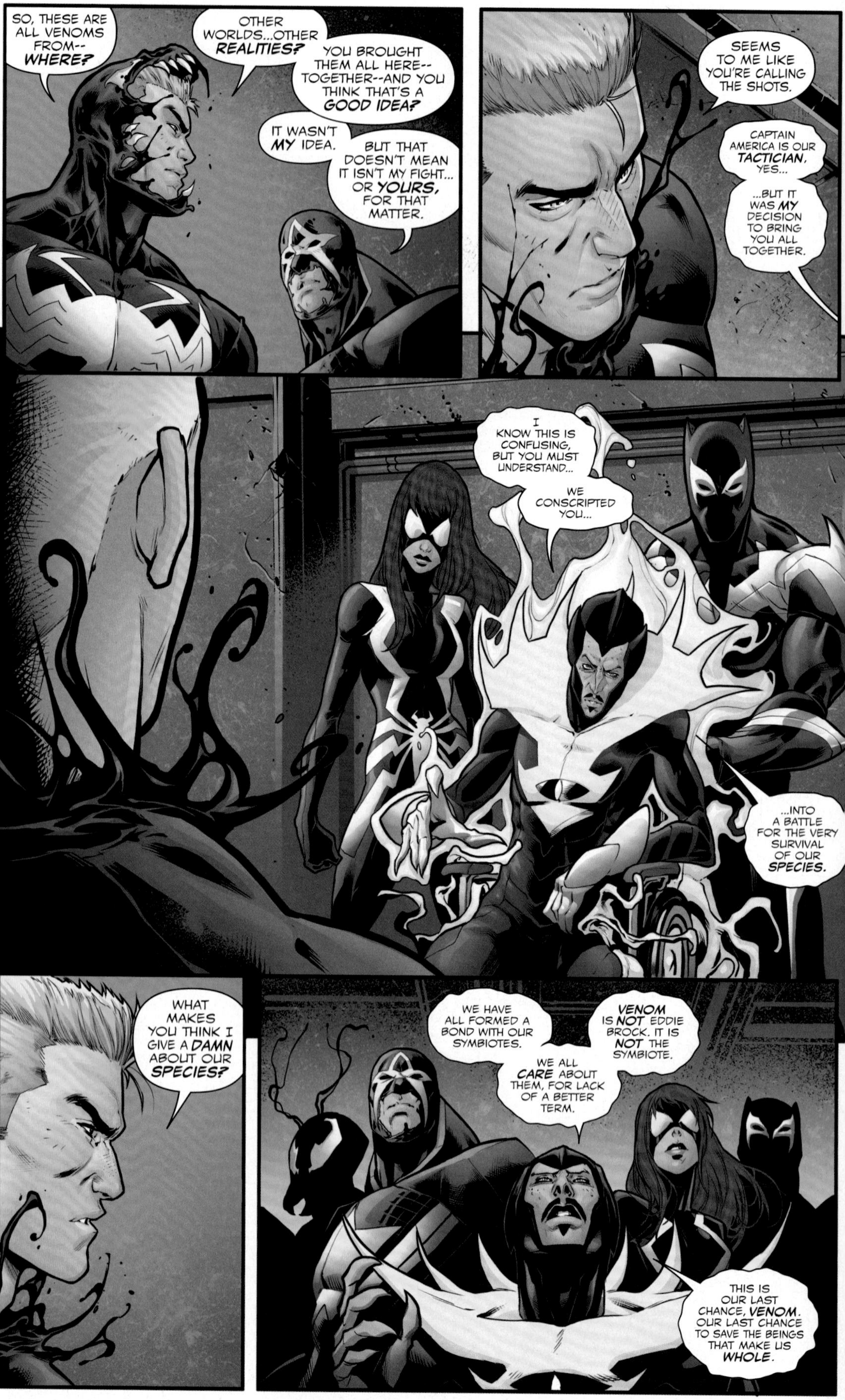
SO, THESE ARE ALL VENOMS FROM-- WHERE?
OTHER WORLDS...OTHER REALITIES?
YOU BROUGHT THEM ALL HERE-- TOGETHER--AND YOU THINK THAT'S A GOOD IDEA?
IT WASN'T MY IDEA.
BUT THAT DOESN'T MEAN IT ISN'T MY FIGHT... OR YOURS, FOR THAT MATTER.
SEEMS TO ME LIKE YOU'RE CALLING THE SHOTS.
CAPTAIN AMERICA IS OUR TACTICIAN, YES...
...BUT IT WAS MY DECISION TO BRING YOU ALL TOGETHER.
I KNOW THIS IS CONFUSING, BUT YOU MUST UNDERSTAND...
WE CONSCRIPTED YOU...
...INTO A BATTLE FOR THE VERY SURVIVAL OF OUR SPECIES.
WHAT MAKES YOU THINK I GIVE A DAMN ABOUT OUR SPECIES?
WE HAVE ALL FORMED A BOND WITH OUR SYMBIOTES.
WE ALL CARE ABOUT THEM, FOR LACK OF A BETTER TERM.
VENOM IS NOT EDDIE BROCK. IT IS NOT THE SYMBIOTE.
THIS IS OUR LAST CHANCE, VENOM. OUR LAST CHANCE TO SAVE THE BEINGS THAT MAKE US WHOLE.

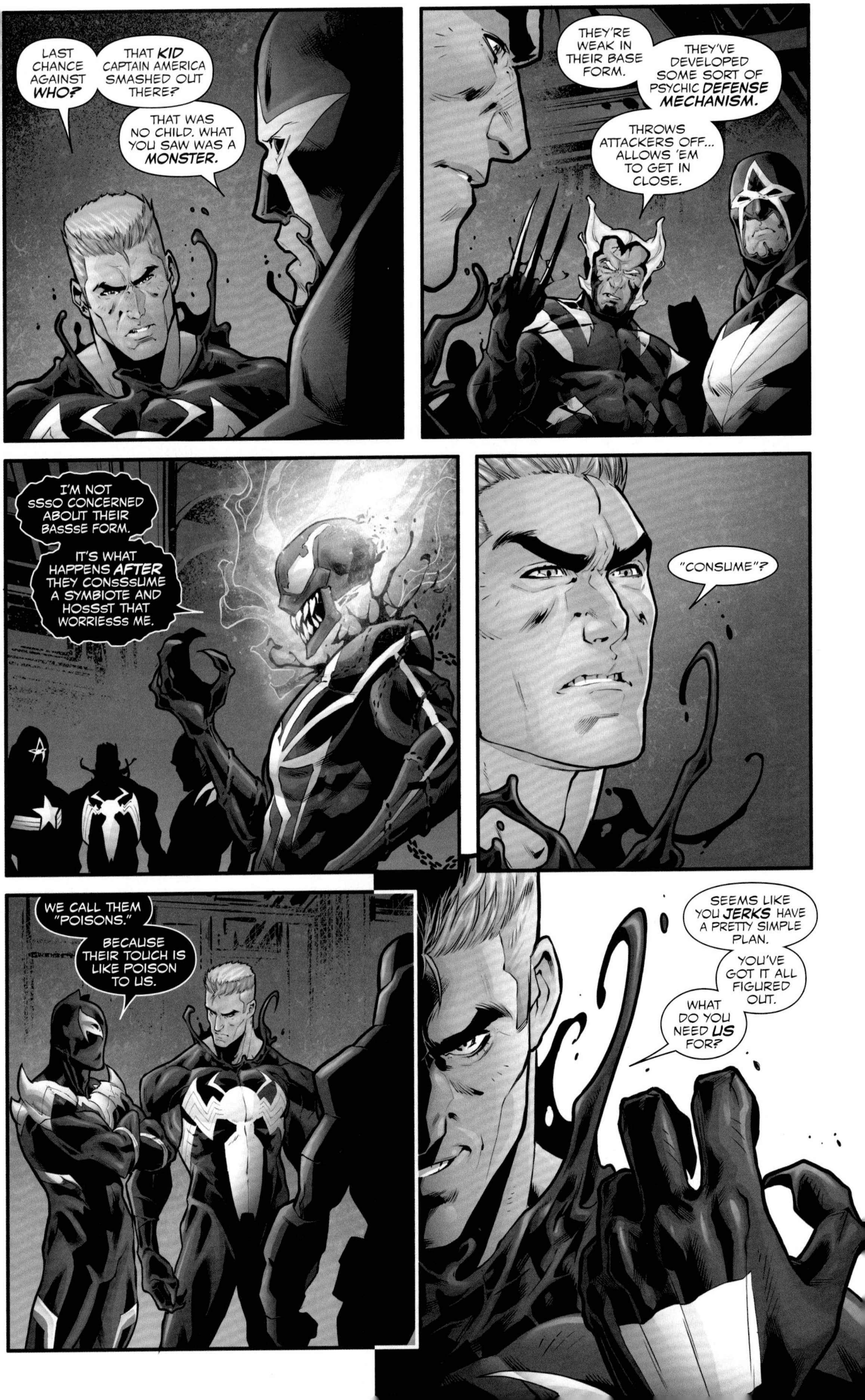
LAST CHANCE AGAINST WHO?
THAT KID CAPTAIN AMERICA SMASHED OUT THERE?
THAT WAS NO CHILD. WHAT YOU SAW WAS A MONSTER.
THEY'RE WEAK IN THEIR BASE FORM.
THEY'VE DEVELOPED SOME SORT OF PSYCHIC DEFENSE MECHANISM.
THROWS ATTACKERS OFF... ALLOWS 'EM TO GET IN CLOSE.
I'M NOT SSSO CONCERNED ABOUT THEIR BASSSE FORM.
IT'S WHAT HAPPENS AFTER THEY CONSSSUME A SYMBIOTE AND HOSSST THAT WORRIESSS ME.
"CONSUME"?
WE CALL THEM "POISONS."
BECAUSE THEIR TOUCH IS LIKE POISON TO US.
SEEMS LIKE YOU JERKS HAVE A PRETTY SIMPLE PLAN.
YOU'VE GOT IT ALL FIGURED OUT.
WHAT DO YOU NEED US FOR?

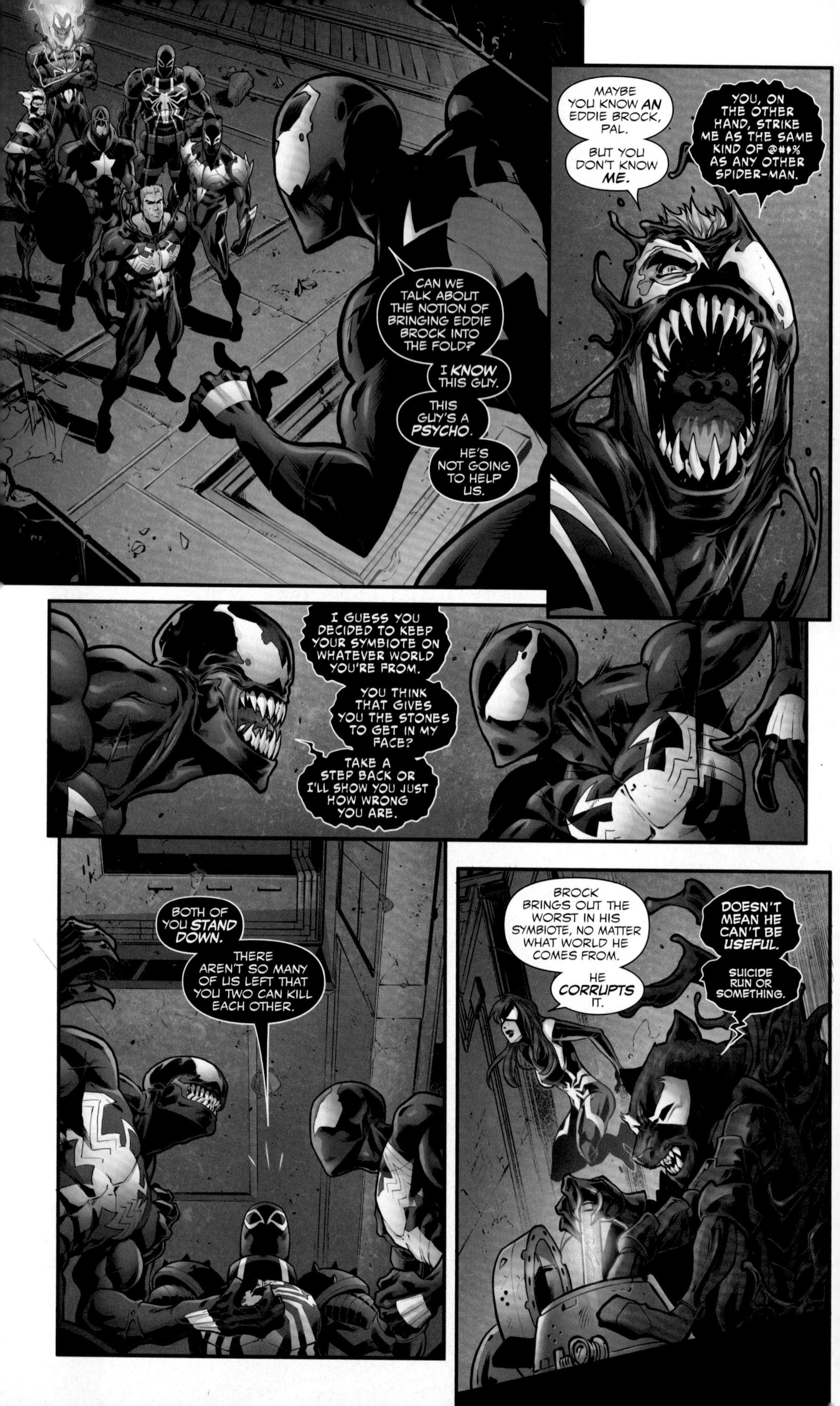
CAN WE TALK ABOUT THE NOTION OF BRINGING EDDIE BROCK INTO THE FOLD?
I KNOW THIS GUY.
THIS GUY'S A PSYCHO.
HE'S NOT GOING TO HELP US.
MAYBE YOU KNOW AN EDDIE BROCK, PAL.
BUT YOU DON'T KNOW ME.
YOU, ON THE OTHER HAND, STRIKE ME AS THE SAME KIND OF @#*% AS ANY OTHER SPIDER-MAN.
I GUESS YOU DECIDED TO KEEP YOUR SYMBIOTE ON WHATEVER WORLD YOU'RE FROM.
YOU THINK THAT GIVES YOU THE STONES TO GET IN MY FACE?
TAKE A STEP BACK OR I'LL SHOW YOU JUST HOW WRONG YOU ARE.
BOTH OF YOU STAND DOWN.
THERE AREN'T SO MANY OF US LEFT THAT YOU TWO CAN KILL EACH OTHER.
BROCK BRINGS OUT THE WORST IN HIS SYMBIOTE, NO MATTER WHAT WORLD HE COMES FROM.
HE CORRUPTS IT.
DOESN'T MEAN HE CAN'T BE USEFUL.
SUICIDE RUN OR SOMETHING.

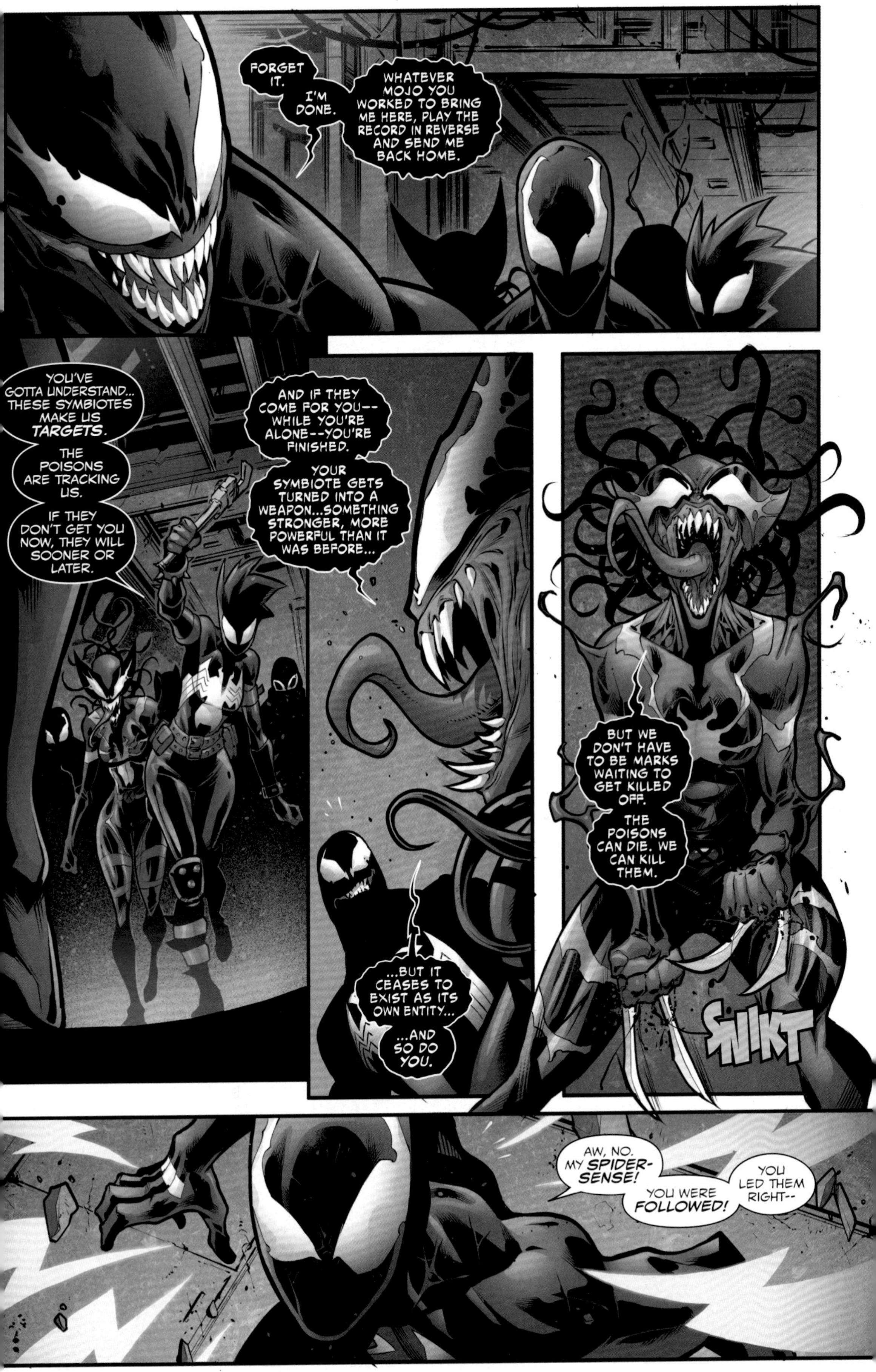

FORGET IT.
I'M DONE.
WHATEVER MOJO YOU WORKED TO BRING ME HERE, PLAY THE RECORD IN REVERSE AND SEND ME BACK HOME.
YOU'VE GOTTA UNDERSTAND... THESE SYMBIOTES MAKE US TARGETS.
THE POISONS ARE TRACKING US.
IF THEY DON'T GET YOU NOW, THEY WILL SOONER OR LATER.
AND IF THEY COME FOR YOU-- WHILE YOU'RE ALONE--YOU'RE FINISHED.
YOUR SYMBIOTE GETS TURNED INTO A WEAPON...SOMETHING STRONGER, MORE POWERFUL THAN IT WAS BEFORE...
...BUT IT CEASES TO EXIST AS ITS OWN ENTITY...
...AND SO DO YOU.
BUT WE DON'T HAVE TO BE MARKS WAITING TO GET KILLED OFF.
THE POISONS CAN DIE. WE CAN KILL THEM.
SNIKT
AW, NO. MY SPIDER-SENSE!
YOU WERE FOLLOWED!
YOU LED THEM RIGHT--

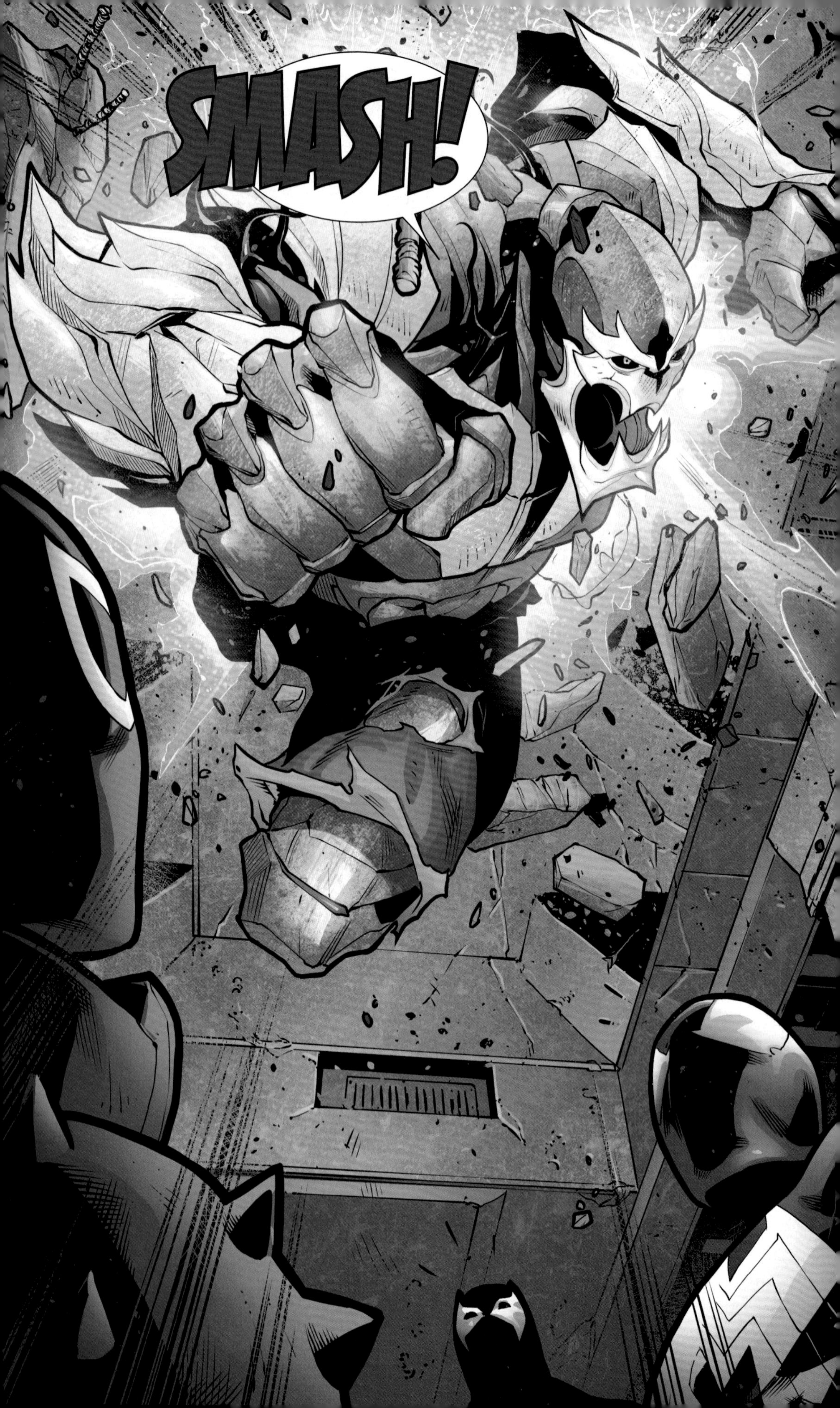
SMASH!

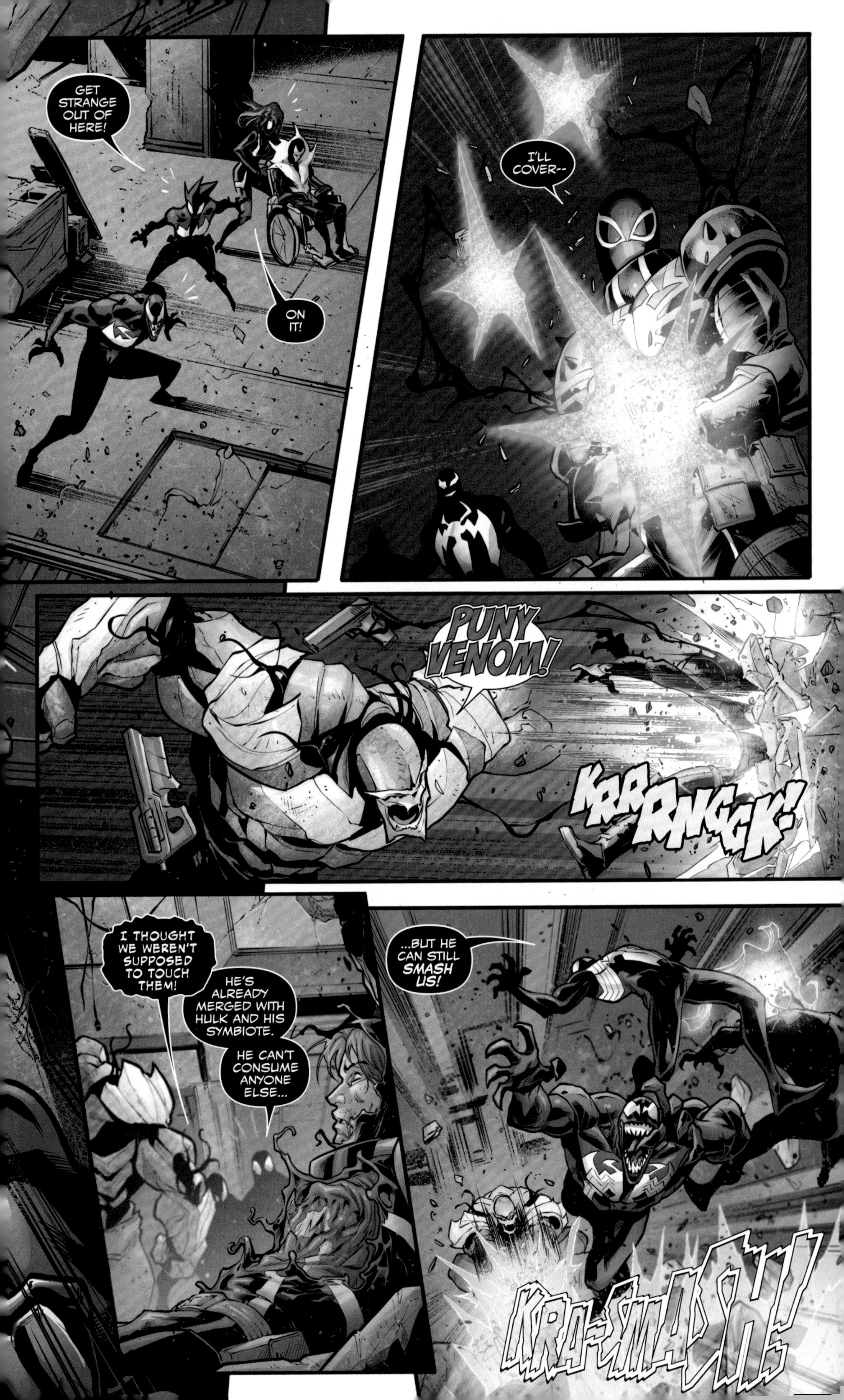

GET STRANGE OUT OF HERE!
ON IT!
I'LL COVER--
PUNY VENOM!
KRRRNGGK!
I THOUGHT WE WEREN'T SUPPOSED TO TOUCH THEM!
HE'S ALREADY MERGED WITH HULK AND HIS SYMBIOTE.
HE CAN'T CONSUME ANYONE ELSE...
...BUT HE CAN STILL SMASH US!
KRA-SMASH!

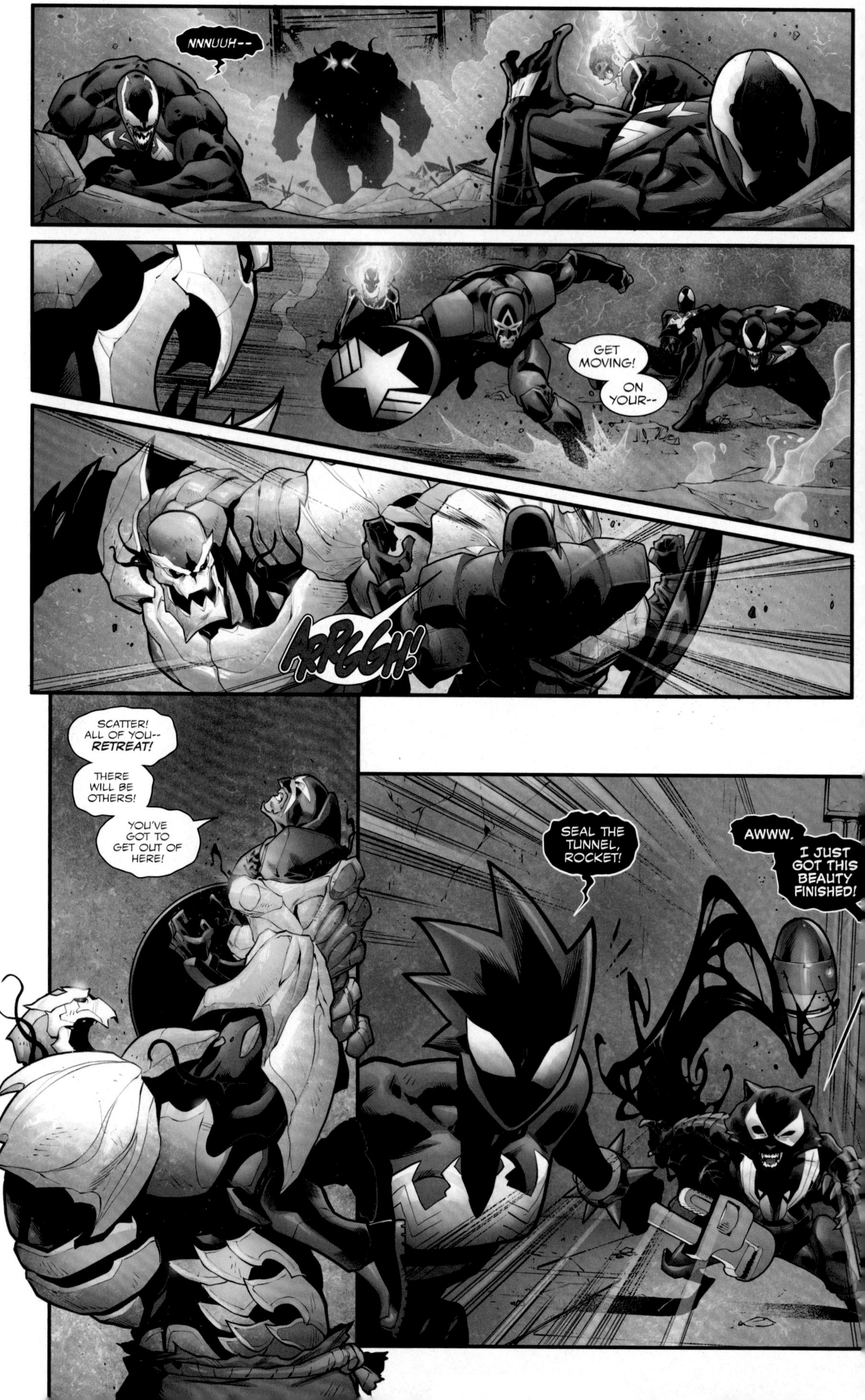
NNNUUH--
GET MOVING!
ON YOUR--
ARRGH!
SCATTER! ALL OF YOU-- RETREAT!
THERE WILL BE OTHERS!
YOU'VE GOT TO GET OUT OF HERE!
SEAL THE TUNNEL, ROCKET!
AWWW.
I JUST GOT THIS BEAUTY FINISHED!

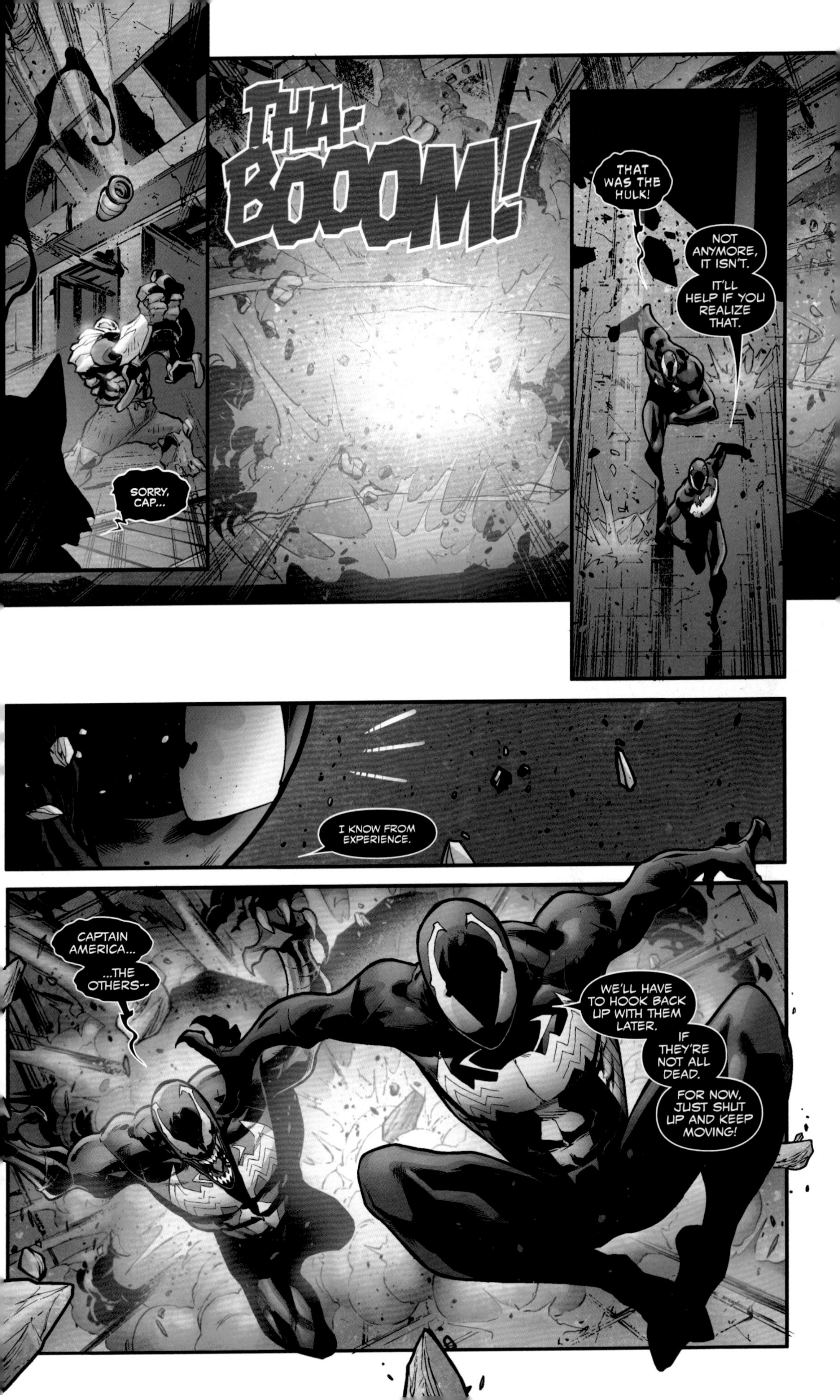

SORRY, CAP...
THA-BOOOM!
THAT WAS THE HULK!
NOT ANYMORE, IT ISN'T.
IT'LL HELP IF YOU REALIZE THAT.
I KNOW FROM EXPERIENCE.
CAPTAIN AMERICA...
...THE OTHERS--
WE'LL HAVE TO HOOK BACK UP WITH THEM LATER.
IF THEY'RE NOT ALL DEAD.
FOR NOW, JUST SHUT UP AND KEEP MOVING!

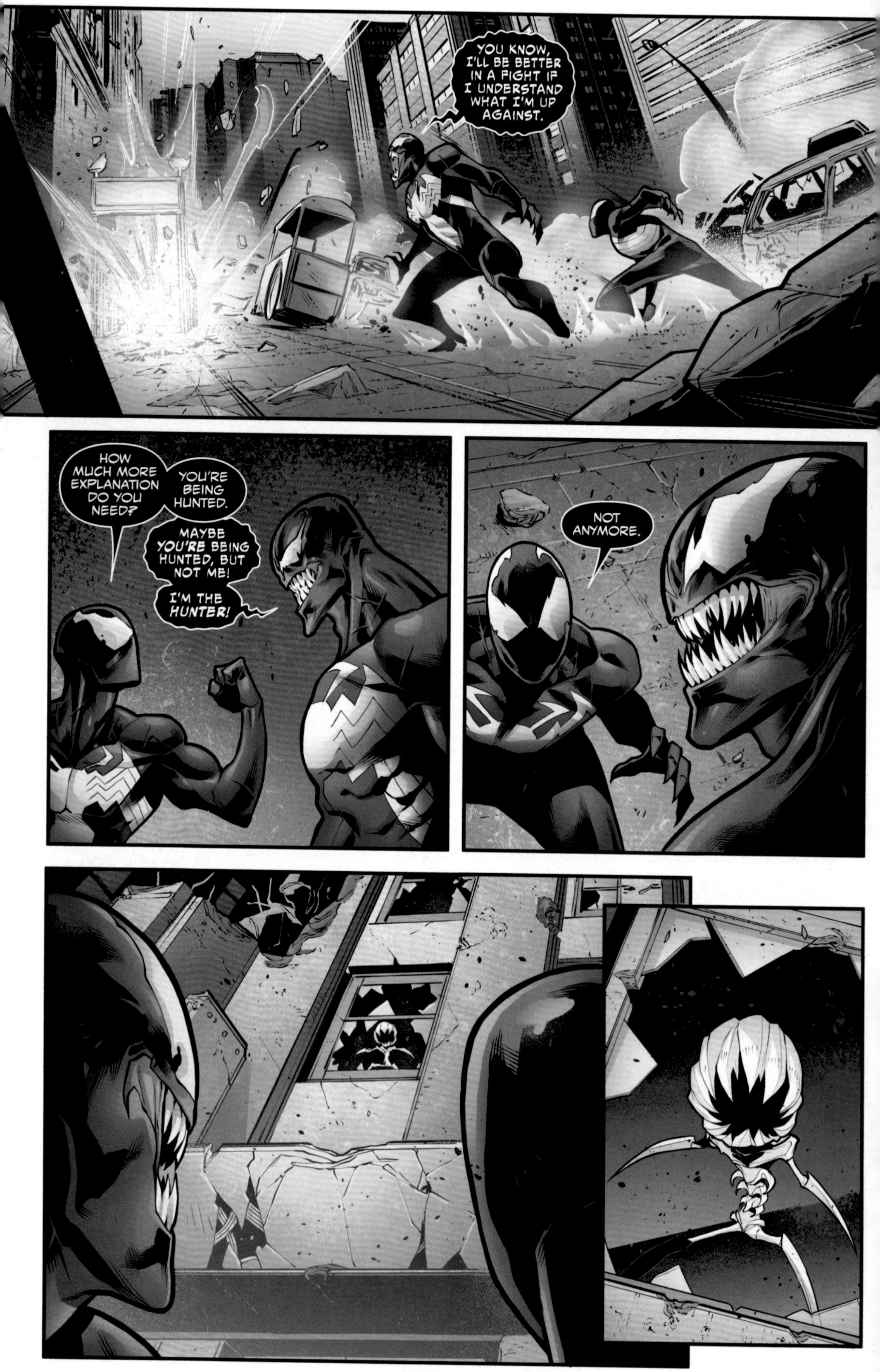

YOU KNOW, I'LL BE BETTER IN A FIGHT IF I UNDERSTAND WHAT I'M UP AGAINST.
HOW MUCH MORE EXPLANATION DO YOU NEED?
YOU'RE BEING HUNTED.
MAYBE YOU'RE BEING HUNTED, BUT NOT ME!
I'M THE HUNTER!
NOT ANYMORE.

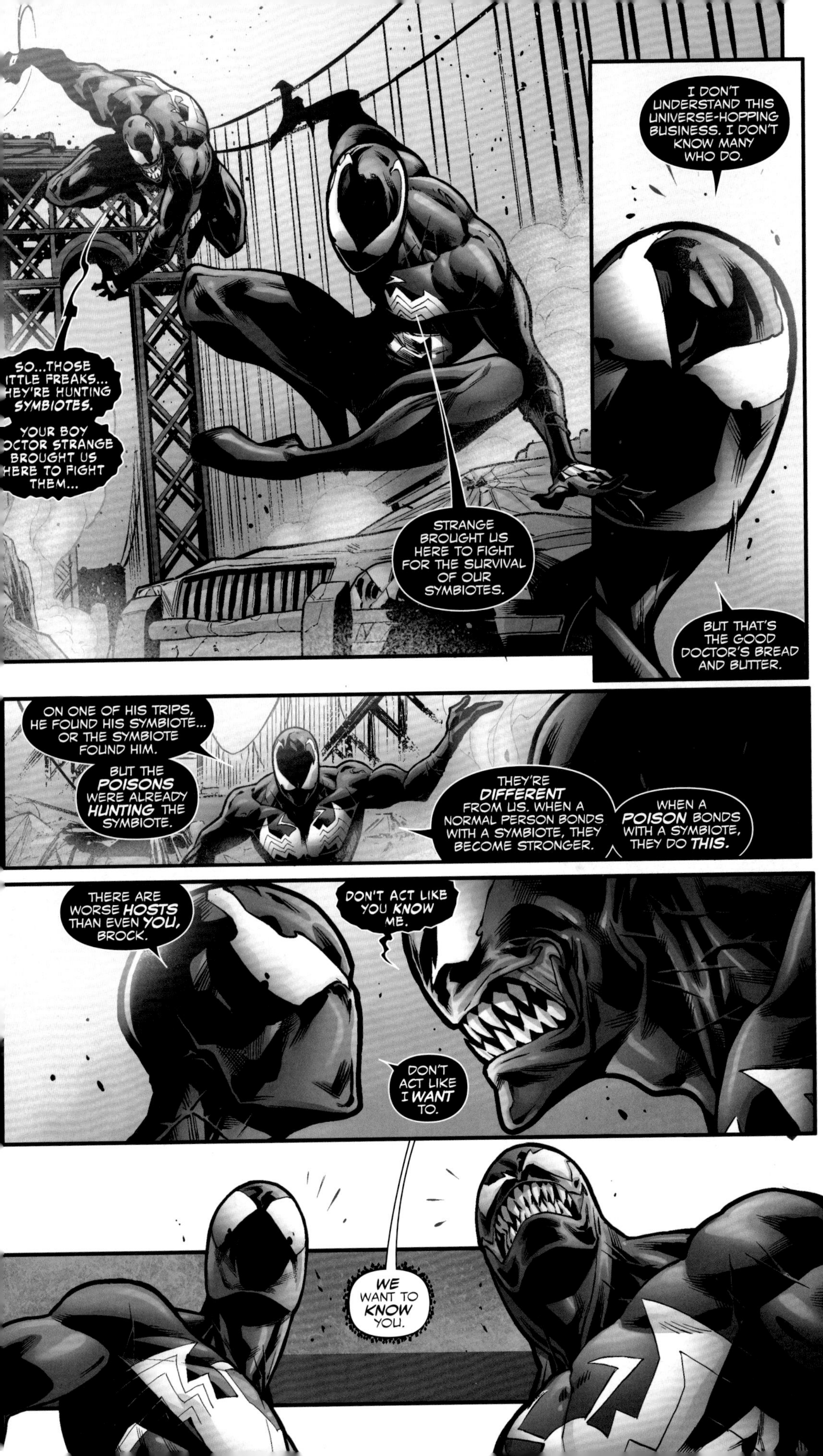
SO...THOSE LITTLE FREAKS... THEY'RE HUNTING SYMBIOTES.
YOUR BOY DOCTOR STRANGE BROUGHT US HERE TO FIGHT THEM...
STRANGE BROUGHT US HERE TO FIGHT FOR THE SURVIVAL OF OUR SYMBIOTES.
I DON'T UNDERSTAND THIS UNIVERSE-HOPPING BUSINESS. I DON'T KNOW MANY WHO DO.
BUT THAT'S THE GOOD DOCTOR'S BREAD AND BUTTER.
ON ONE OF HIS TRIPS, HE FOUND HIS SYMBIOTE... OR THE SYMBIOTE FOUND HIM.
BUT THE POISONS WERE ALREADY HUNTING THE SYMBIOTE.
THEY'RE DIFFERENT FROM US. WHEN A NORMAL PERSON BONDS WITH A SYMBIOTE, THEY BECOME STRONGER.
WHEN A POISON BONDS WITH A SYMBIOTE, THEY DO THIS.
THERE ARE WORSE HOSTS THAN EVEN YOU, BROCK.
DON'T ACT LIKE YOU KNOW ME.
DON'T ACT LIKE I WANT TO.
WE WANT TO KNOW YOU.

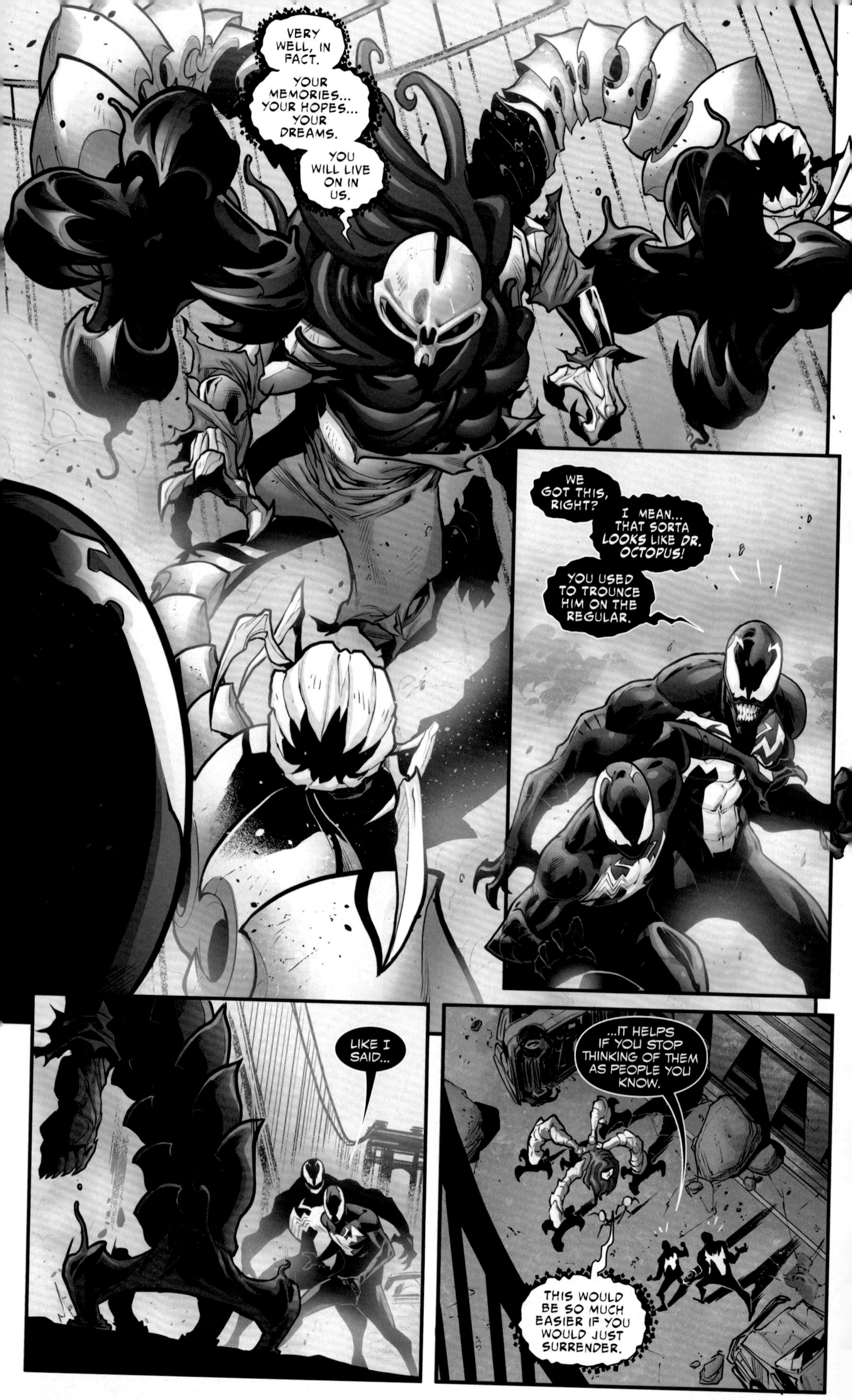
VERY WELL, IN FACT.
YOUR MEMORIES... YOUR HOPES... YOUR DREAMS.
YOU WILL LIVE ON IN US.
WE GOT THIS, RIGHT?
I MEAN... THAT SORTA LOOKS LIKE DR. OCTOPUS!
YOU USED TO TROUNCE HIM ON THE REGULAR.
LIKE I SAID...
...IT HELPS IF YOU STOP THINKING OF THEM AS PEOPLE YOU KNOW.
THIS WOULD BE SO MUCH EASIER IF YOU WOULD JUST SURRENDER.

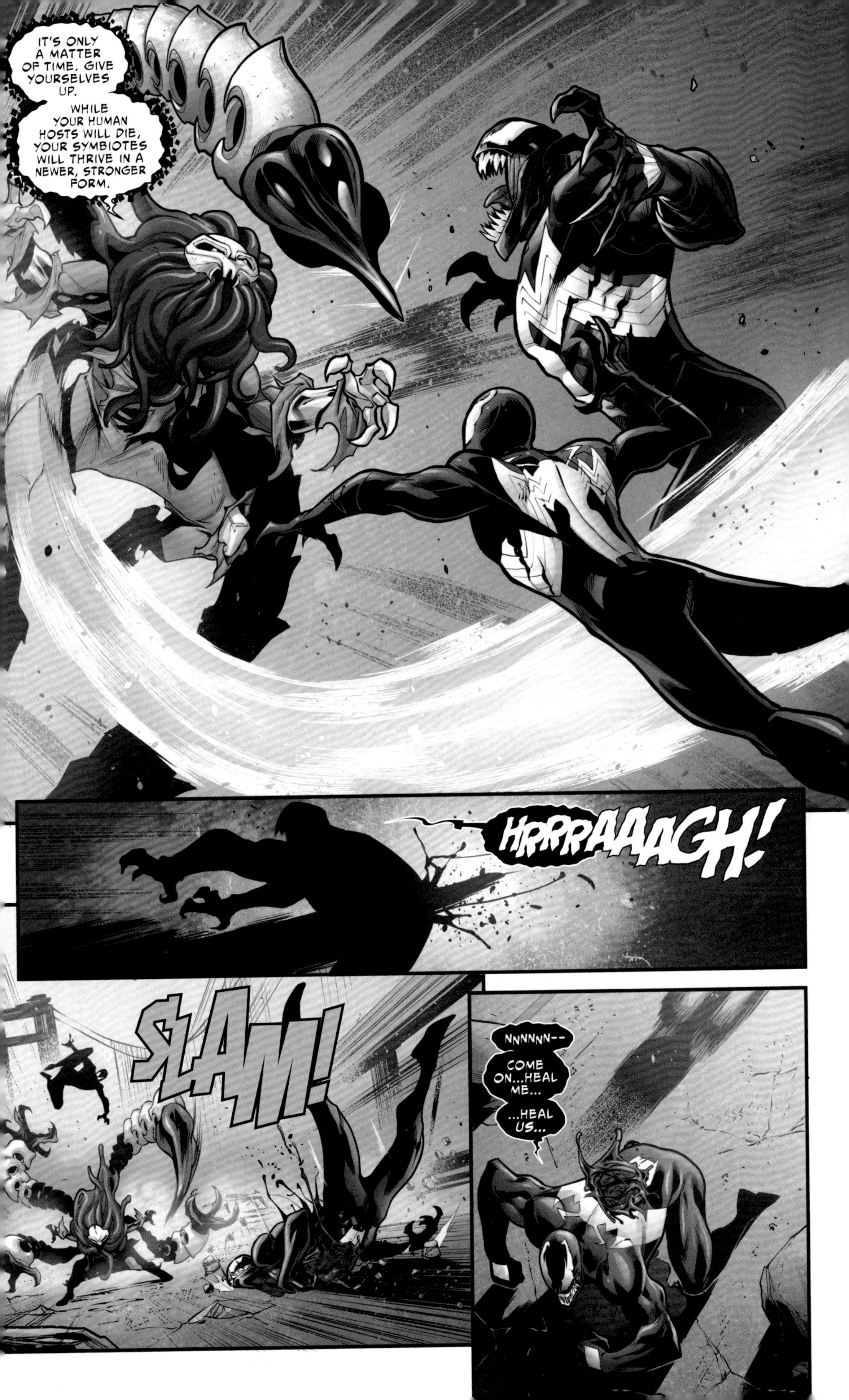

IT'S ONLY A MATTER OF TIME. GIVE YOURSELVES UP.
WHILE YOUR HUMAN HOSTS WILL DIE, YOUR SYMBIOTES WILL THRIVE IN A NEWER, STRONGER FORM.
HRRRAAAGH!
SLAM!
NNNNNN--
COME ON...HEAL ME...
...HEAL US...

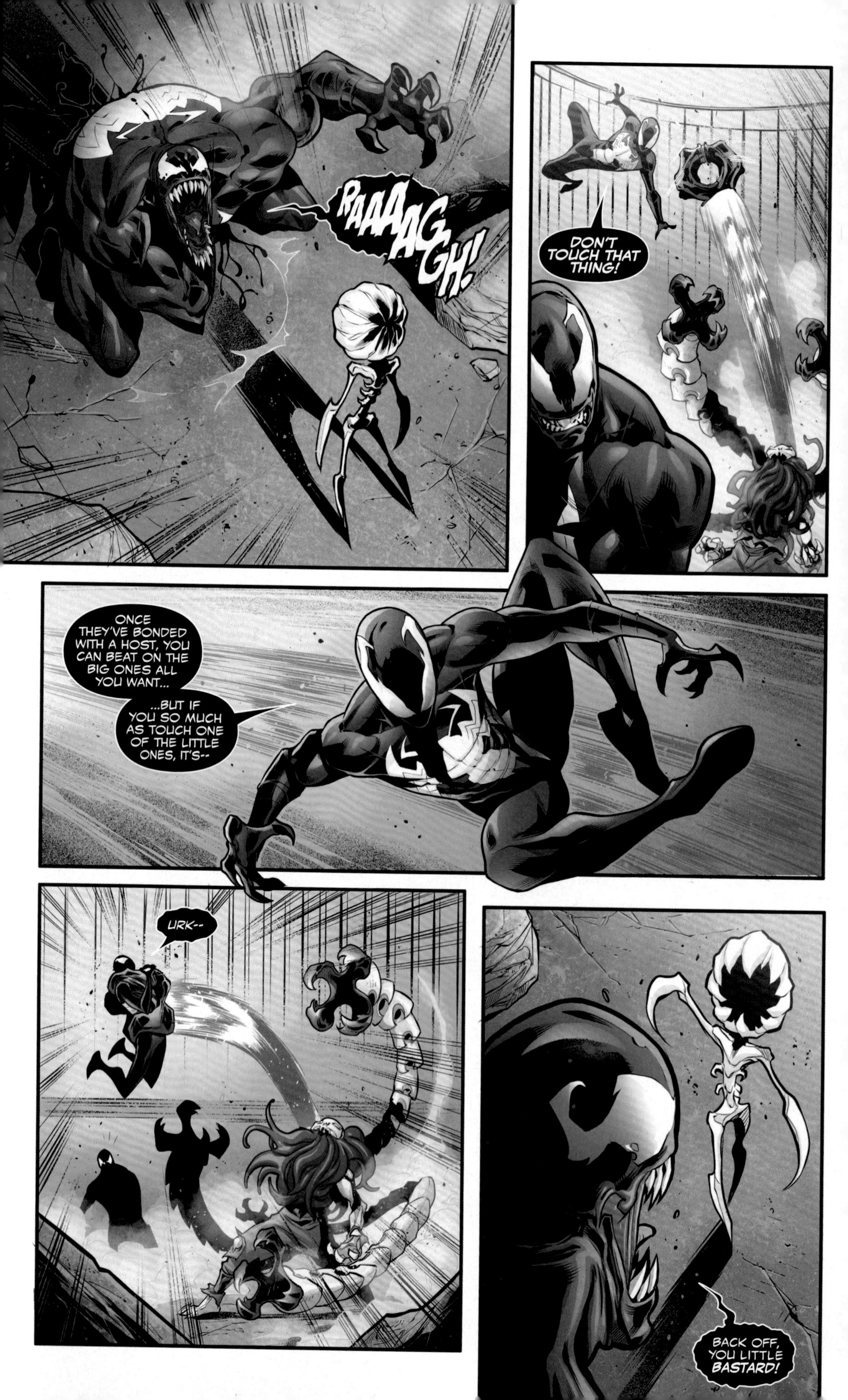
RAAAAGH!
DON'T TOUCH THAT THING!
ONCE THEY'VE BONDED WITH A HOST, YOU CAN BEAT ON THE BIG ONES ALL YOU WANT...
...BUT IF YOU SO MUCH AS TOUCH ONE OF THE LITTLE ONES, IT'S--
URK--
BACK OFF, YOU LITTLE BASTARD!

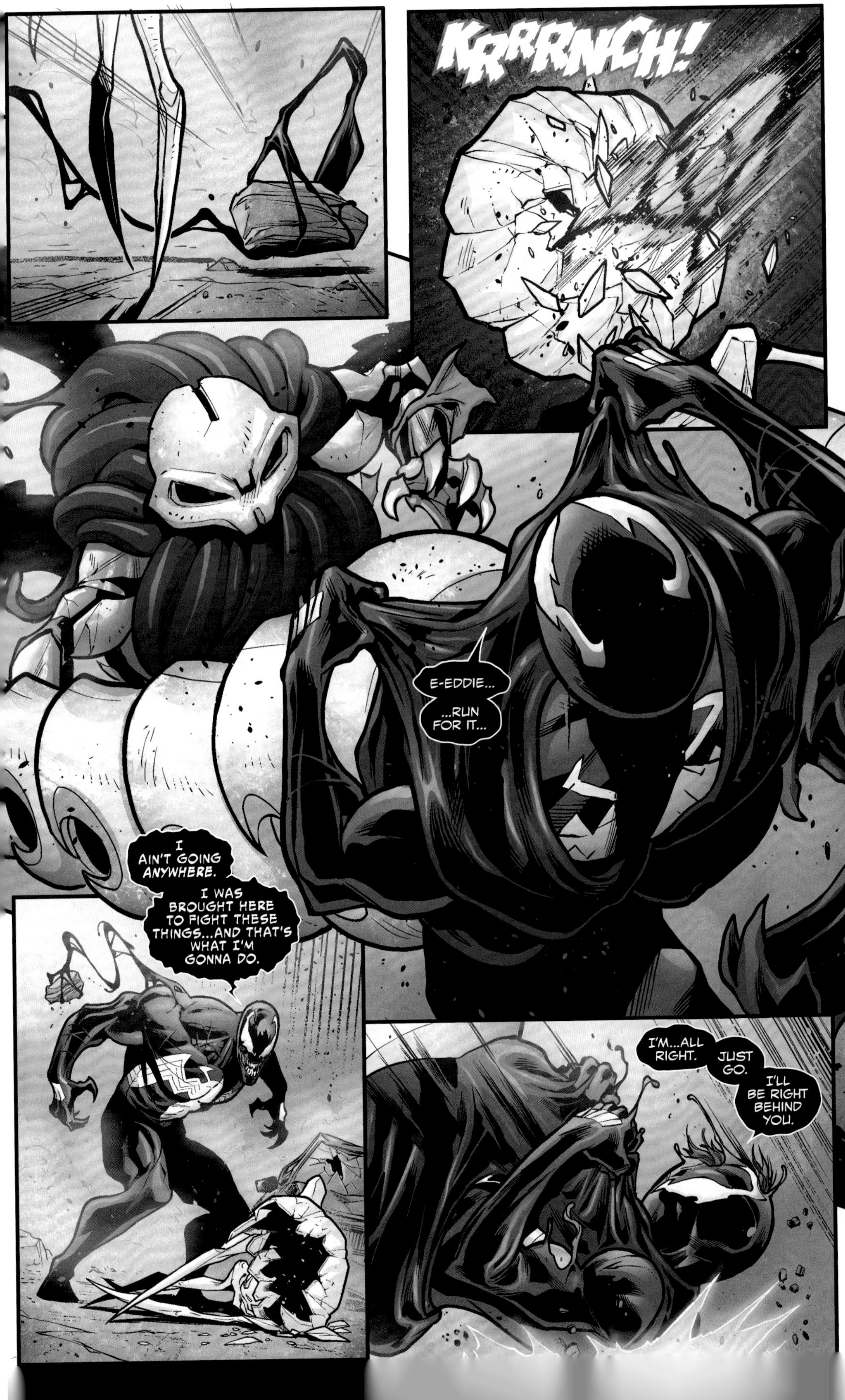
KRRRNCH!
E-EDDIE...
...RUN FOR IT...
I AIN'T GOING ANYWHERE.
I WAS BROUGHT HERE TO FIGHT THESE THINGS...AND THAT'S WHAT I'M GONNA DO.
I'M...ALL RIGHT.
JUST GO.
I'LL BE RIGHT BEHIND YOU.

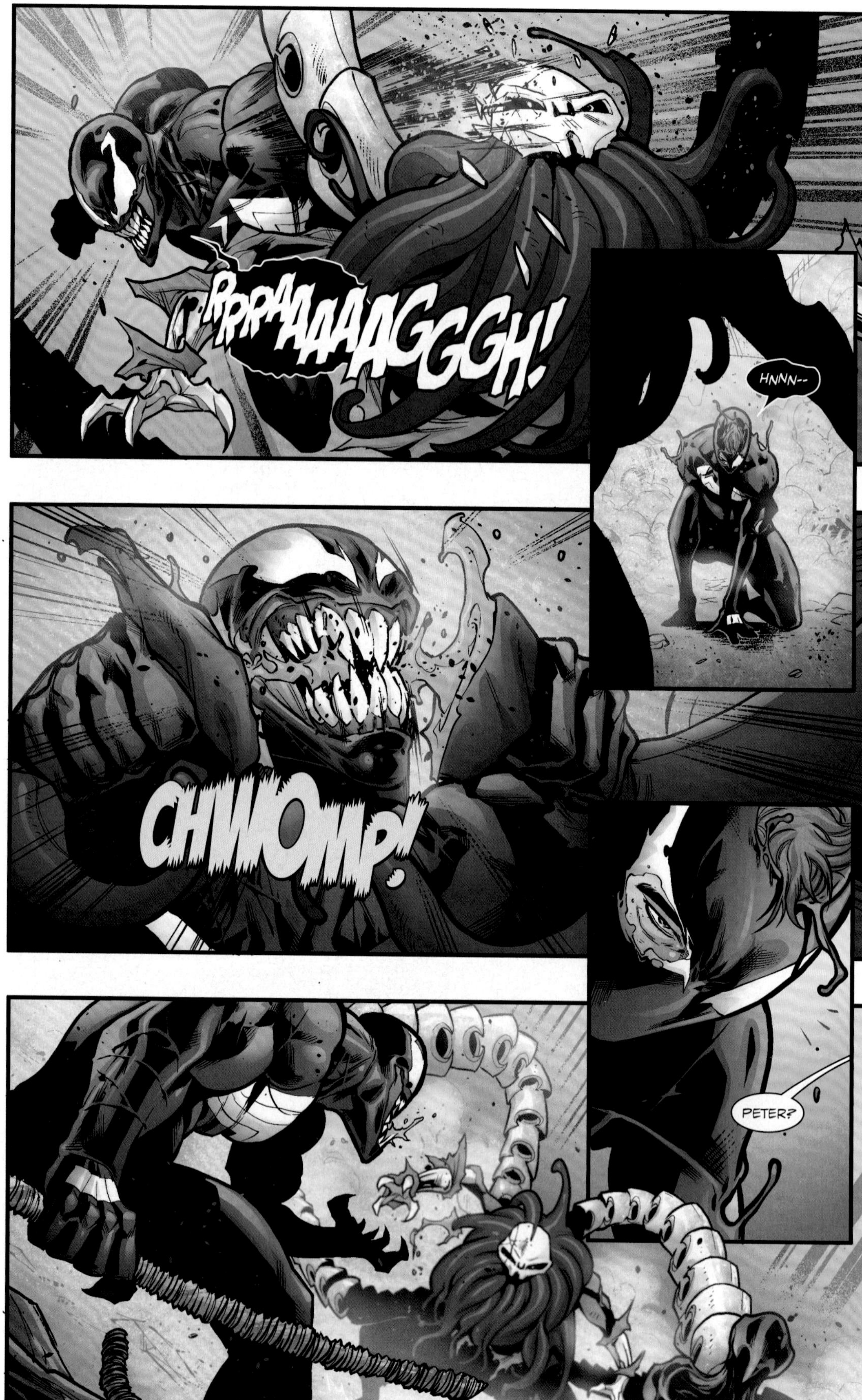
RRRRAAAAAAGGGH!
HNNN--
CHWOMP!
PETER?

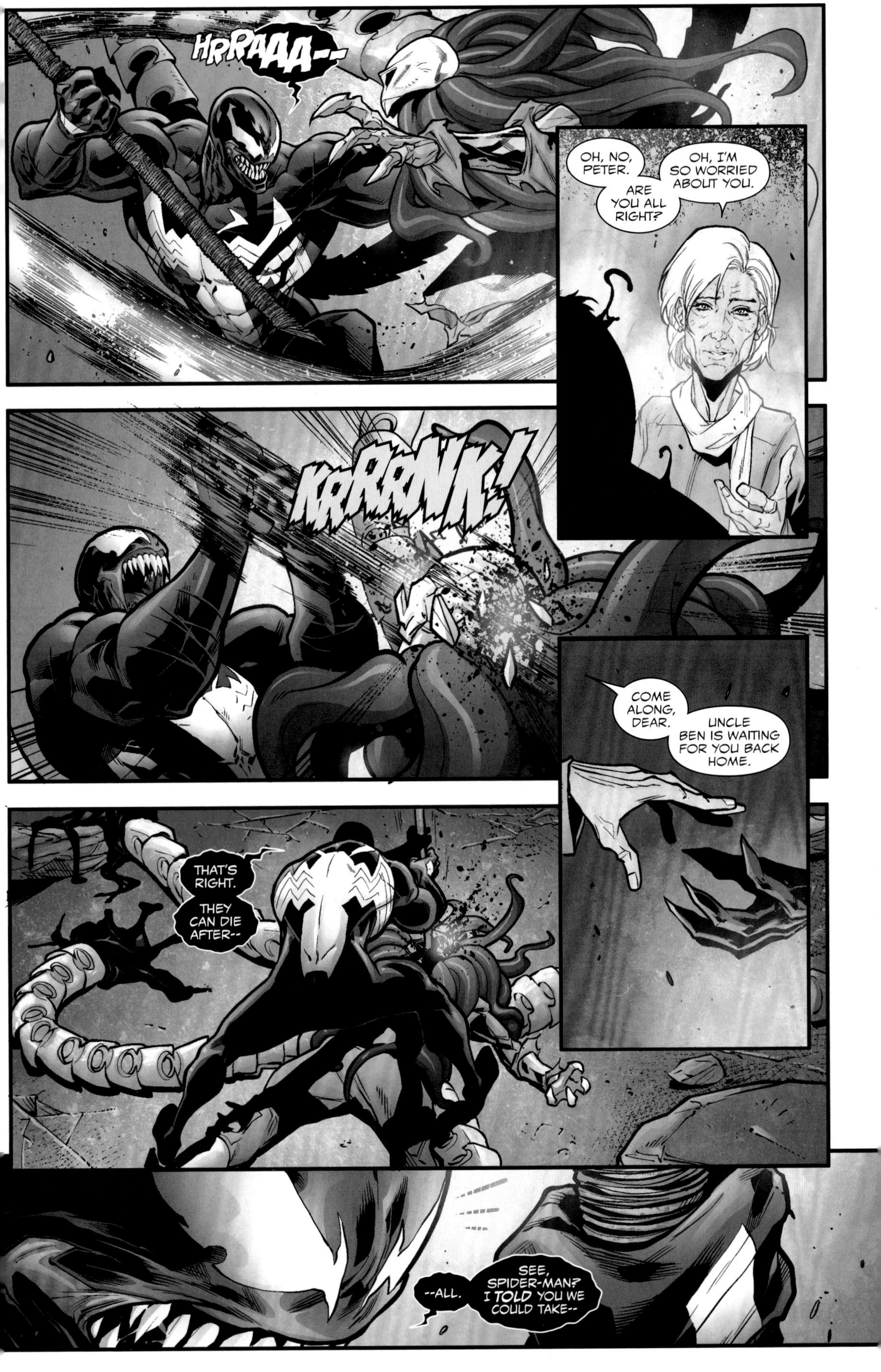
HRRAAA--
OH, NO, PETER.
ARE YOU ALL RIGHT?
OH, I'M SO WORRIED ABOUT YOU.
KRRONK!
COME ALONG, DEAR.
UNCLE BEN IS WAITING FOR YOU BACK HOME.
THAT'S RIGHT.
THEY CAN DIE AFTER--
--ALL.
SEE, SPIDER-MAN? I TOLD YOU WE COULD TAKE--

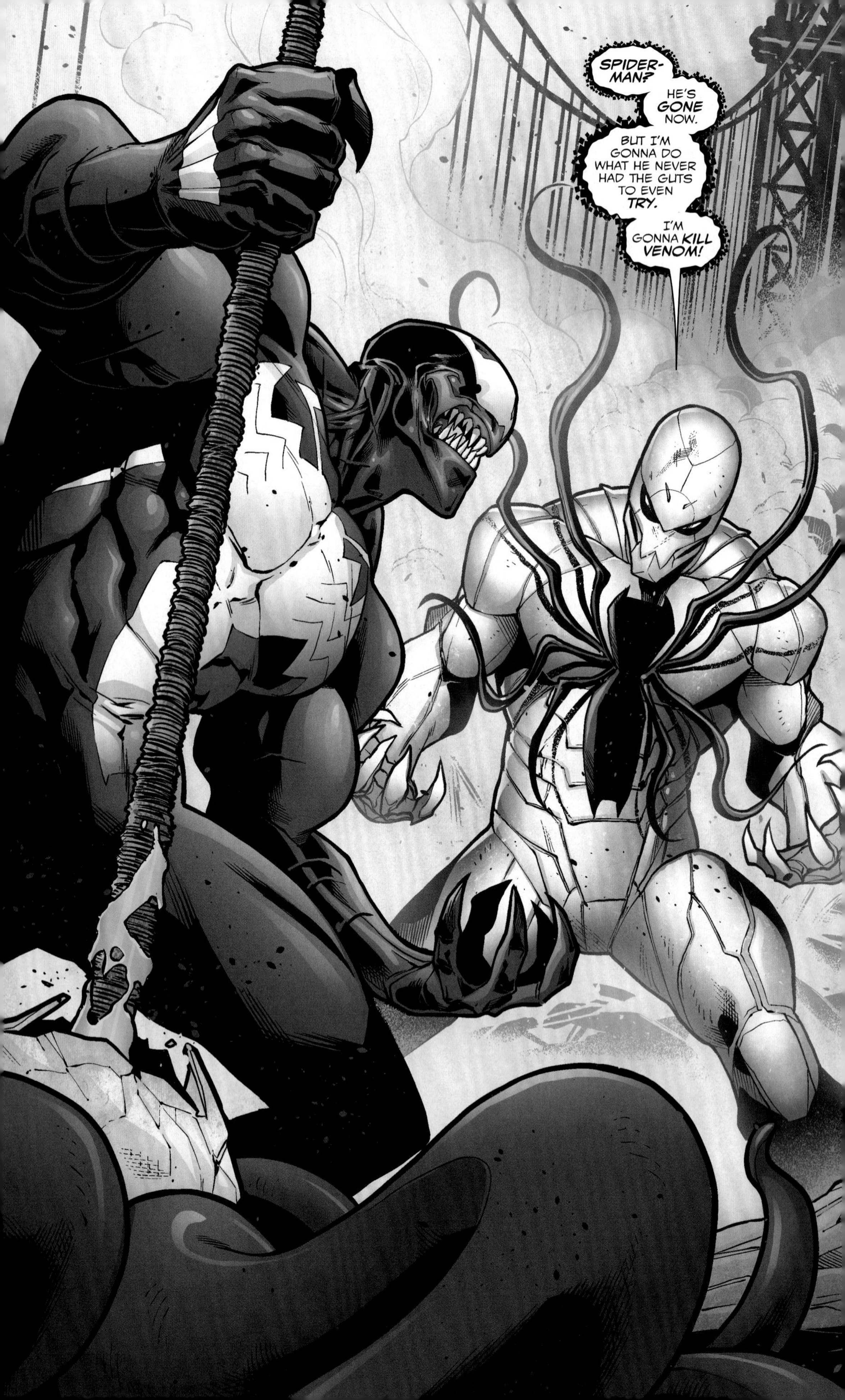
SPIDER-MAN?
HE'S GONE NOW.
BUT I'M GONNA DO WHAT HE NEVER HAD THE GUTS TO EVEN TRY.
I'M GONNA KILL VENOM!

2

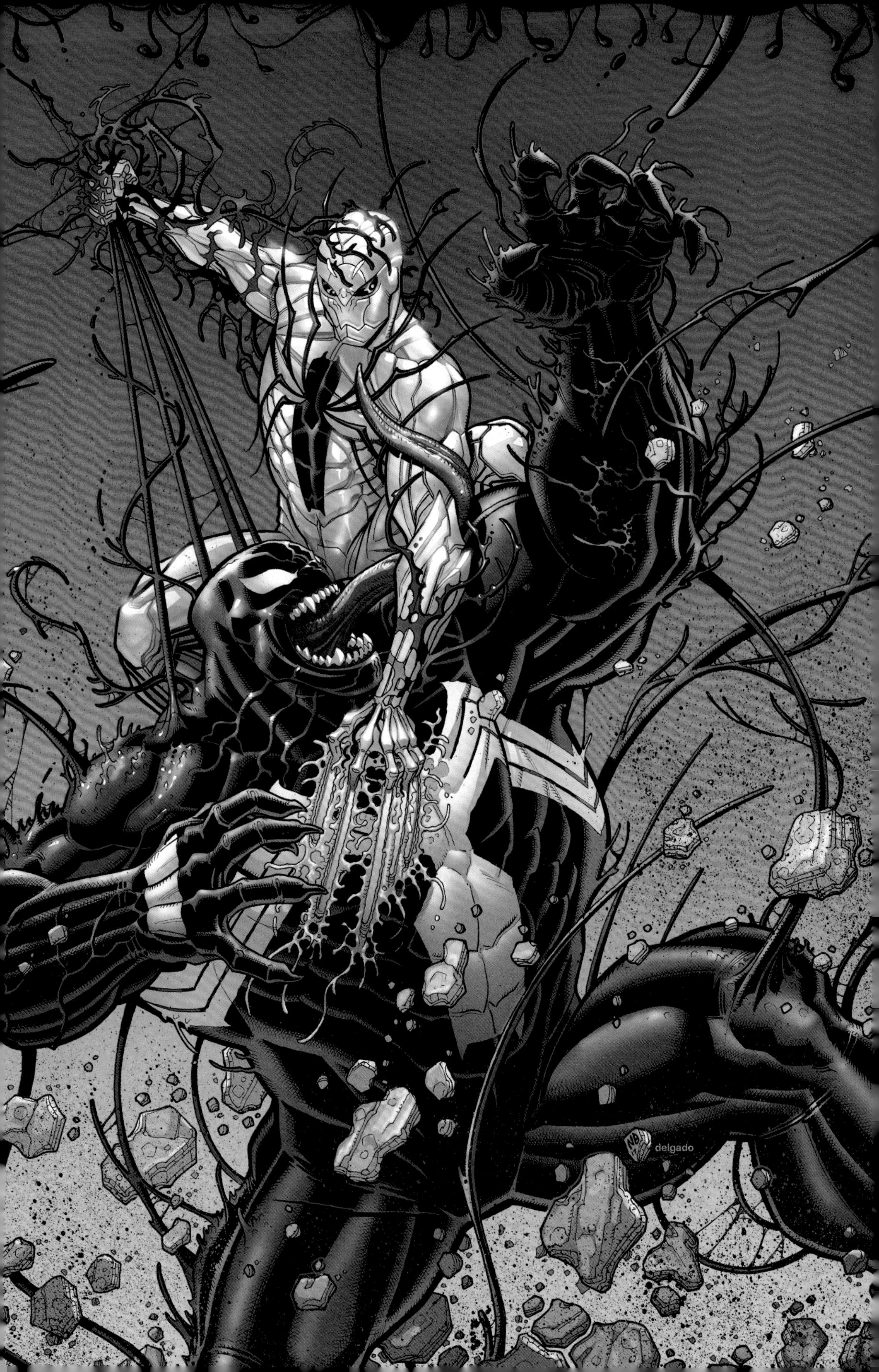

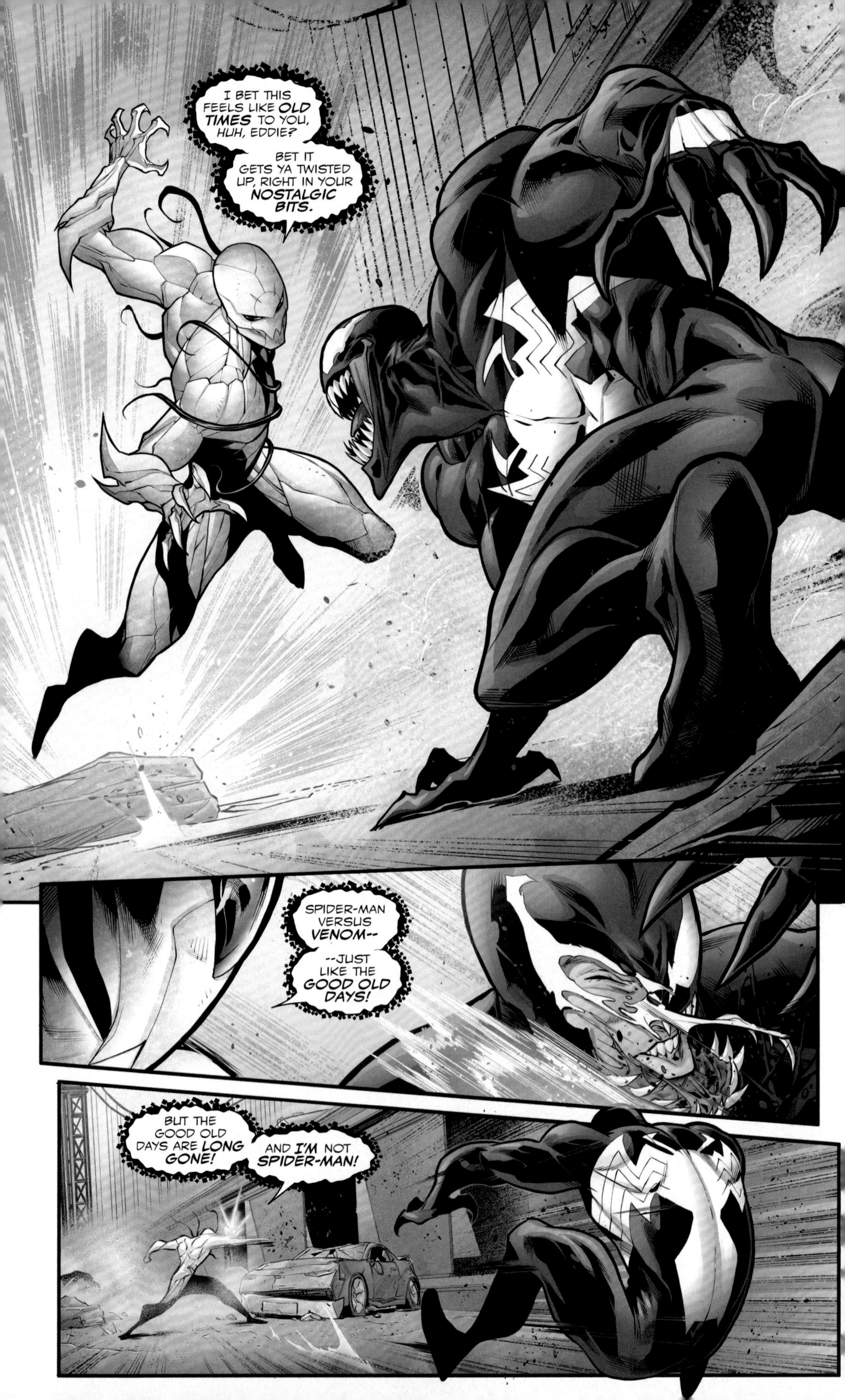
I BET THIS FEELS LIKE OLD TIMES TO YOU, HUH, EDDIE?
BET IT GETS YA TWISTED UP, RIGHT IN YOUR NOSTALGIC BITS.
SPIDER-MAN VERSUS VENOM--
--JUST LIKE THE GOOD OLD DAYS!
BUT THE GOOD OLD DAYS ARE LONG GONE!
AND I'M NOT SPIDER-MAN!

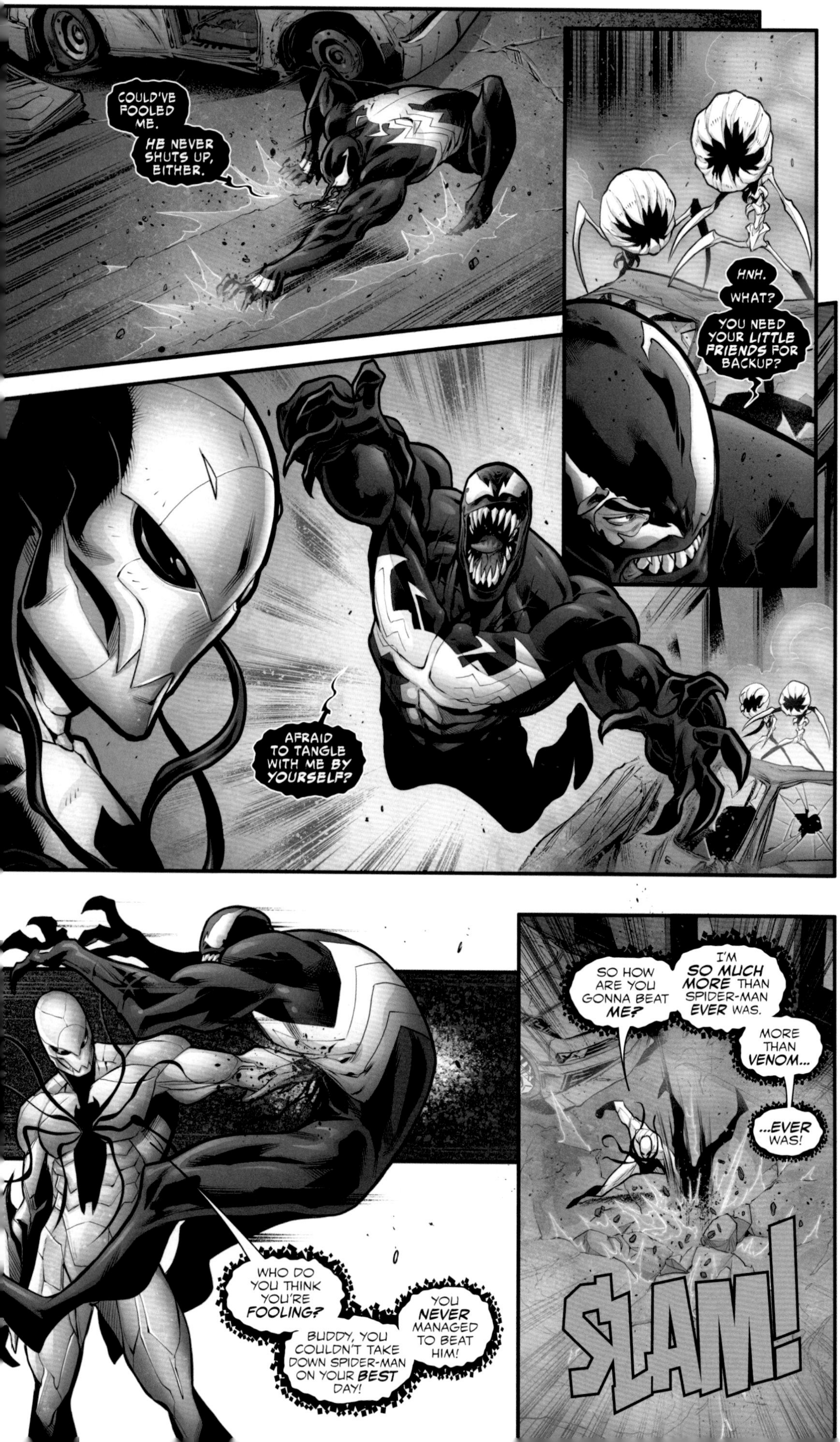
COULD'VE FOOLED ME.
HE NEVER SHUTS UP, EITHER.
HNH.
WHAT?
YOU NEED YOUR LITTLE FRIENDS FOR BACKUP?
AFRAID TO TANGLE WITH ME BY YOURSELF?
WHO DO YOU THINK YOU'RE FOOLING?
BUDDY, YOU COULDN'T TAKE DOWN SPIDER-MAN ON YOUR BEST DAY!
YOU NEVER MANAGED TO BEAT HIM!
SO HOW ARE YOU GONNA BEAT ME?
I'M SO MUCH MORE THAN SPIDER-MAN EVER WAS.
MORE THAN VENOM...
...EVER WAS!
SLAM!

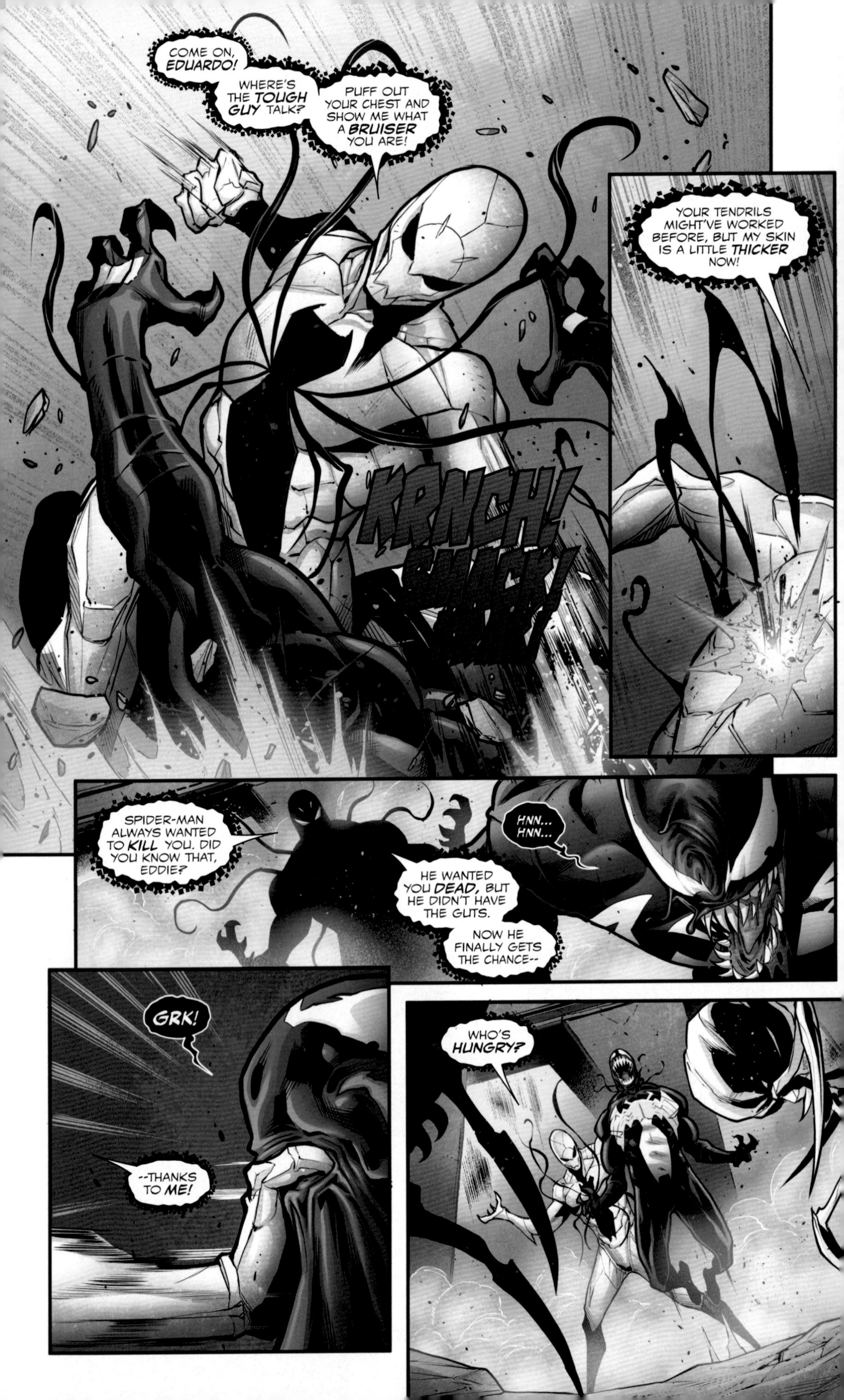
COME ON, EDUARDO!
WHERE'S THE TOUGH GUY TALK?
PUFF OUT YOUR CHEST AND SHOW ME WHAT A BRUISER YOU ARE!
KRNCH!
YOUR TENDRILS MIGHT'VE WORKED BEFORE, BUT MY SKIN IS A LITTLE THICKER NOW!
SPIDER-MAN ALWAYS WANTED TO KILL YOU. DID YOU KNOW THAT, EDDIE?
HNN... HNN...
HE WANTED YOU DEAD, BUT HE DIDN'T HAVE THE GUTS.
NOW HE FINALLY GETS THE CHANCE--
GRK!
--THANKS TO ME!
WHO'S HUNGRY?

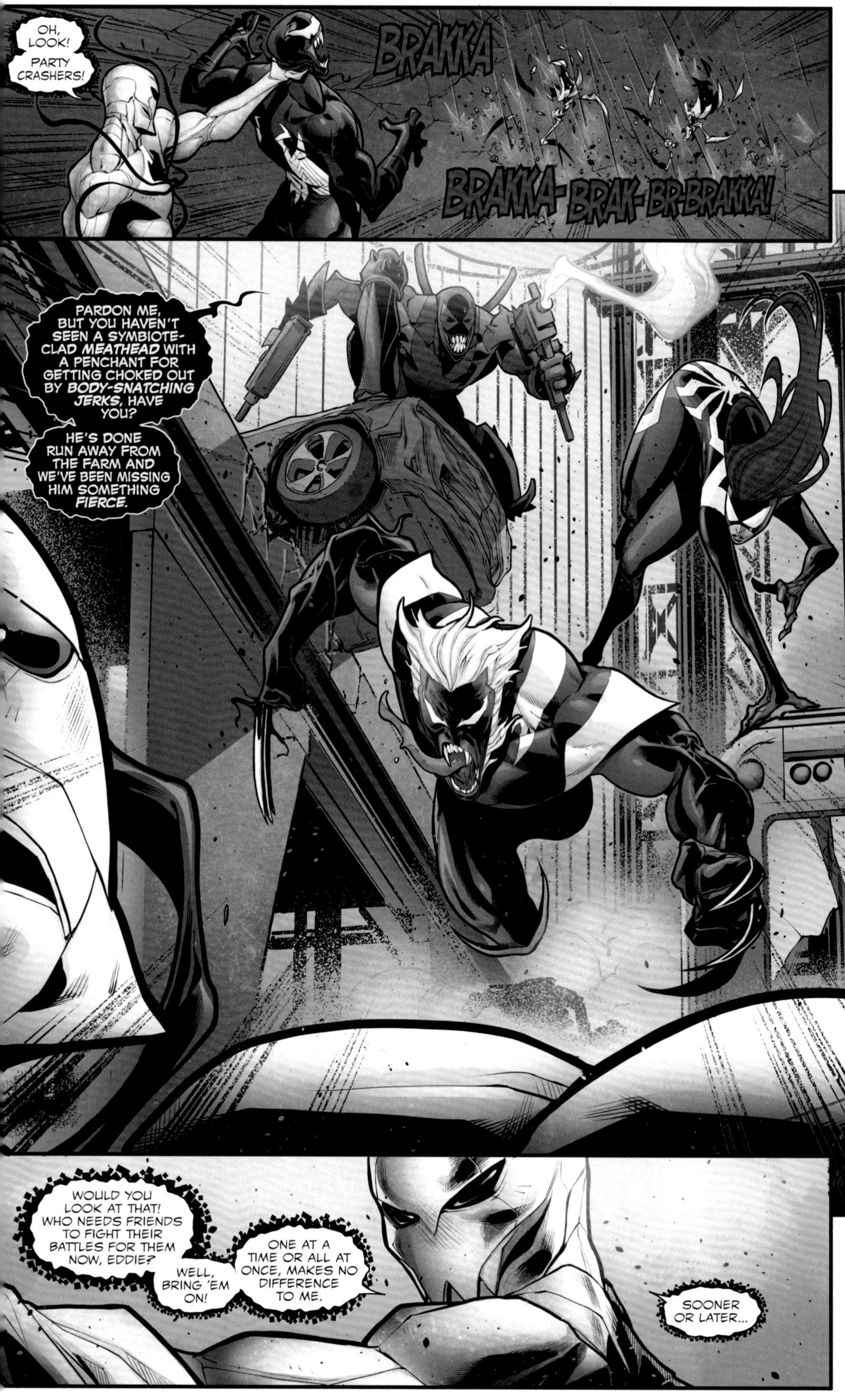
OH, LOOK! PARTY CRASHERS!
BRAKKA
BRAKKA-BRAK-BR-BRAKKA!
PARDON ME, BUT YOU HAVEN'T SEEN A SYMBIOTE-CLAD *MEATHEAD* WITH A PENCHANT FOR GETTING CHOKED OUT BY *BODY-SNATCHING JERKS*, HAVE YOU?
HE'S DONE RUN AWAY FROM THE FARM AND WE'VE BEEN MISSING HIM SOMETHING *FIERCE*.
WOULD YOU LOOK AT THAT! WHO NEEDS FRIENDS TO FIGHT THEIR BATTLES FOR THEM NOW, EDDIE?
WELL, BRING 'EM ON!
ONE AT A TIME OR ALL AT ONCE, MAKES NO DIFFERENCE TO ME.
SOONER OR LATER...

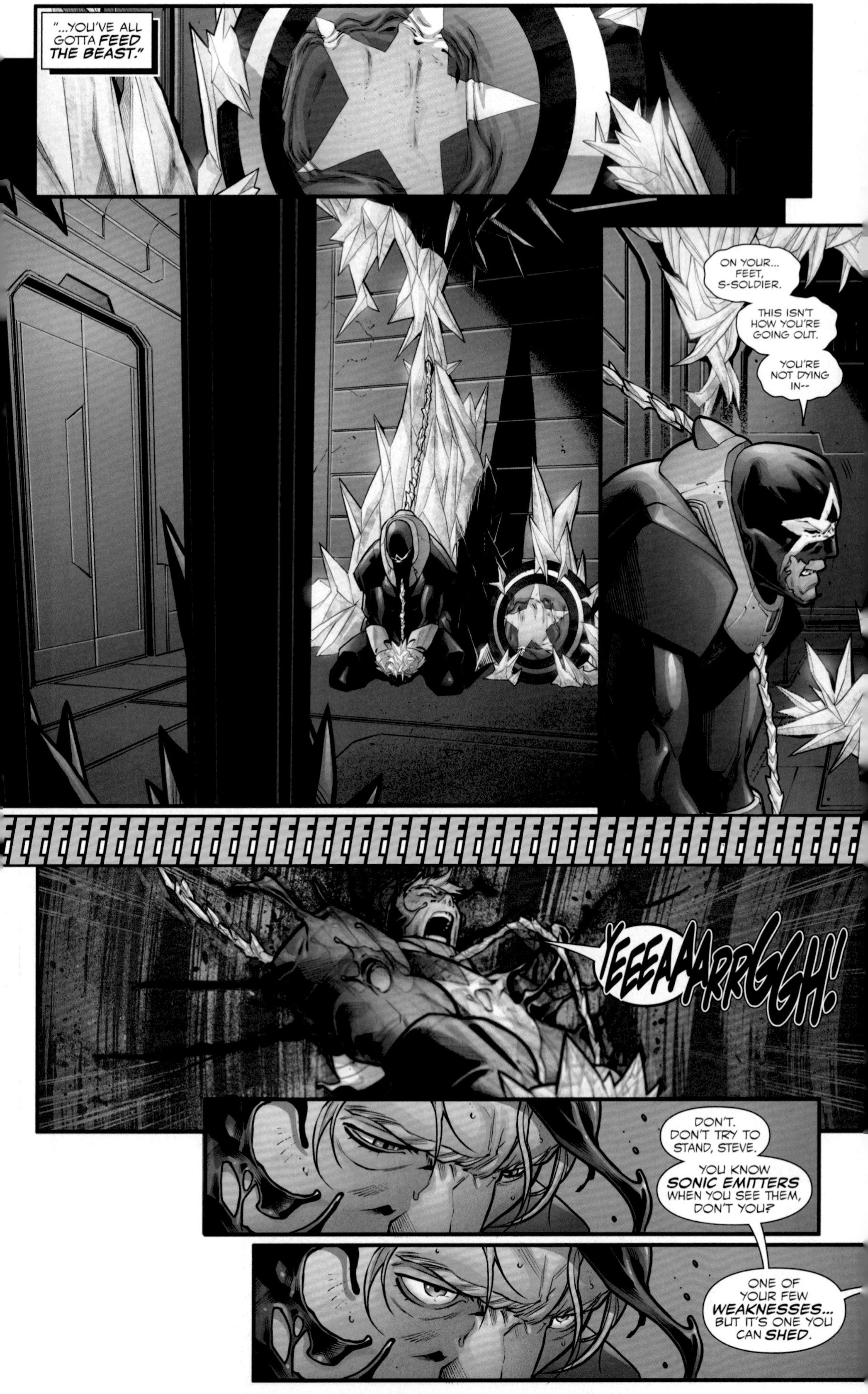

"...YOU'VE ALL GOTTA *FEED THE BEAST.*"
ON YOUR... FEET, S-SOLDIER.
THIS ISN'T HOW YOU'RE GOING OUT.
YOU'RE NOT DYING IN--
EEEEEEEEEEEEEEEEEEEEEEEEEEEEEEEEEEEEEEEEEEEEEEEEEEEEEEEEE
YEEEAAARRGGH!
DON'T. DON'T TRY TO STAND, STEVE.
YOU KNOW **SONIC EMITTERS** WHEN YOU SEE THEM, DON'T YOU?
ONE OF YOUR FEW **WEAKNESSES...** BUT IT'S ONE YOU CAN **SHED**.

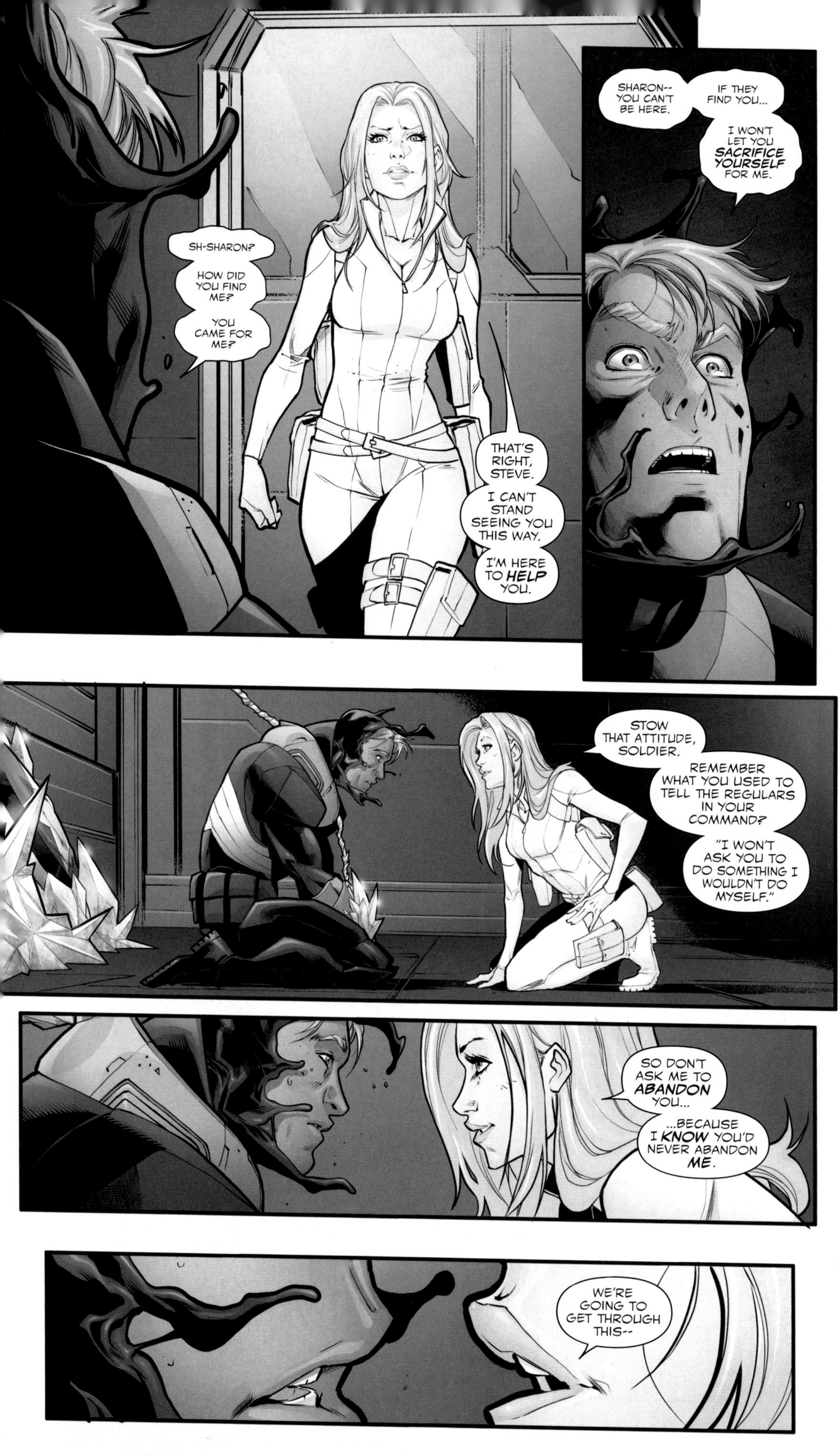
SH-SHARON?
HOW DID YOU FIND ME?
YOU CAME FOR ME?
THAT'S RIGHT, STEVE.
I CAN'T STAND SEEING YOU THIS WAY.
I'M HERE TO HELP YOU.
SHARON-- YOU CAN'T BE HERE.
IF THEY FIND YOU...
I WON'T LET YOU SACRIFICE YOURSELF FOR ME.
STOW THAT ATTITUDE, SOLDIER.
REMEMBER WHAT YOU USED TO TELL THE REGULARS IN YOUR COMMAND?
"I WON'T ASK YOU TO DO SOMETHING I WOULDN'T DO MYSELF."
SO DON'T ASK ME TO ABANDON YOU...
...BECAUSE I KNOW YOU'D NEVER ABANDON ME.
WE'RE GOING TO GET THROUGH THIS--

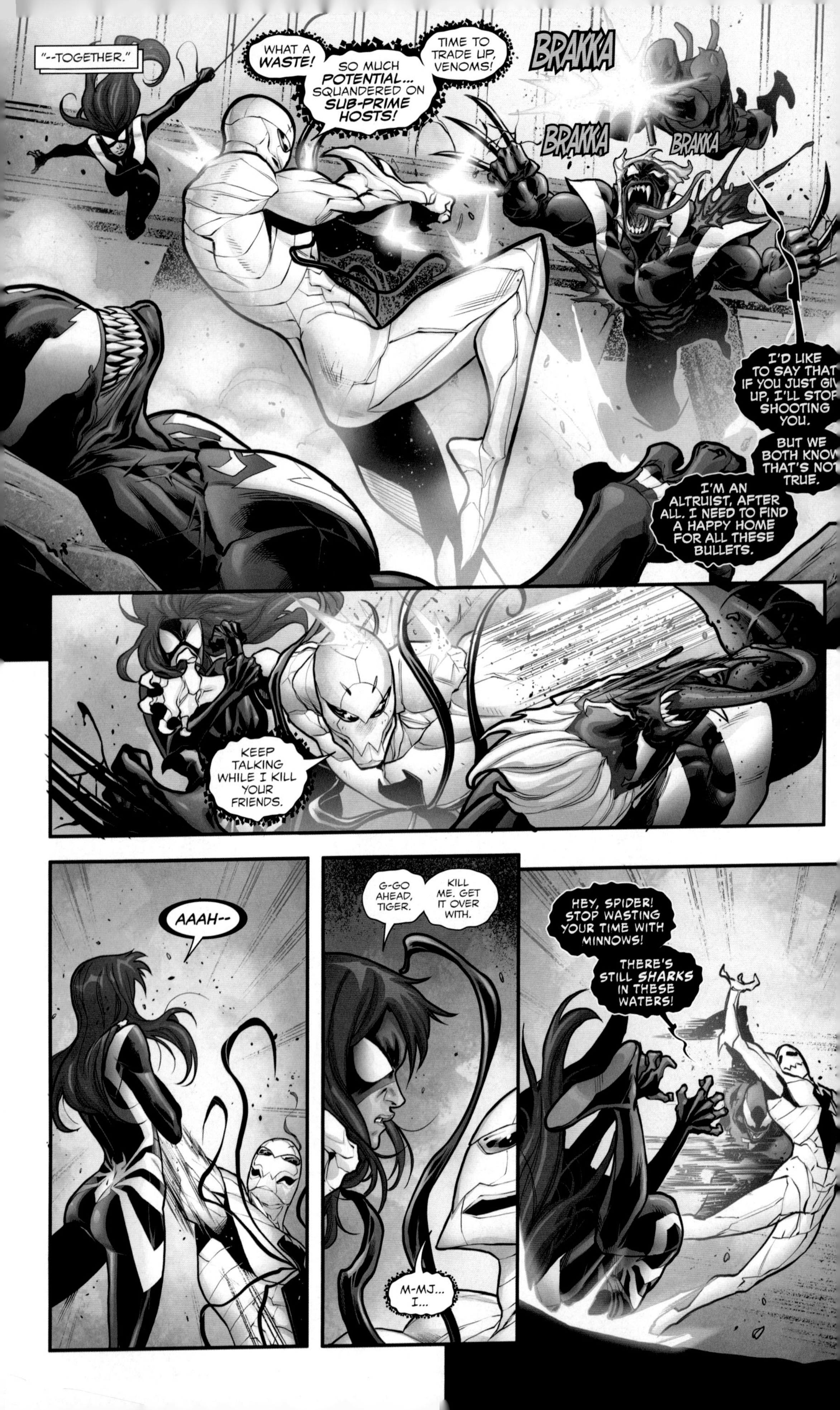
"--TOGETHER."
WHAT A WASTE!
SO MUCH POTENTIAL... SQUANDERED ON SUB-PRIME HOSTS!
TIME TO TRADE UP, VENOMS!
BRAKKA
BRAKKA
BRAKKA
I'D LIKE TO SAY THAT IF YOU JUST GIV UP, I'LL STOP SHOOTING YOU.
BUT WE BOTH KNOW THAT'S NOT TRUE.
I'M AN ALTRUIST, AFTER ALL. I NEED TO FIND A HAPPY HOME FOR ALL THESE BULLETS.
KEEP TALKING WHILE I KILL YOUR FRIENDS.
AAAH--
G-GO AHEAD, TIGER.
KILL ME. GET IT OVER WITH.
M-MJ... I...
HEY, SPIDER! STOP WASTING YOUR TIME WITH MINNOWS!
THERE'S STILL SHARKS IN THESE WATERS!

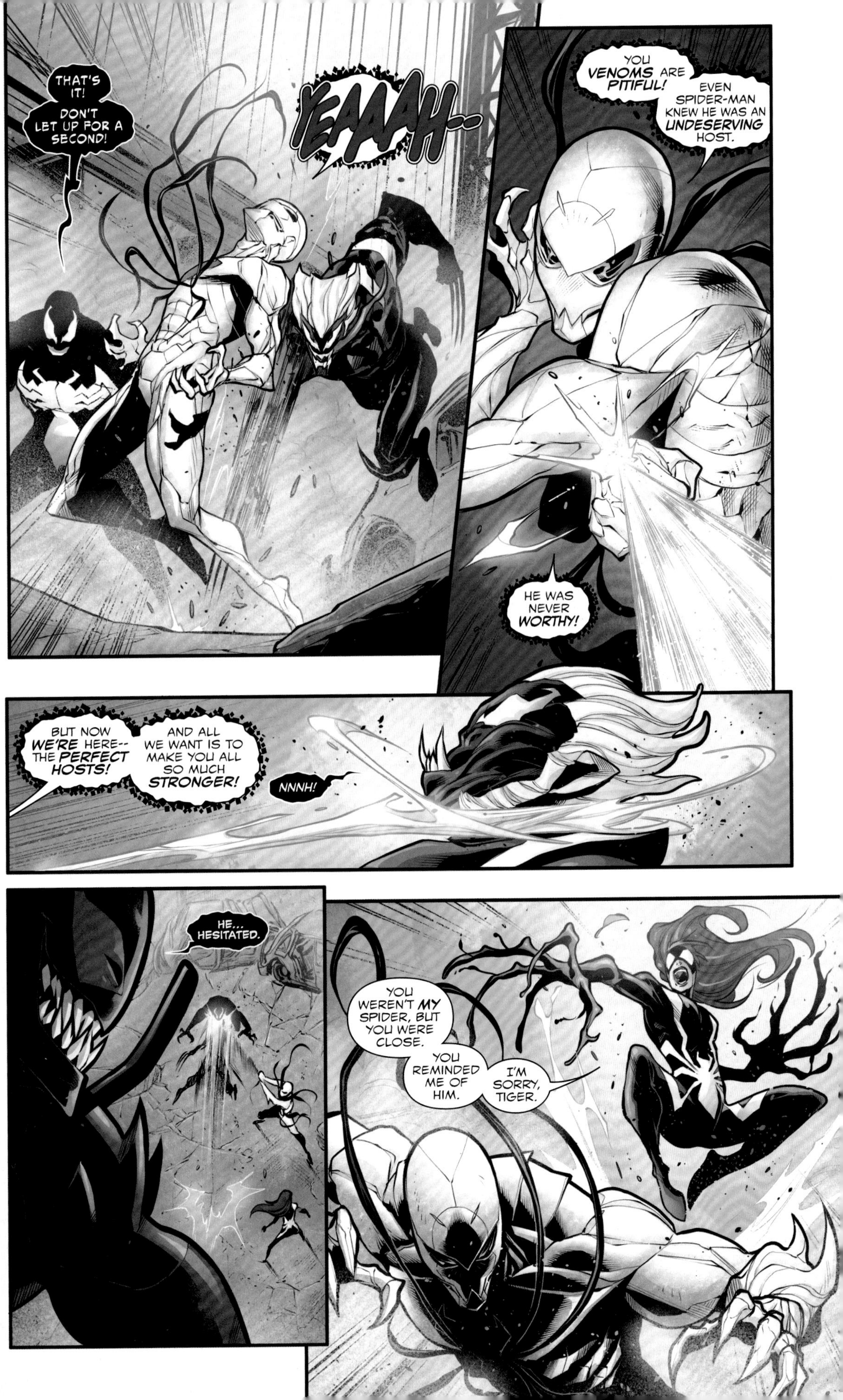
THAT'S IT! DON'T LET UP FOR A SECOND!
YEAAAH--
YOU VENOMS ARE PITIFUL!
EVEN SPIDER-MAN KNEW HE WAS AN UNDESERVING HOST.
HE WAS NEVER WORTHY!
BUT NOW WE'RE HERE-- THE PERFECT HOSTS!
AND ALL WE WANT IS TO MAKE YOU ALL SO MUCH STRONGER!
NNNH!
HE... HESITATED.
YOU WEREN'T MY SPIDER, BUT YOU WERE CLOSE.
YOU REMINDED ME OF HIM.
I'M SORRY, TIGER.

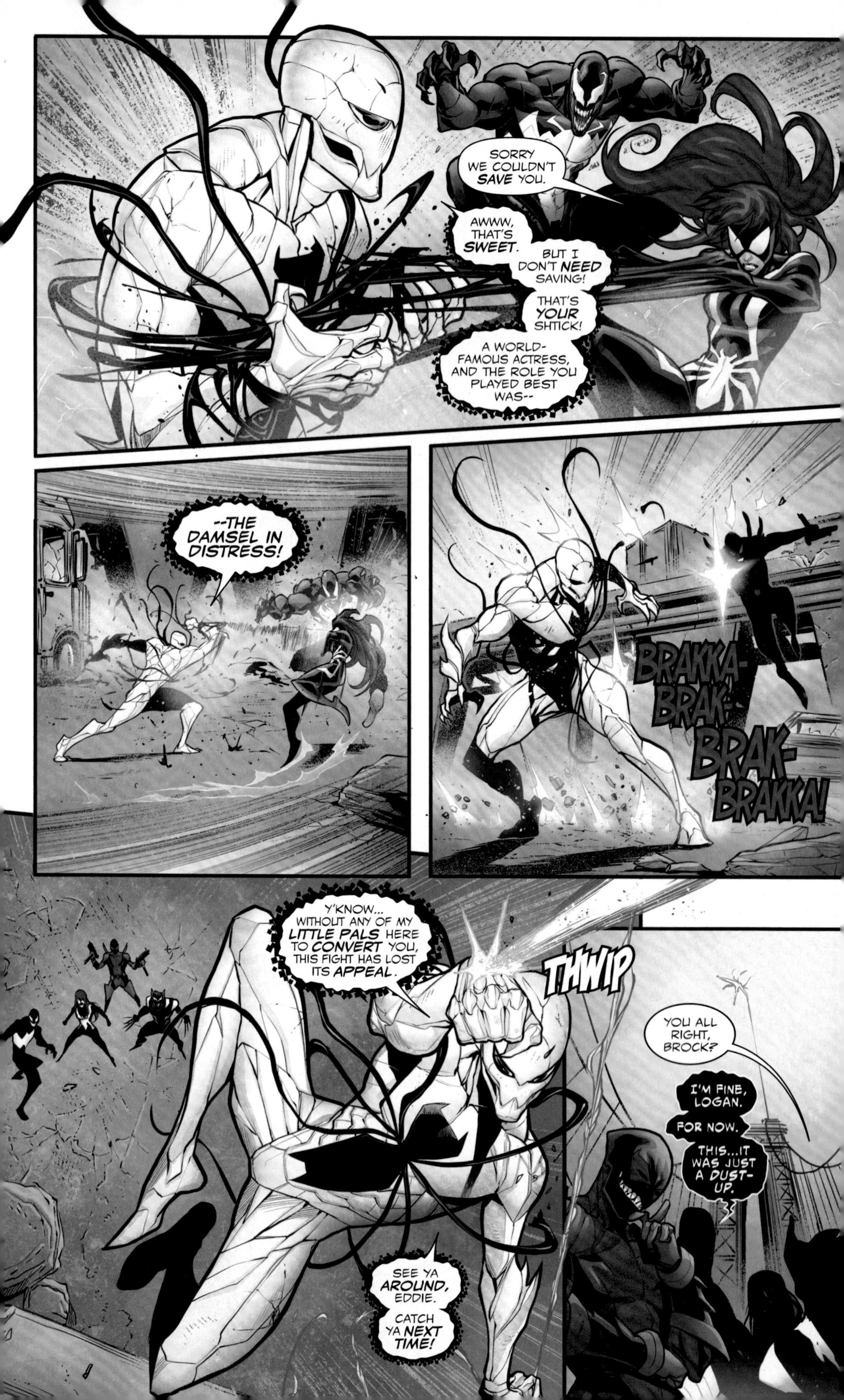
SORRY WE COULDN'T SAVE YOU.
AWWW, THAT'S SWEET.
BUT I DON'T NEED SAVING!
THAT'S YOUR SHTICK!
A WORLD-FAMOUS ACTRESS, AND THE ROLE YOU PLAYED BEST WAS--
--THE DAMSEL IN DISTRESS!
BRAKKA-BRAK-BRAK-BRAKKA!
Y'KNOW... WITHOUT ANY OF MY LITTLE PALS HERE TO CONVERT YOU, THIS FIGHT HAS LOST ITS APPEAL.
THWIP
SEE YA AROUND, EDDIE.
CATCH YA NEXT TIME!
YOU ALL RIGHT, BROCK?
I'M FINE, LOGAN.
FOR NOW.
THIS...IT WAS JUST A DUST-UP.

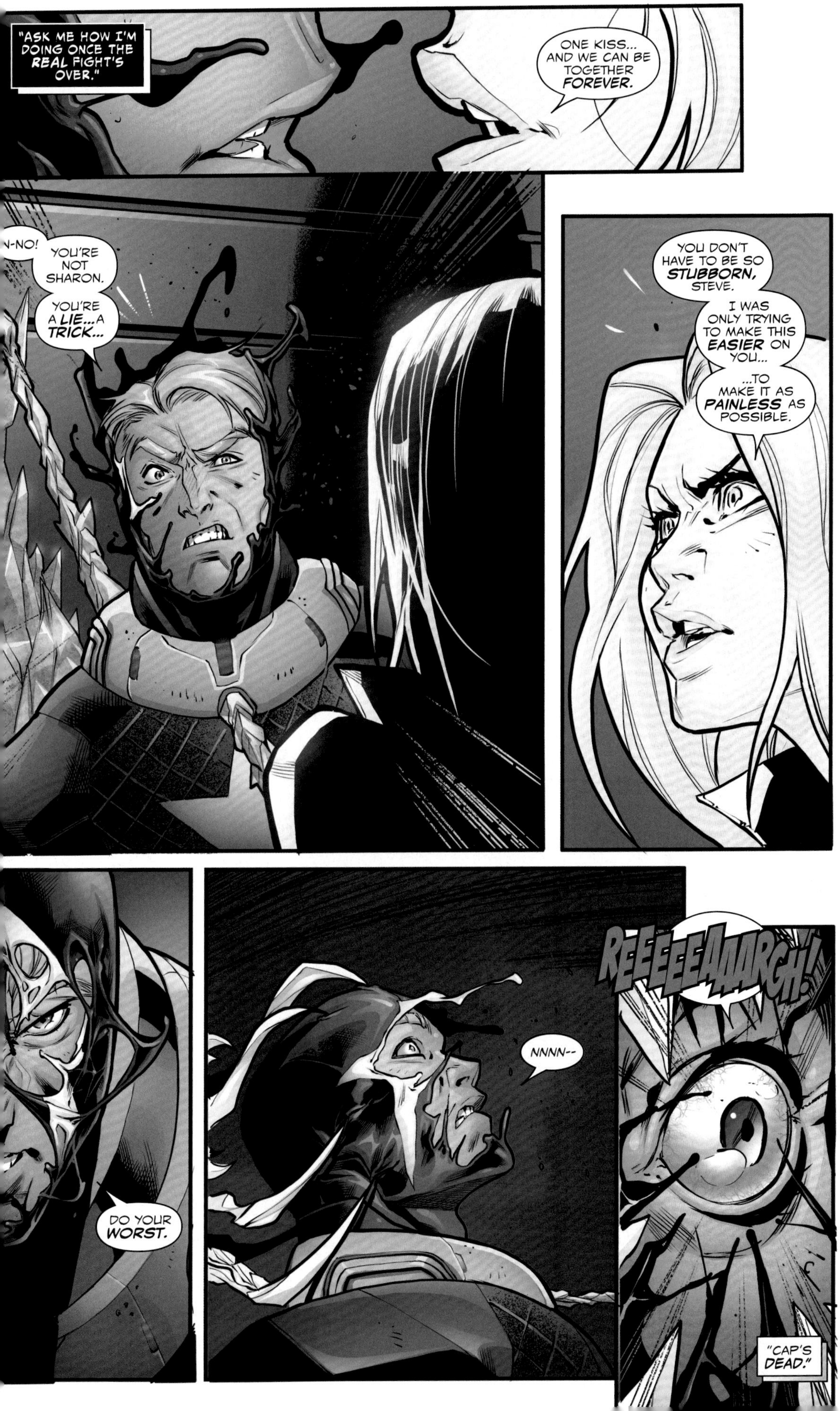
"ASK ME HOW I'M DOING ONCE THE REAL FIGHT'S OVER."
ONE KISS... AND WE CAN BE TOGETHER FOREVER.
N-NO!
YOU'RE NOT SHARON.
YOU'RE A LIE...A TRICK...
YOU DON'T HAVE TO BE SO STUBBORN, STEVE.
I WAS ONLY TRYING TO MAKE THIS EASIER ON YOU...
...TO MAKE IT AS PAINLESS AS POSSIBLE.
DO YOUR WORST.
NNNN--
REEEEEAAARGH!
"CAP'S DEAD."

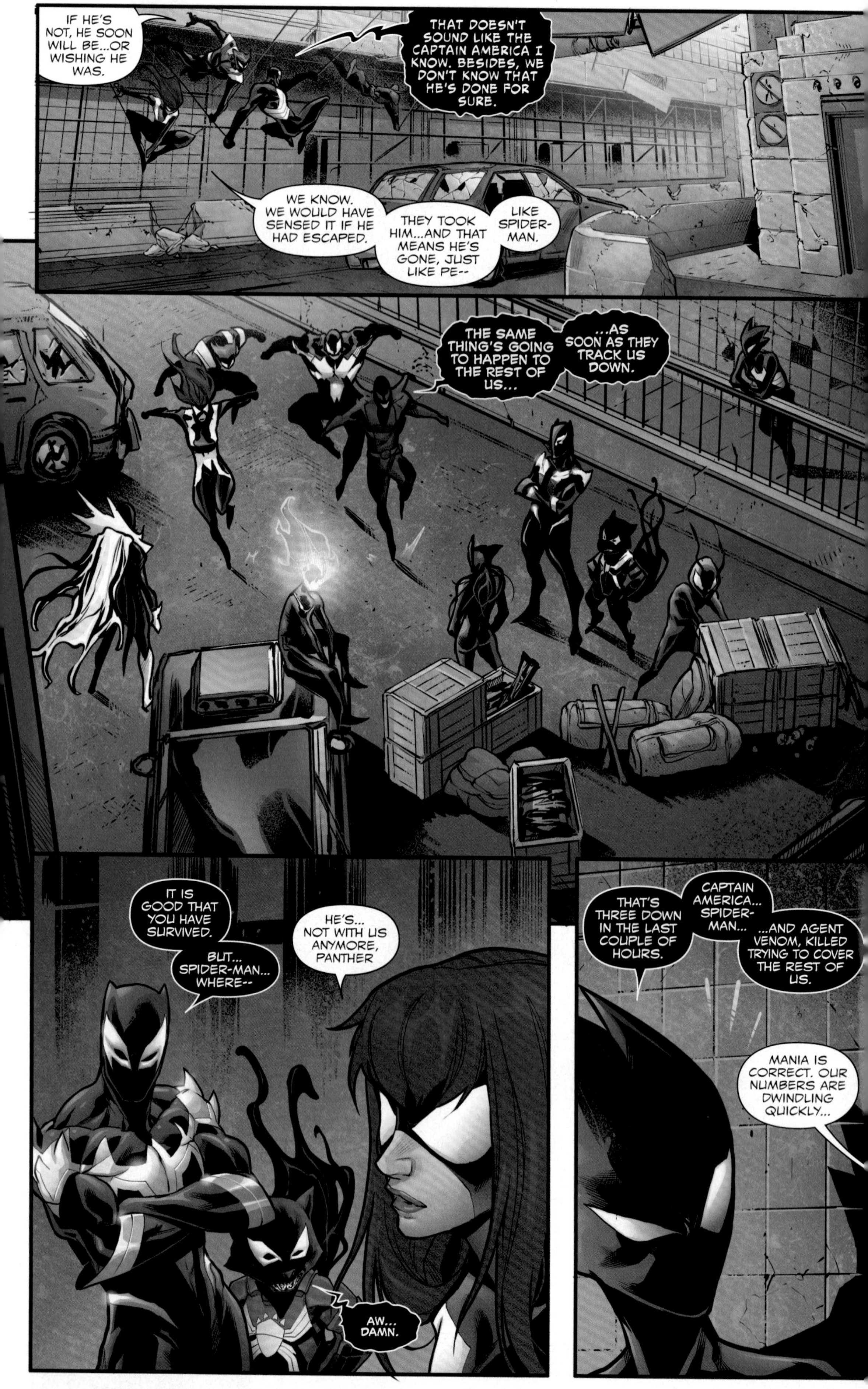
IF HE'S NOT, HE SOON WILL BE...OR WISHING HE WAS.
THAT DOESN'T SOUND LIKE THE CAPTAIN AMERICA I KNOW. BESIDES, WE DON'T KNOW THAT HE'S DONE FOR SURE.
WE KNOW. WE WOULD HAVE SENSED IT IF HE HAD ESCAPED.
THEY TOOK HIM...AND THAT MEANS HE'S GONE, JUST LIKE PE--
LIKE SPIDER-MAN.
THE SAME THING'S GOING TO HAPPEN TO THE REST OF US...
...AS SOON AS THEY TRACK US DOWN.
IT IS GOOD THAT YOU HAVE SURVIVED.
BUT... SPIDER-MAN... WHERE--
HE'S... NOT WITH US ANYMORE, PANTHER
AW... DAMN.
THAT'S THREE DOWN IN THE LAST COUPLE OF HOURS.
CAPTAIN AMERICA... SPIDER-MAN...
...AND AGENT VENOM, KILLED TRYING TO COVER THE REST OF US.
MANIA IS CORRECT. OUR NUMBERS ARE DWINDLING QUICKLY...

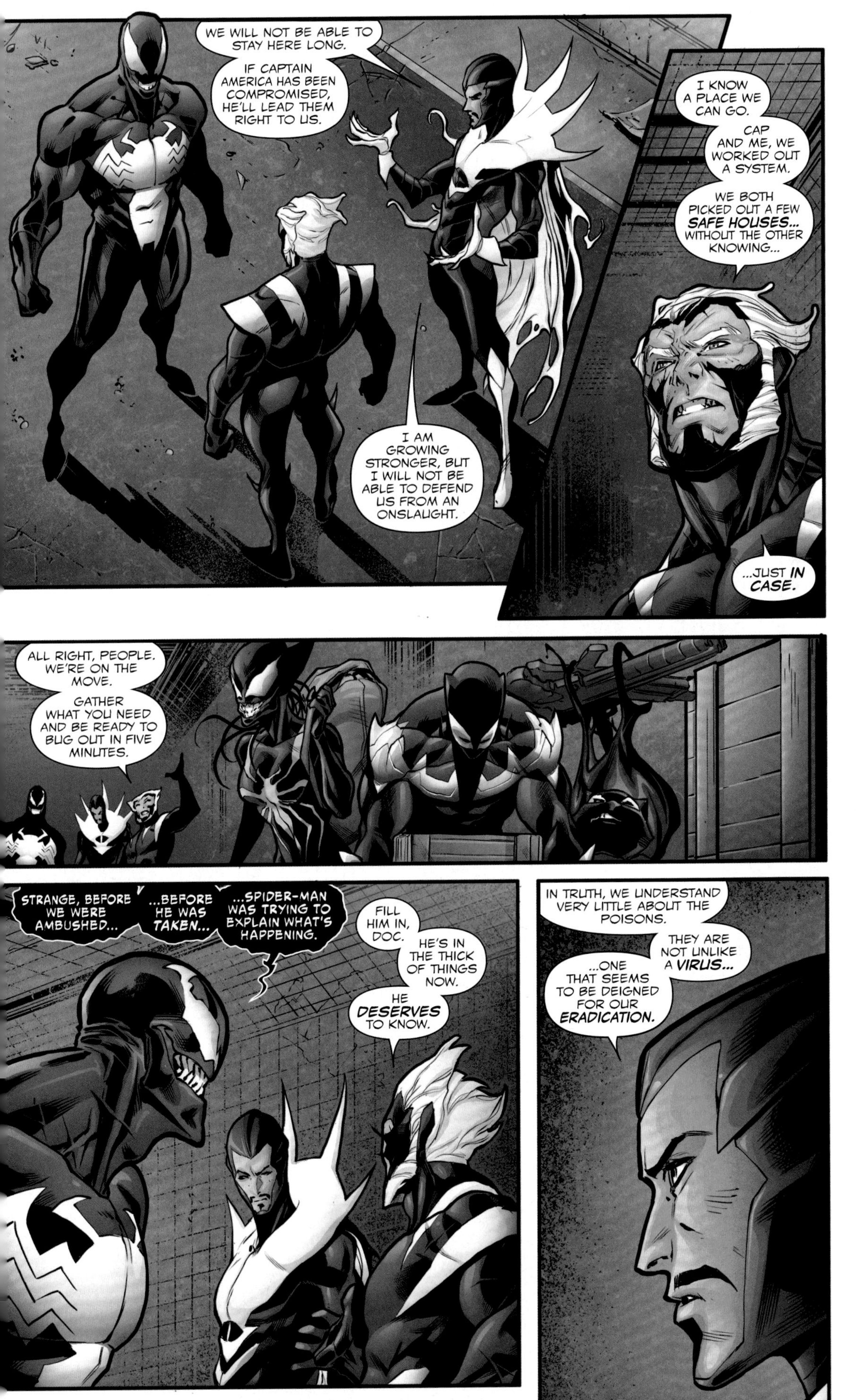

WE WILL NOT BE ABLE TO STAY HERE LONG.
IF CAPTAIN AMERICA HAS BEEN COMPROMISED, HE'LL LEAD THEM RIGHT TO US.
I AM GROWING STRONGER, BUT I WILL NOT BE ABLE TO DEFEND US FROM AN ONSLAUGHT.
I KNOW A PLACE WE CAN GO.
CAP AND ME, WE WORKED OUT A SYSTEM.
WE BOTH PICKED OUT A FEW SAFE HOUSES... WITHOUT THE OTHER KNOWING...
...JUST IN CASE.
ALL RIGHT, PEOPLE. WE'RE ON THE MOVE.
GATHER WHAT YOU NEED AND BE READY TO BUG OUT IN FIVE MINUTES.
STRANGE, BEFORE WE WERE AMBUSHED...
...BEFORE HE WAS TAKEN...
...SPIDER-MAN WAS TRYING TO EXPLAIN WHAT'S HAPPENING.
FILL HIM IN, DOC.
HE'S IN THE THICK OF THINGS NOW.
HE DESERVES TO KNOW.
IN TRUTH, WE UNDERSTAND VERY LITTLE ABOUT THE POISONS.
THEY ARE NOT UNLIKE A VIRUS...
...ONE THAT SEEMS TO BE DEIGNED FOR OUR ERADICATION.

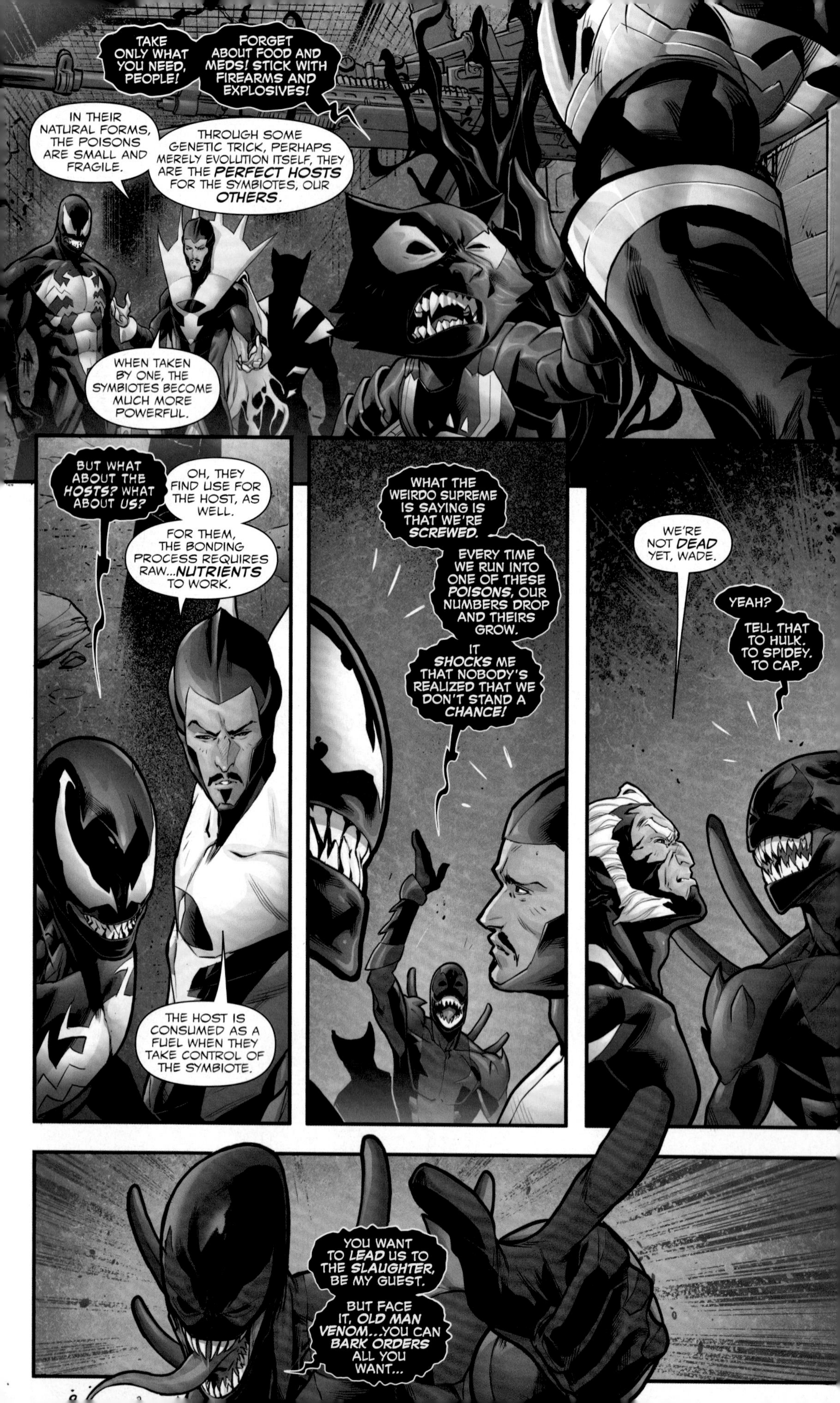
TAKE ONLY WHAT YOU NEED, PEOPLE!
FORGET ABOUT FOOD AND MEDS! STICK WITH FIREARMS AND EXPLOSIVES!
IN THEIR NATURAL FORMS, THE POISONS ARE SMALL AND FRAGILE.
THROUGH SOME GENETIC TRICK, PERHAPS MERELY EVOLUTION ITSELF, THEY ARE THE PERFECT HOSTS FOR THE SYMBIOTES, OUR OTHERS.
WHEN TAKEN BY ONE, THE SYMBIOTES BECOME MUCH MORE POWERFUL.
BUT WHAT ABOUT THE HOSTS? WHAT ABOUT US?
OH, THEY FIND USE FOR THE HOST, AS WELL.
FOR THEM, THE BONDING PROCESS REQUIRES RAW...NUTRIENTS TO WORK.
THE HOST IS CONSUMED AS A FUEL WHEN THEY TAKE CONTROL OF THE SYMBIOTE.
WHAT THE WEIRDO SUPREME IS SAYING IS THAT WE'RE SCREWED.
EVERY TIME WE RUN INTO ONE OF THESE POISONS, OUR NUMBERS DROP AND THEIRS GROW.
IT SHOCKS ME THAT NOBODY'S REALIZED THAT WE DON'T STAND A CHANCE!
WE'RE NOT DEAD YET, WADE.
YEAH?
TELL THAT TO HULK. TO SPIDEY. TO CAP.
YOU WANT TO LEAD US TO THE SLAUGHTER, BE MY GUEST.
BUT FACE IT, OLD MAN VENOM...YOU CAN BARK ORDERS ALL YOU WANT...

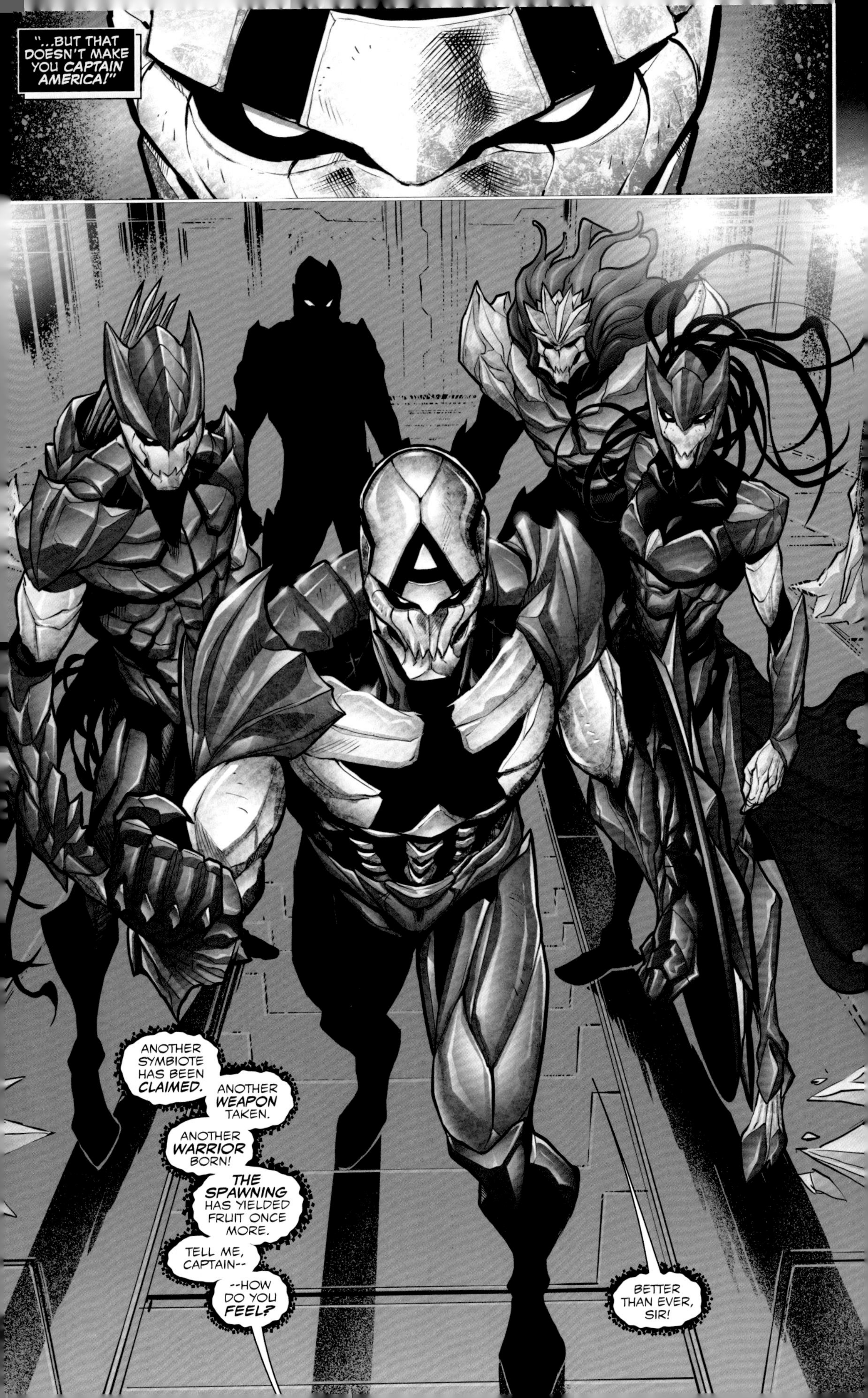
"...BUT THAT DOESN'T MAKE YOU CAPTAIN AMERICA!"
ANOTHER SYMBIOTE HAS BEEN CLAIMED.
ANOTHER WEAPON TAKEN.
ANOTHER WARRIOR BORN!
THE SPAWNING HAS YIELDED FRUIT ONCE MORE.
TELL ME, CAPTAIN--
--HOW DO YOU FEEL?
BETTER THAN EVER, SIR!

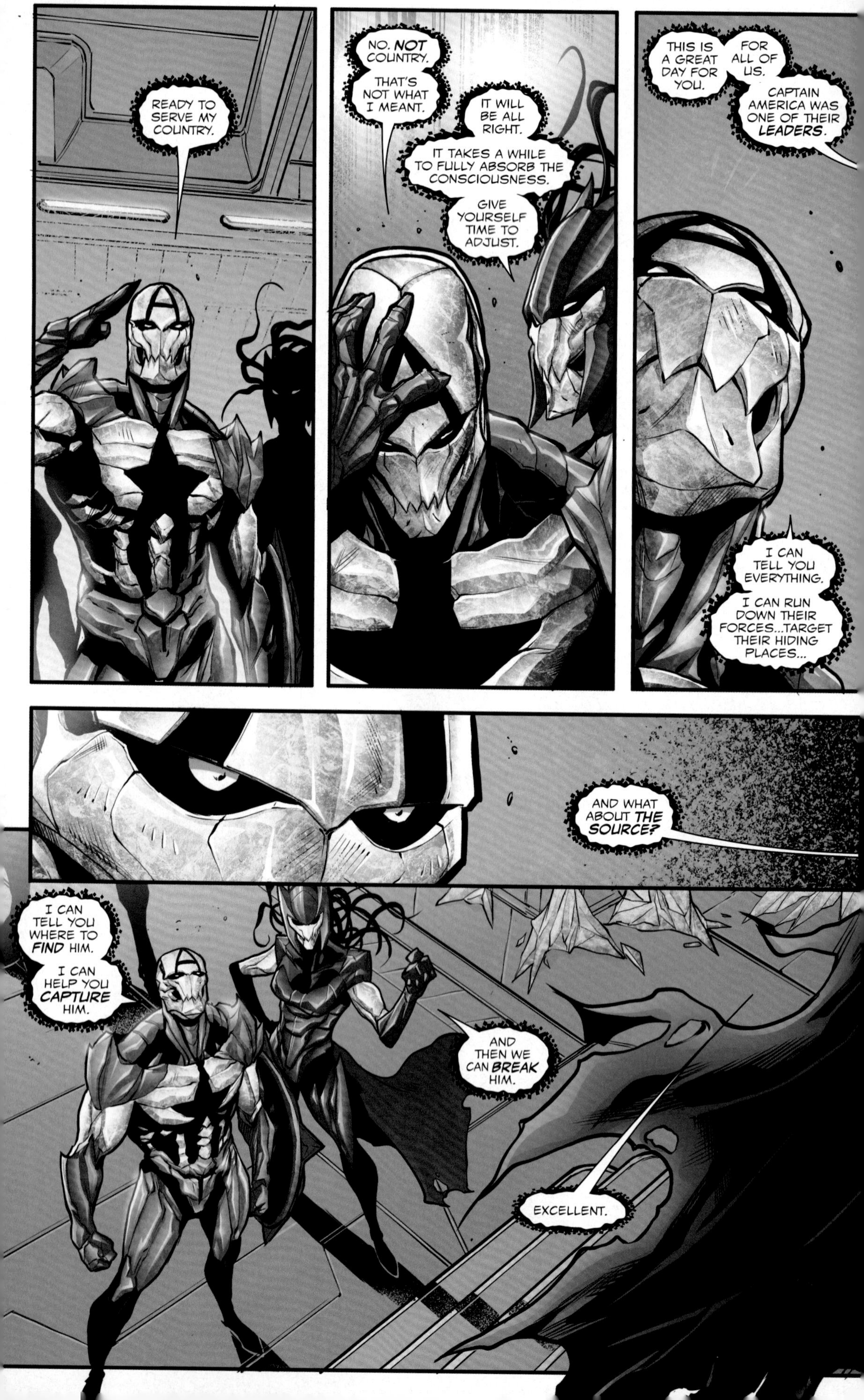
READY TO SERVE MY COUNTRY.
NO. NOT COUNTRY.
THAT'S NOT WHAT I MEANT.
IT WILL BE ALL RIGHT.
IT TAKES A WHILE TO FULLY ABSORB THE CONSCIOUSNESS.
GIVE YOURSELF TIME TO ADJUST.
THIS IS A GREAT DAY FOR YOU.
FOR ALL OF US.
CAPTAIN AMERICA WAS ONE OF THEIR LEADERS.
I CAN TELL YOU EVERYTHING.
I CAN RUN DOWN THEIR FORCES...TARGET THEIR HIDING PLACES...
AND WHAT ABOUT THE SOURCE?
I CAN TELL YOU WHERE TO FIND HIM.
I CAN HELP YOU CAPTURE HIM.
AND THEN WE CAN BREAK HIM.
EXCELLENT.

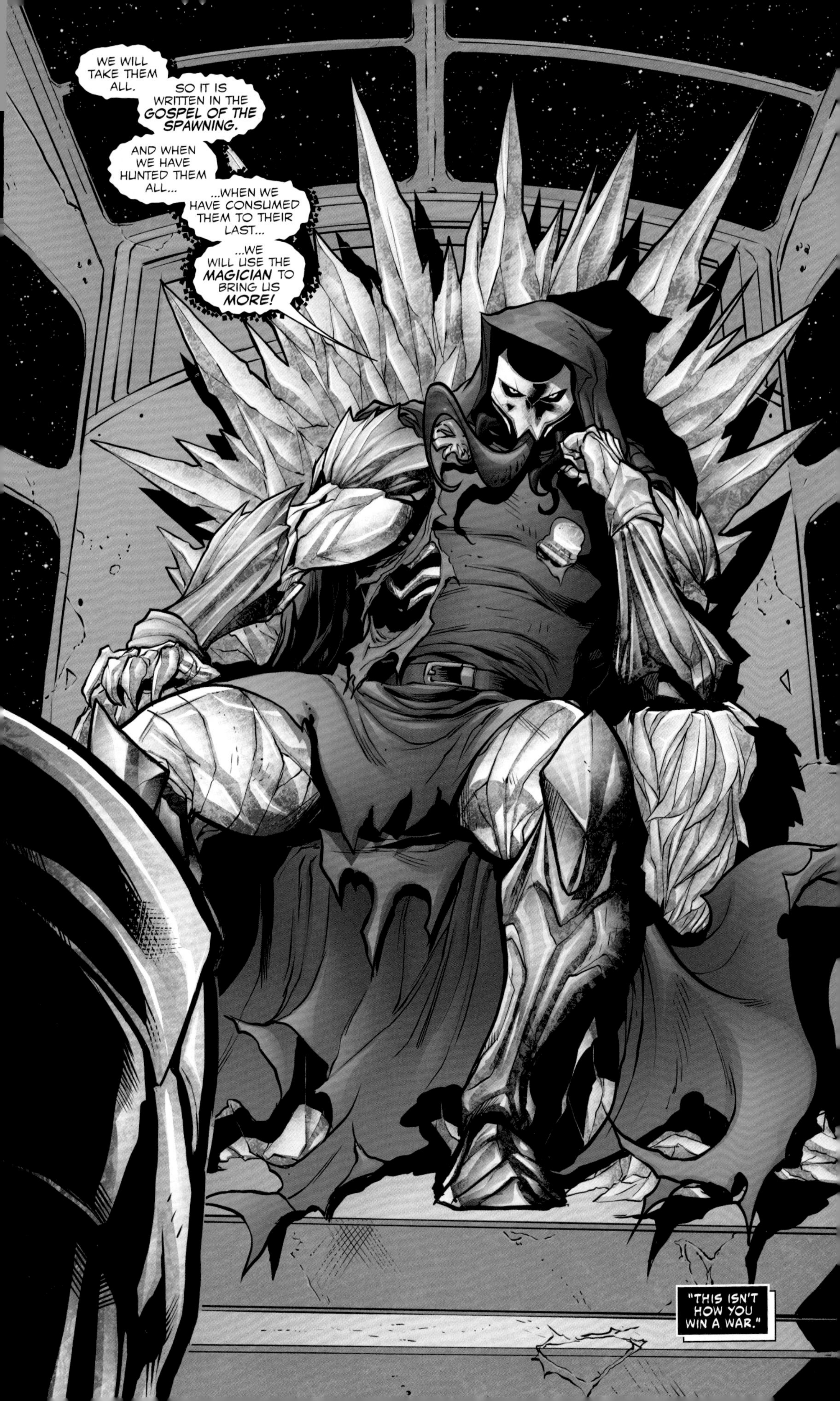

WE WILL TAKE THEM ALL.
SO IT IS WRITTEN IN THE GOSPEL OF THE SPAWNING.
AND WHEN WE HAVE HUNTED THEM ALL...
...WHEN WE HAVE CONSUMED THEM TO THEIR LAST...
...WE WILL USE THE MAGICIAN TO BRING US MORE!
"THIS ISN'T HOW YOU WIN A WAR."

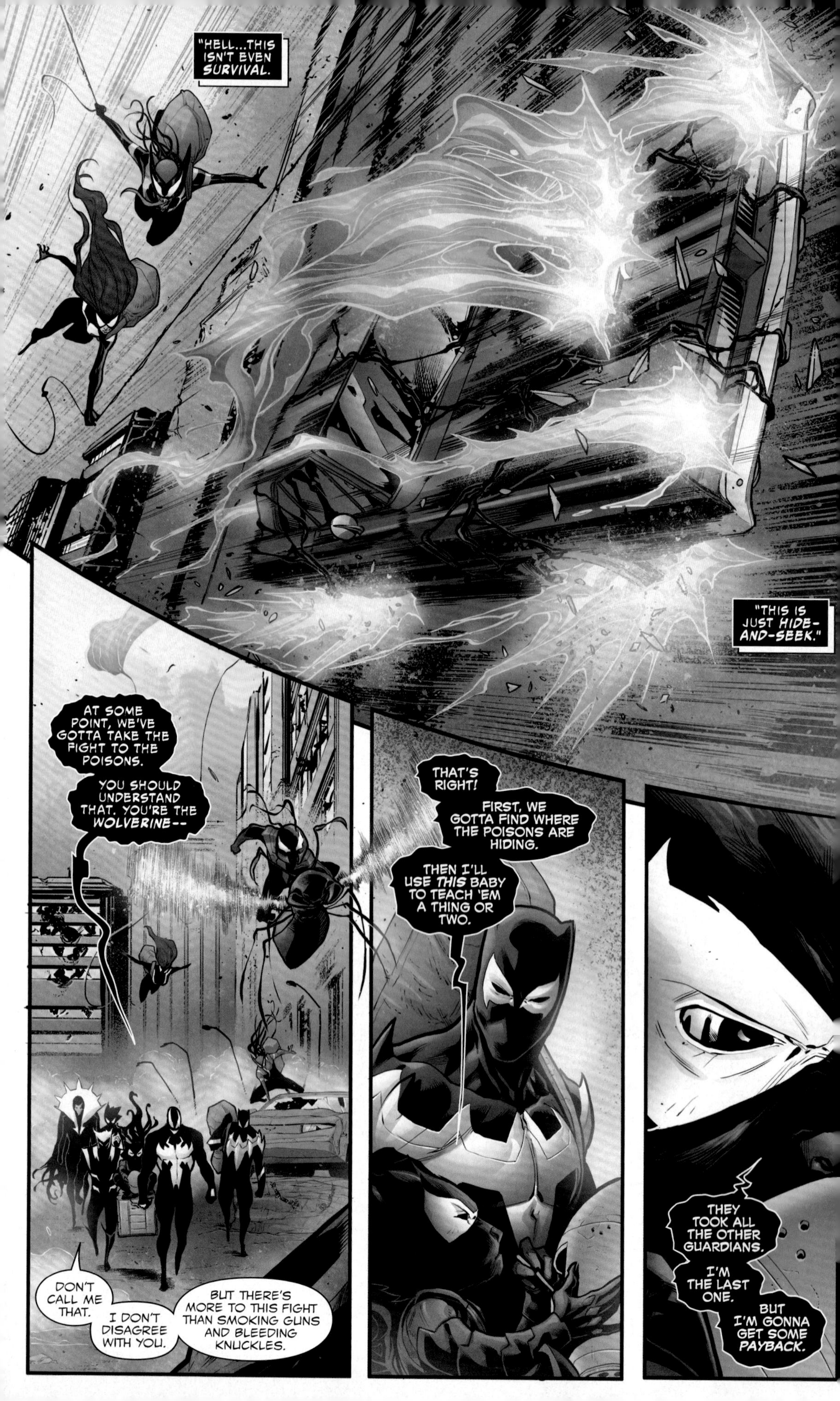
"HELL...THIS ISN'T EVEN SURVIVAL.
"THIS IS JUST HIDE-AND-SEEK."
AT SOME POINT, WE'VE GOTTA TAKE THE FIGHT TO THE POISONS.
YOU SHOULD UNDERSTAND THAT. YOU'RE THE WOLVERINE--
DON'T CALL ME THAT.
I DON'T DISAGREE WITH YOU.
BUT THERE'S MORE TO THIS FIGHT THAN SMOKING GUNS AND BLEEDING KNUCKLES.
THAT'S RIGHT!
FIRST, WE GOTTA FIND WHERE THE POISONS ARE HIDING.
THEN I'LL USE THIS BABY TO TEACH 'EM A THING OR TWO.
THEY TOOK ALL THE OTHER GUARDIANS.
I'M THE LAST ONE.
BUT I'M GONNA GET SOME PAYBACK.

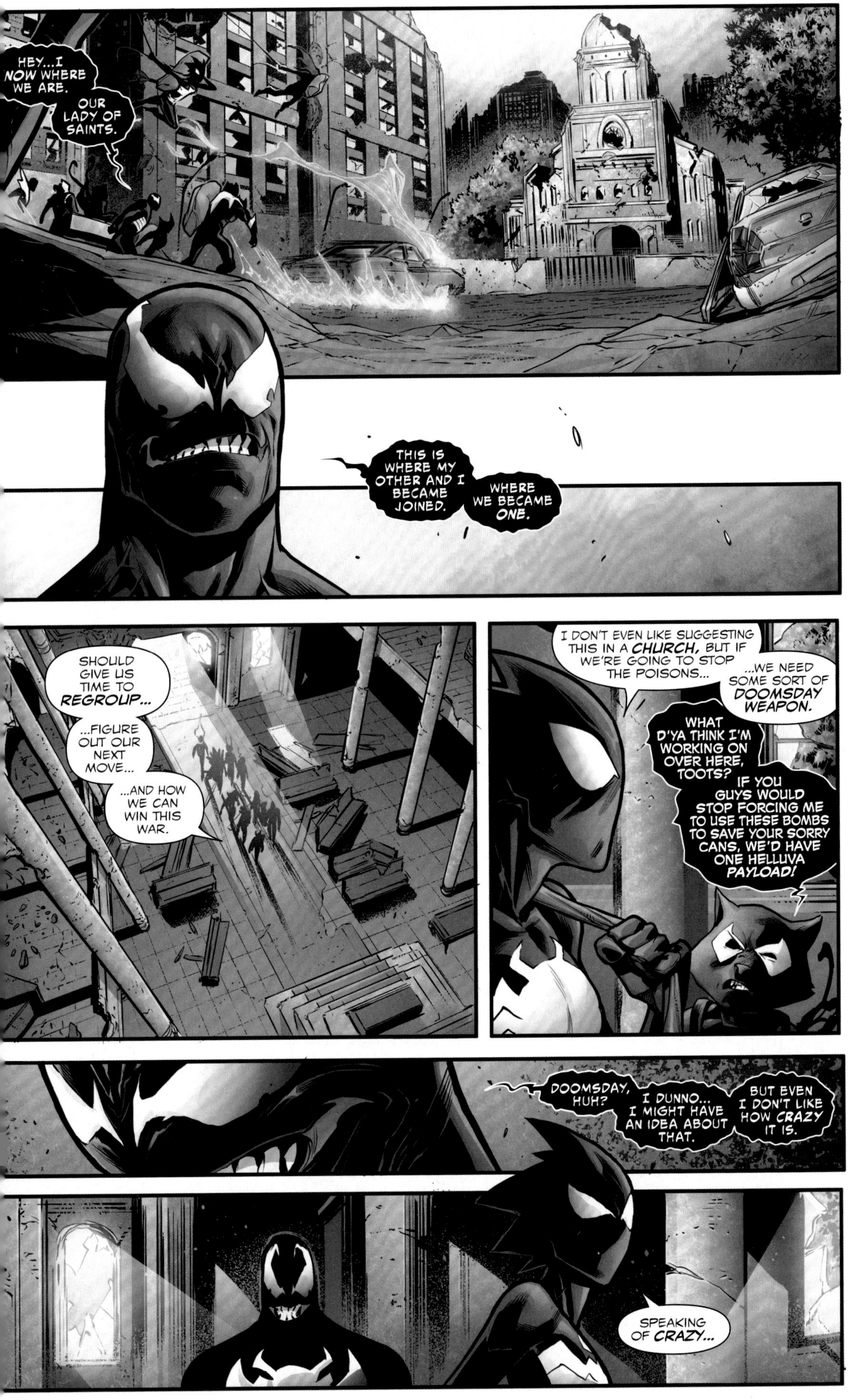
HEY...I NOW WHERE WE ARE.
OUR LADY OF SAINTS.
THIS IS WHERE MY OTHER AND I BECAME JOINED.
WHERE WE BECAME ONE.
SHOULD GIVE US TIME TO REGROUP...
...FIGURE OUT OUR NEXT MOVE...
...AND HOW WE CAN WIN THIS WAR.
I DON'T EVEN LIKE SUGGESTING THIS IN A CHURCH, BUT IF WE'RE GOING TO STOP THE POISONS...
...WE NEED SOME SORT OF DOOMSDAY WEAPON.
WHAT D'YA THINK I'M WORKING ON OVER HERE, TOOTS?
IF YOU GUYS WOULD STOP FORCING ME TO USE THESE BOMBS TO SAVE YOUR SORRY CANS, WE'D HAVE ONE HELLUVA PAYLOAD!
DOOMSDAY, HUH?
I DUNNO... I MIGHT HAVE AN IDEA ABOUT THAT.
BUT EVEN I DON'T LIKE HOW CRAZY IT IS.
SPEAKING OF CRAZY...

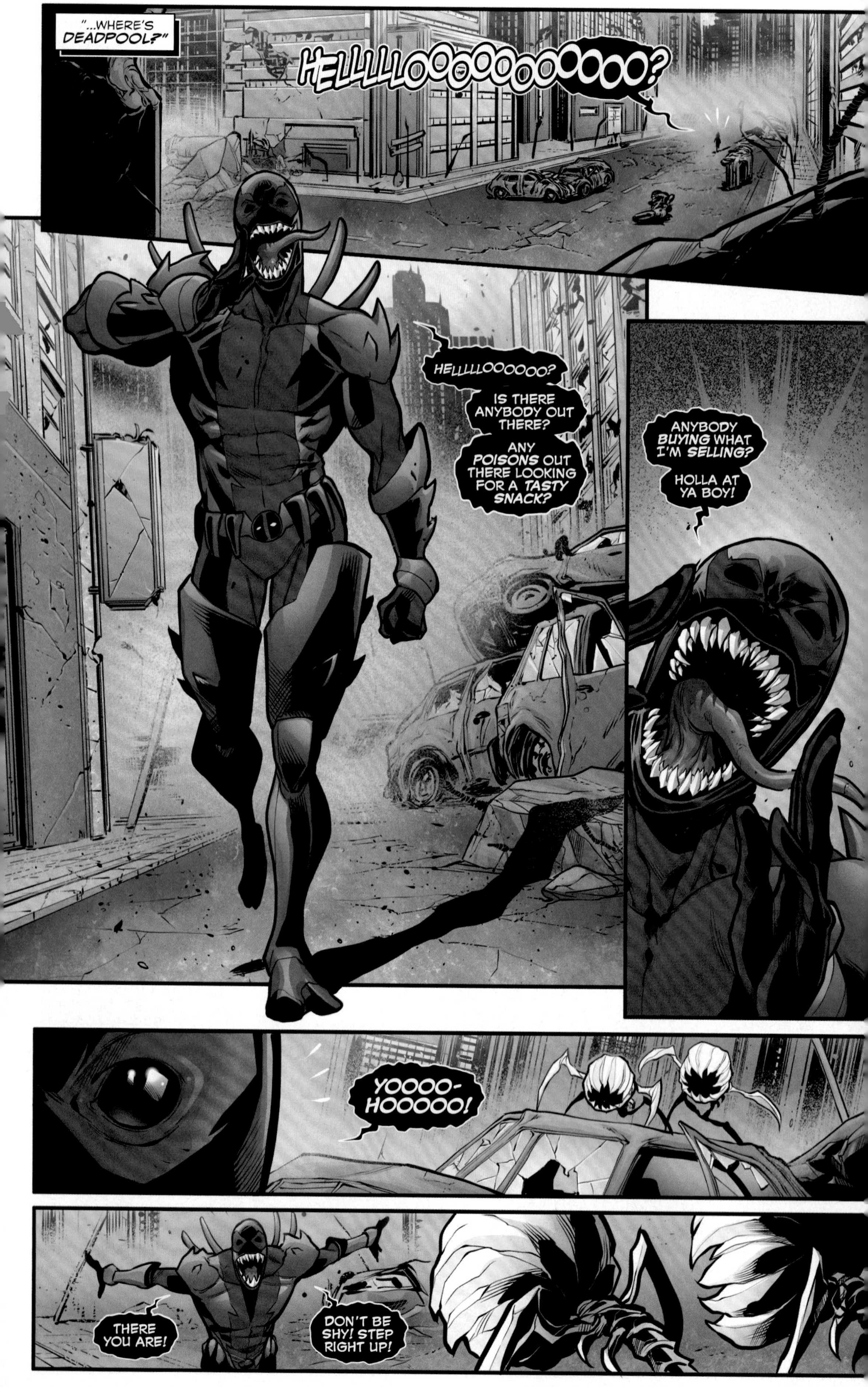
"...WHERE'S DEADPOOL?"
HELLLLLOOOOOOOOOOO?
HELLLLLOOOOOOO?
IS THERE ANYBODY OUT THERE?
ANY POISONS OUT THERE LOOKING FOR A TASTY SNACK?
ANYBODY BUYING WHAT I'M SELLING?
HOLLA AT YA BOY!
YOOOO-HOOOOO!
THERE YOU ARE!
DON'T BE SHY! STEP RIGHT UP!

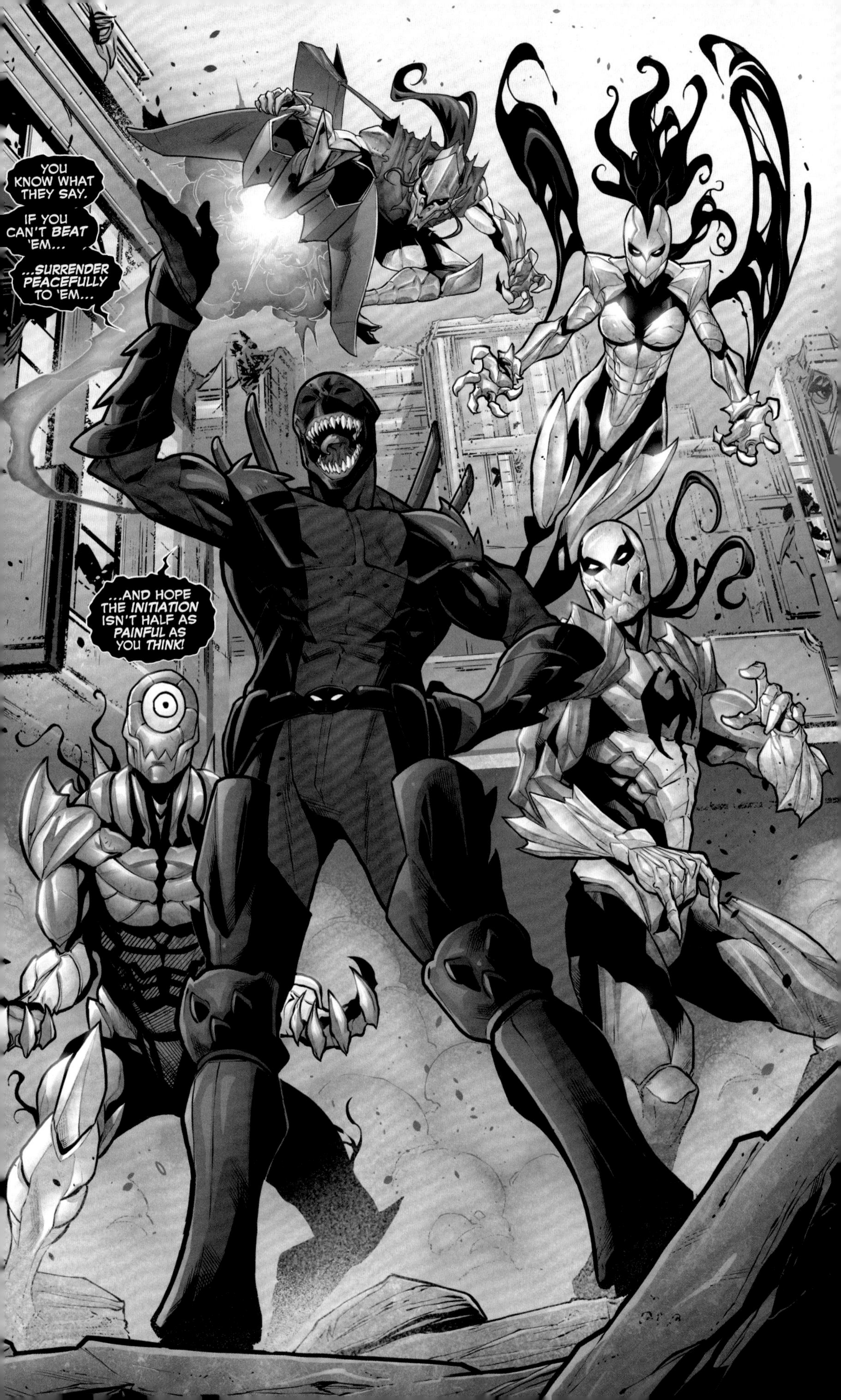

YOU KNOW WHAT THEY SAY.
IF YOU CAN'T BEAT 'EM...
...SURRENDER PEACEFULLY TO 'EM...
...AND HOPE THE INITIATION ISN'T HALF AS PAINFUL AS YOU THINK!

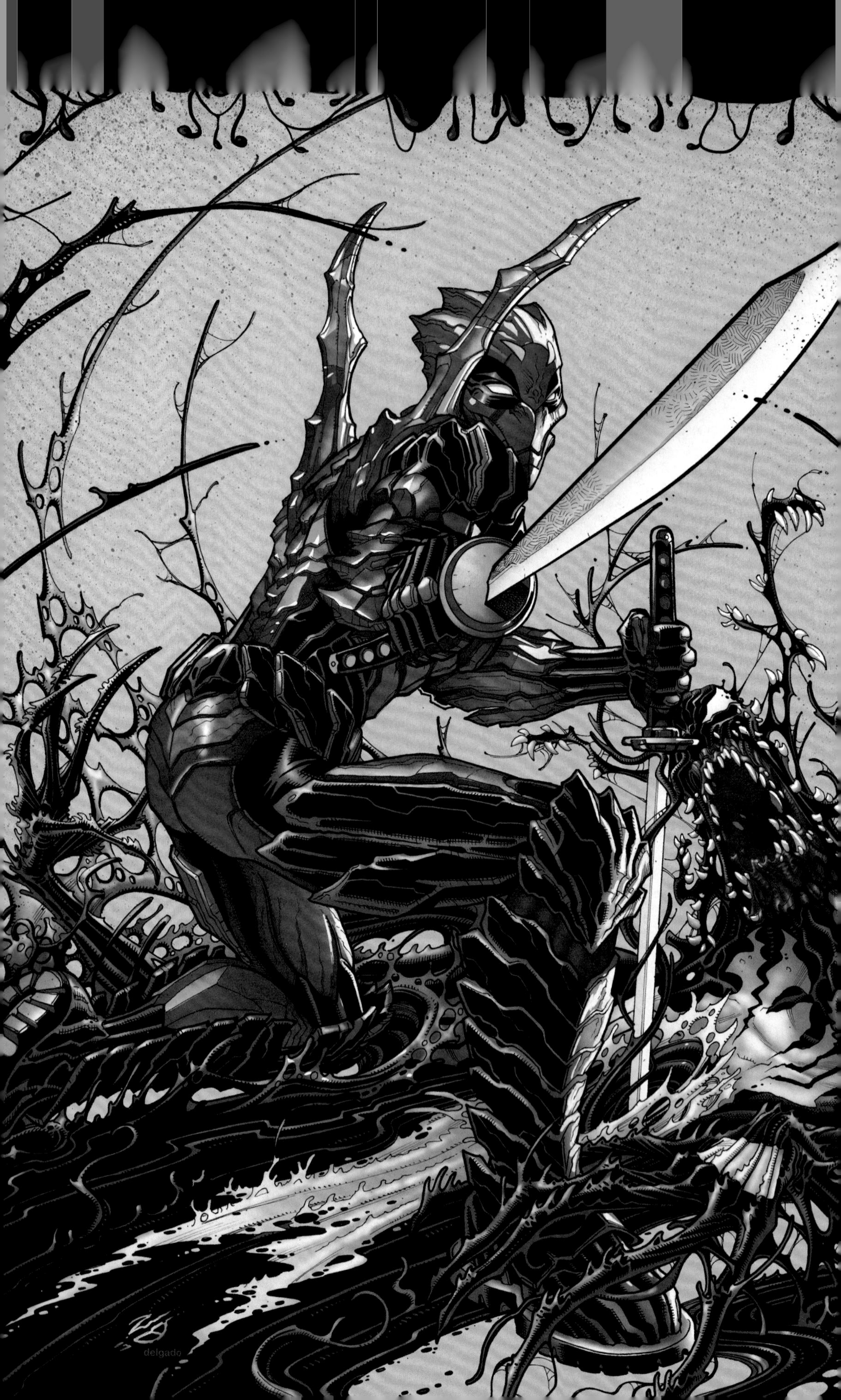
delgado

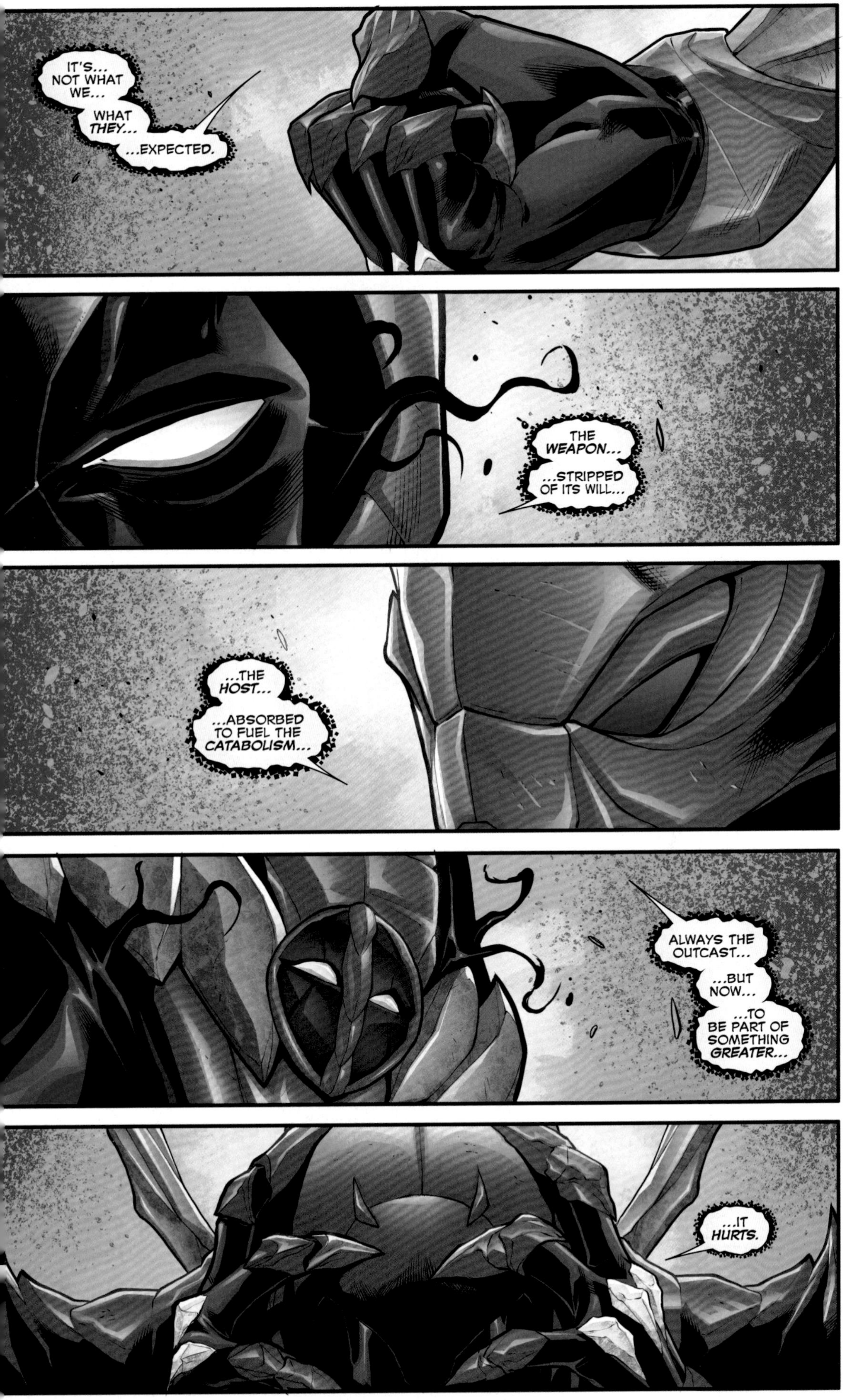
IT'S... NOT WHAT WE...
WHAT THEY...
...EXPECTED.
THE WEAPON...
...STRIPPED OF ITS WILL...
...THE HOST...
...ABSORBED TO FUEL THE CATABOLISM...
ALWAYS THE OUTCAST...
...BUT NOW...
...TO BE PART OF SOMETHING GREATER...
...IT HURTS.

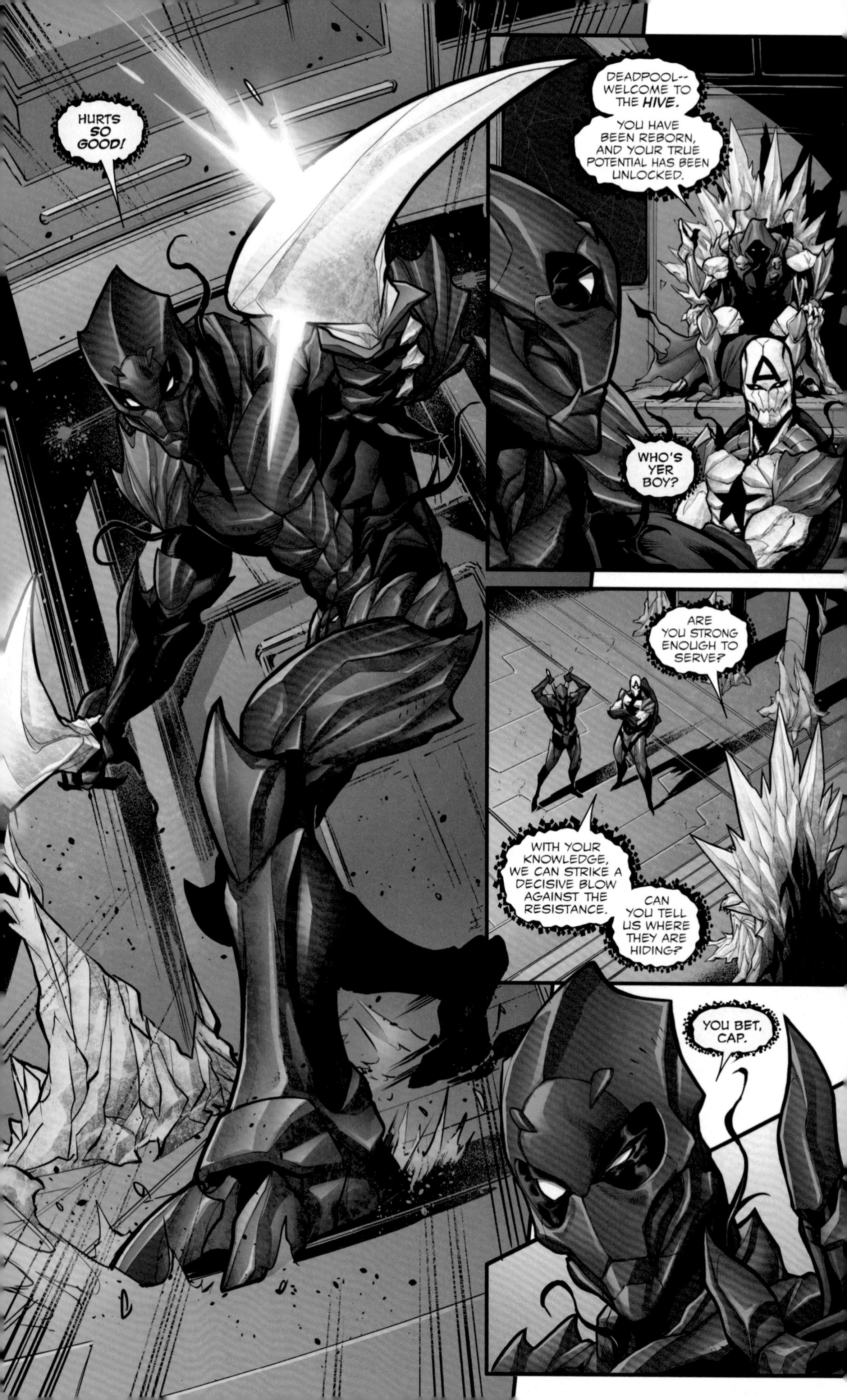
HURTS SO GOOD!
DEADPOOL-- WELCOME TO THE HIVE.
YOU HAVE BEEN REBORN, AND YOUR TRUE POTENTIAL HAS BEEN UNLOCKED.
WHO'S YER BOY?
ARE YOU STRONG ENOUGH TO SERVE?
WITH YOUR KNOWLEDGE, WE CAN STRIKE A DECISIVE BLOW AGAINST THE RESISTANCE.
CAN YOU TELL US WHERE THEY ARE HIDING?
YOU BET, CAP.

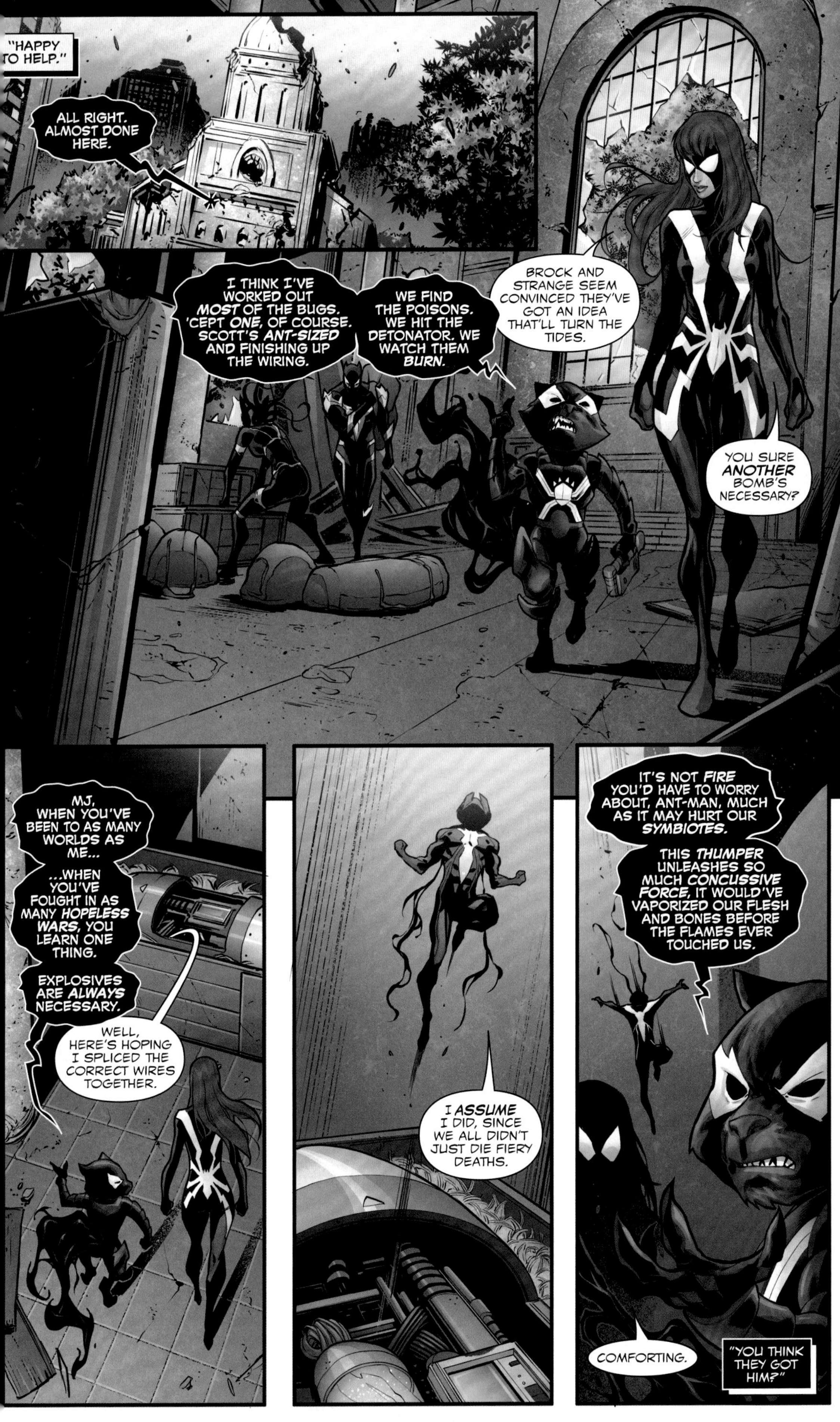

"HAPPY TO HELP."
ALL RIGHT. ALMOST DONE HERE.
I THINK I'VE WORKED OUT MOST OF THE BUGS. 'CEPT ONE, OF COURSE. SCOTT'S ANT-SIZED AND FINISHING UP THE WIRING.
WE FIND THE POISONS. WE HIT THE DETONATOR. WE WATCH THEM BURN.
BROCK AND STRANGE SEEM CONVINCED THEY'VE GOT AN IDEA THAT'LL TURN THE TIDES.
YOU SURE ANOTHER BOMB'S NECESSARY?
MJ, WHEN YOU'VE BEEN TO AS MANY WORLDS AS ME...
...WHEN YOU'VE FOUGHT IN AS MANY HOPELESS WARS, YOU LEARN ONE THING.
EXPLOSIVES ARE ALWAYS NECESSARY.
WELL, HERE'S HOPING I SPLICED THE CORRECT WIRES TOGETHER.
I ASSUME I DID, SINCE WE ALL DIDN'T JUST DIE FIERY DEATHS.
IT'S NOT FIRE YOU'D HAVE TO WORRY ABOUT, ANT-MAN, MUCH AS IT MAY HURT OUR SYMBIOTES.
THIS THUMPER UNLEASHES SO MUCH CONCUSSIVE FORCE, IT WOULD'VE VAPORIZED OUR FLESH AND BONES BEFORE THE FLAMES EVER TOUCHED US.
COMFORTING.
"YOU THINK THEY GOT HIM?"

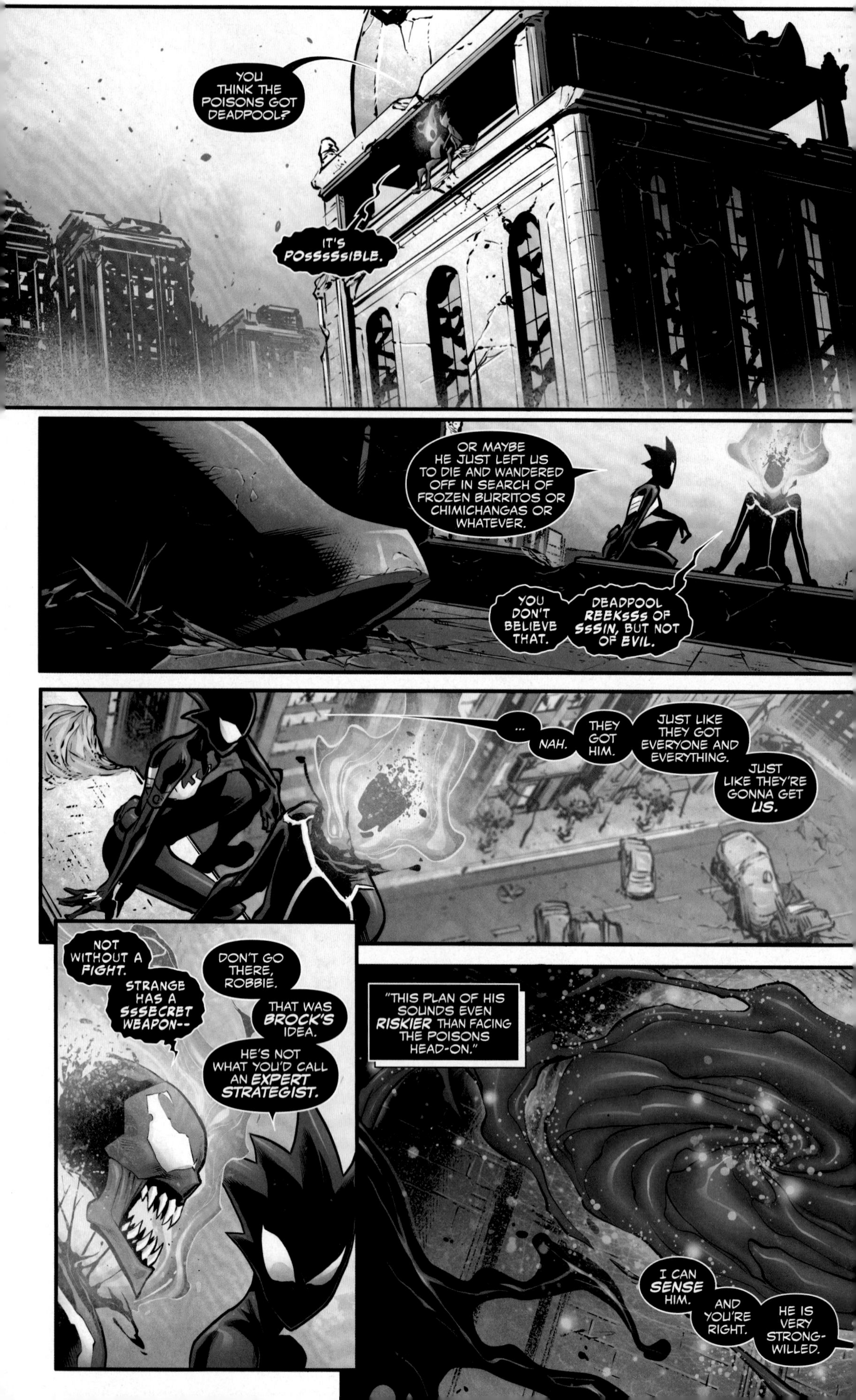
YOU THINK THE POISONS GOT DEADPOOL?
IT'S POSSSSSIBLE.
OR MAYBE HE JUST LEFT US TO DIE AND WANDERED OFF IN SEARCH OF FROZEN BURRITOS OR CHIMICHANGAS OR WHATEVER.
YOU DON'T BELIEVE THAT.
DEADPOOL REEKSSS OF SSSIN, BUT NOT OF EVIL.
...
NAH.
THEY GOT HIM.
JUST LIKE THEY GOT EVERYONE AND EVERYTHING.
JUST LIKE THEY'RE GONNA GET US.
NOT WITHOUT A FIGHT.
STRANGE HAS A SSSECRET WEAPON--
DON'T GO THERE, ROBBIE.
THAT WAS BROCK'S IDEA.
HE'S NOT WHAT YOU'D CALL AN EXPERT STRATEGIST.
"THIS PLAN OF HIS SOUNDS EVEN RISKIER THAN FACING THE POISONS HEAD-ON."
I CAN SENSE HIM.
AND YOU'RE RIGHT.
HE IS VERY STRONG-WILLED.

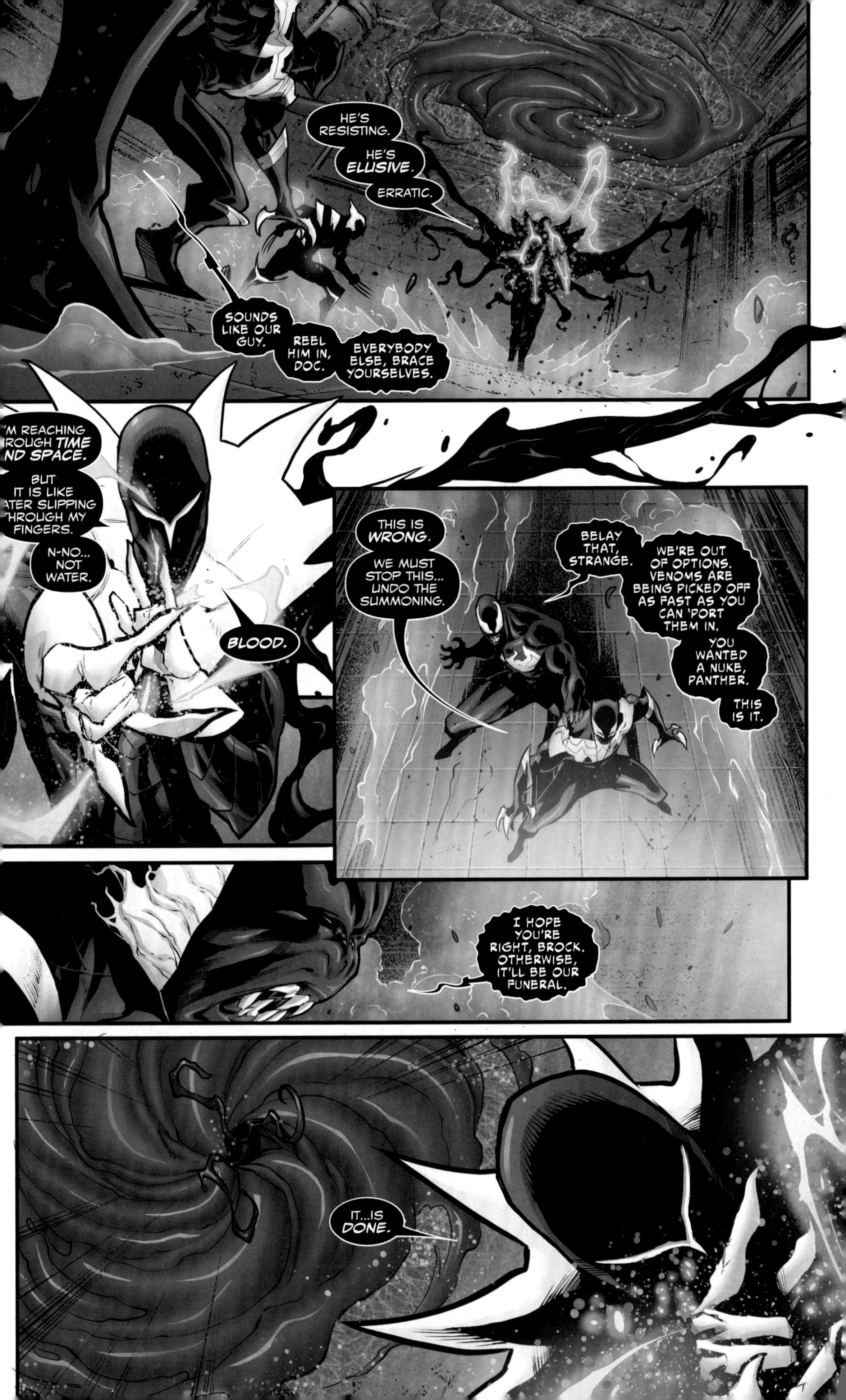
HE'S RESISTING.
HE'S ELUSIVE.
ERRATIC.
SOUNDS LIKE OUR GUY.
REEL HIM IN, DOC.
EVERYBODY ELSE, BRACE YOURSELVES.
'M REACHING ROUGH TIME ND SPACE.
BUT IT IS LIKE ATER SLIPPING HROUGH MY FINGERS.
N-NO... NOT WATER.
BLOOD.
THIS IS WRONG.
WE MUST STOP THIS... UNDO THE SUMMONING.
BELAY THAT, STRANGE.
WE'RE OUT OF OPTIONS. VENOMS ARE BEING PICKED OFF AS FAST AS YOU CAN 'PORT THEM IN.
YOU WANTED A NUKE, PANTHER.
THIS IS IT.
I HOPE YOU'RE RIGHT, BROCK. OTHERWISE, IT'LL BE OUR FUNERAL.
IT...IS DONE.

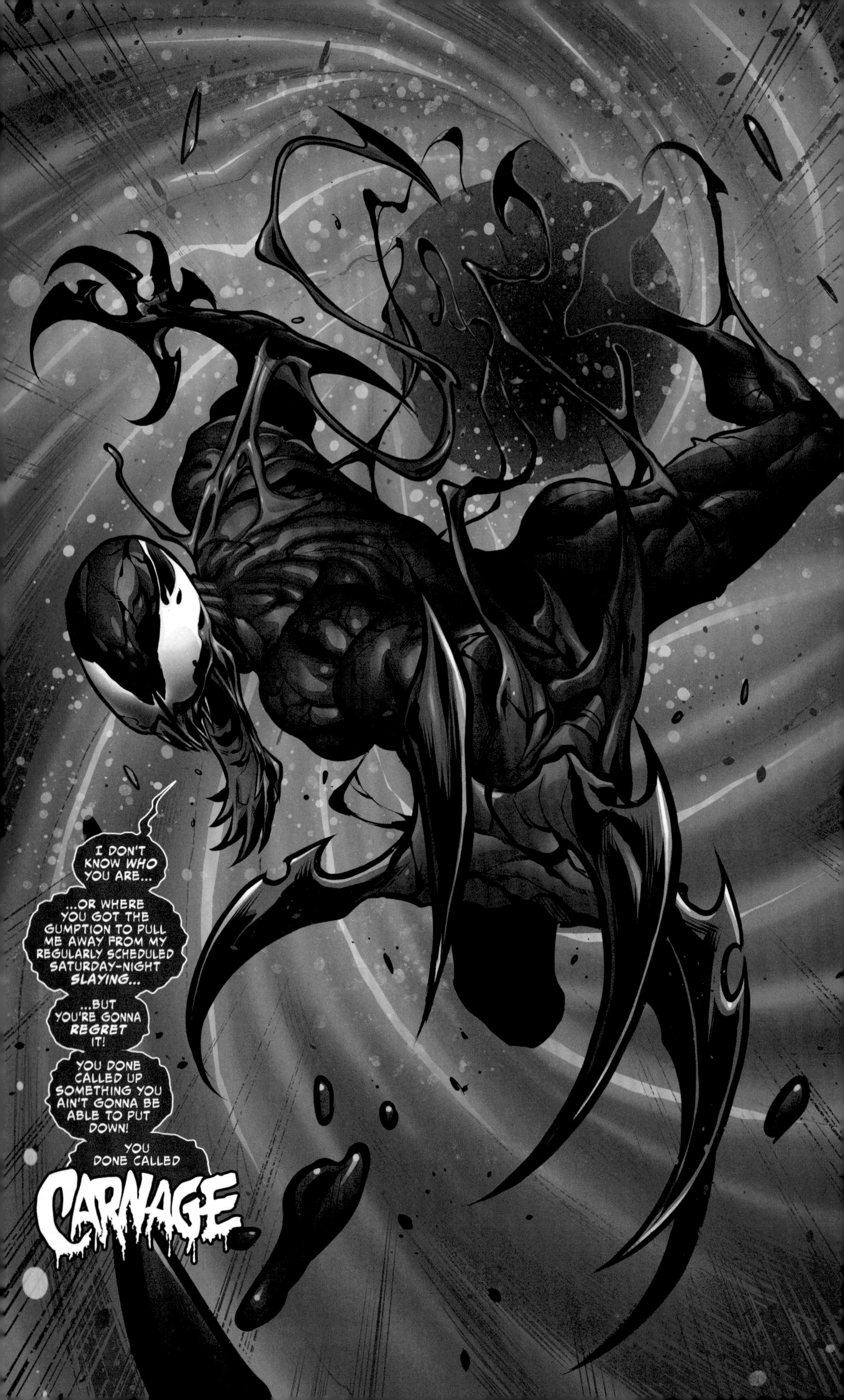
I DON'T KNOW WHO YOU ARE...
...OR WHERE YOU GOT THE GUMPTION TO PULL ME AWAY FROM MY REGULARLY SCHEDULED SATURDAY-NIGHT SLAYING...
...BUT YOU'RE GONNA REGRET IT!
YOU DONE CALLED UP SOMETHING YOU AIN'T GONNA BE ABLE TO PUT DOWN!
YOU DONE CALLED
CARNAGE

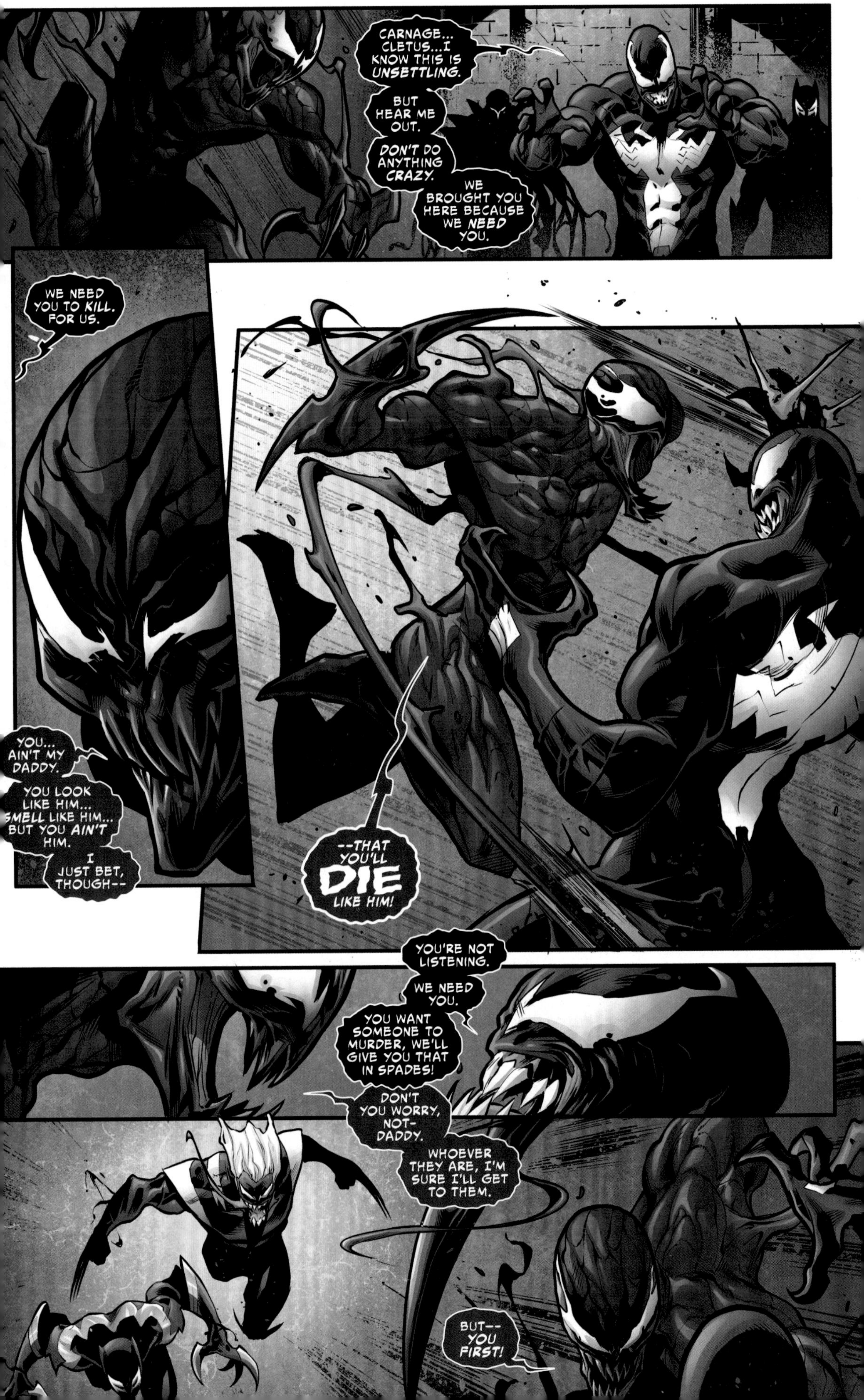
CARNAGE... CLETUS...I KNOW THIS IS UNSETTLING.
BUT HEAR ME OUT.
DON'T DO ANYTHING CRAZY.
WE BROUGHT YOU HERE BECAUSE WE NEED YOU.
WE NEED YOU TO KILL. FOR US.
YOU... AIN'T MY DADDY.
YOU LOOK LIKE HIM... SMELL LIKE HIM... BUT YOU AIN'T HIM.
I JUST BET, THOUGH--
--THAT YOU'LL DIE LIKE HIM!
YOU'RE NOT LISTENING.
WE NEED YOU.
YOU WANT SOMEONE TO MURDER, WE'LL GIVE YOU THAT IN SPADES!
DON'T YOU WORRY, NOT-DADDY.
WHOEVER THEY ARE, I'M SURE I'LL GET TO THEM.
BUT-- YOU FIRST!

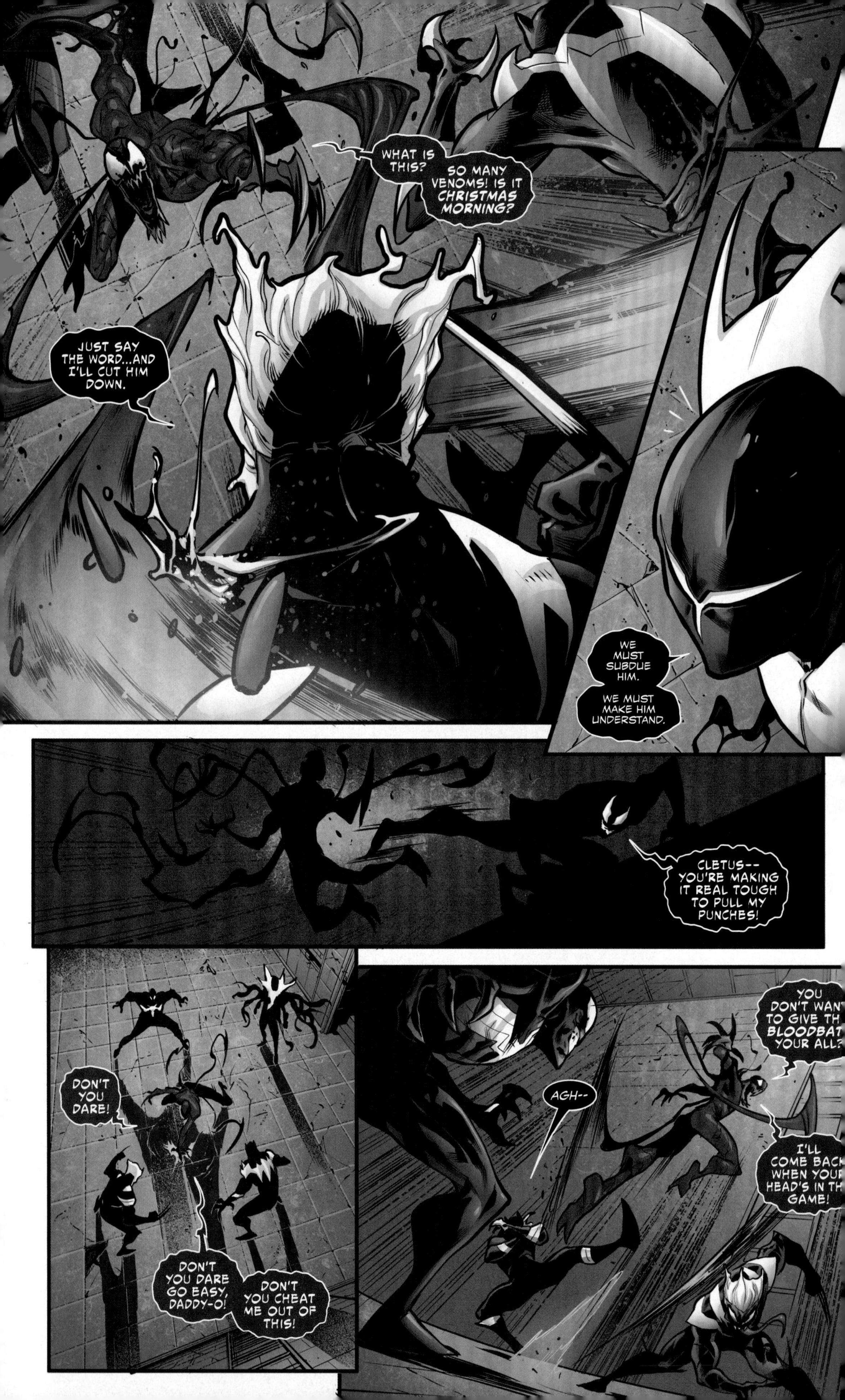
WHAT IS THIS?
SO MANY VENOMS! IS IT CHRISTMAS MORNING?
JUST SAY THE WORD...AND I'LL CUT HIM DOWN.
WE MUST SUBDUE HIM.
WE MUST MAKE HIM UNDERSTAND.
CLETUS-- YOU'RE MAKING IT REAL TOUGH TO PULL MY PUNCHES!
DON'T YOU DARE!
DON'T YOU DARE GO EASY, DADDY-O!
DON'T YOU CHEAT ME OUT OF THIS!
YOU DON'T WAN TO GIVE TH BLOODBAT YOUR ALL?
AGH--
I'LL COME BACK WHEN YOUR HEAD'S IN TH GAME!

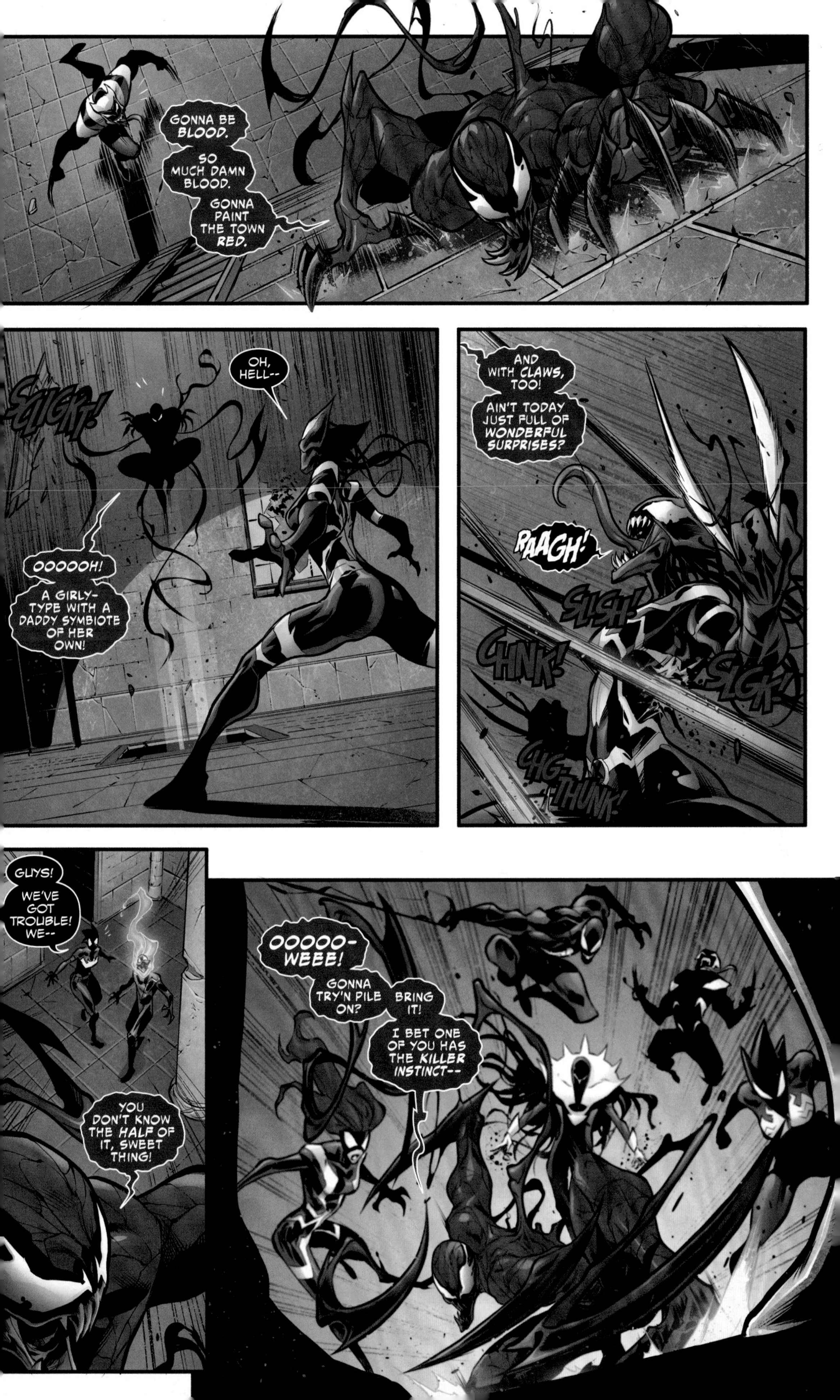
GONNA BE BLOOD.
SO MUCH DAMN BLOOD.
GONNA PAINT THE TOWN RED.
SCLICK!
OH, HELL--
OOOOOH!
A GIRLY-TYPE WITH A DADDY SYMBIOTE OF HER OWN!
AND WITH CLAWS, TOO!
AIN'T TODAY JUST FULL OF WONDERFUL SURPRISES?
RAAGH!
SLISH!
CHNK!
SLICK!
CHG-THUNK!
GUYS!
WE'VE GOT TROUBLE! WE--
YOU DON'T KNOW THE HALF OF IT, SWEET THING!
OOOOO-WEEE!
GONNA TRY'N PILE ON?
BRING IT!
I BET ONE OF YOU HAS THE KILLER INSTINCT--

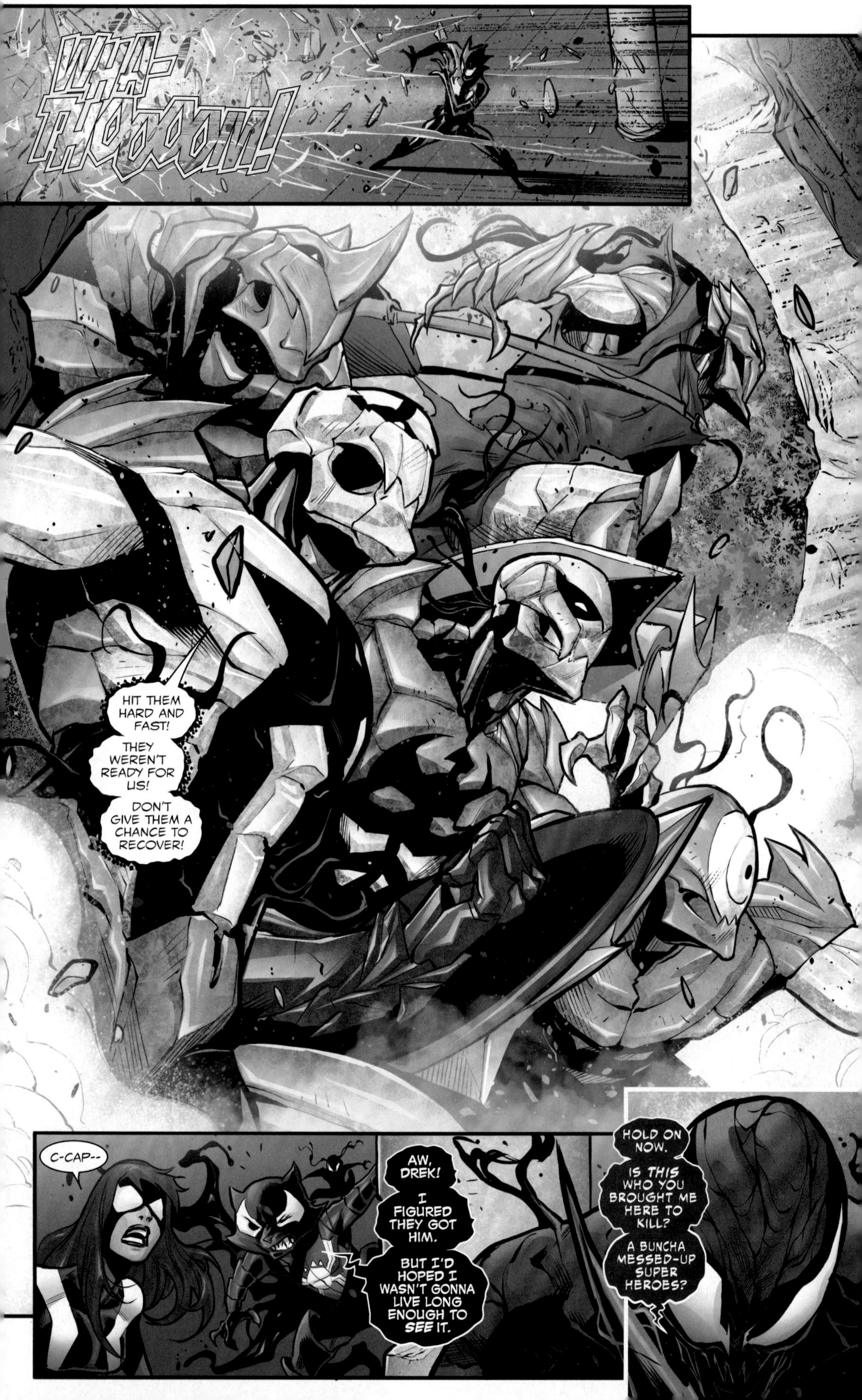

WHA-THOOOM!
HIT THEM HARD AND FAST!
THEY WEREN'T READY FOR US!
DON'T GIVE THEM A CHANCE TO RECOVER!
C-CAP--
AW, DREK!
I FIGURED THEY GOT HIM.
BUT I'D HOPED I WASN'T GONNA LIVE LONG ENOUGH TO SEE IT.
HOLD ON NOW.
IS THIS WHO YOU BROUGHT ME HERE TO KILL?
A BUNCHA MESSED-UP SUPER HEROES?

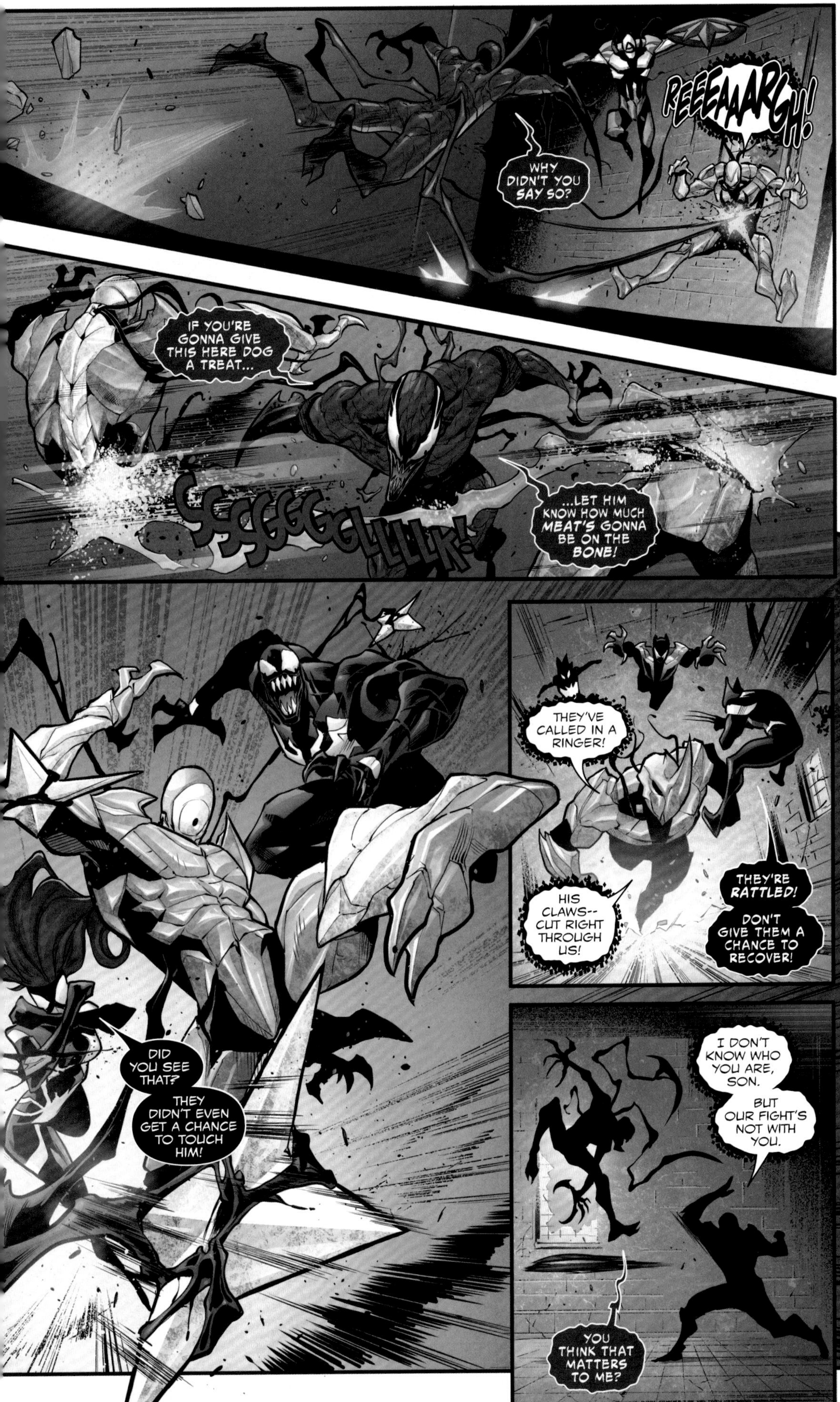

WHY DIDN'T YOU SAY SO?
REEEAAARGH!
IF YOU'RE GONNA GIVE THIS HERE DOG A TREAT...
SSSGGGGLLLLLK!
...LET HIM KNOW HOW MUCH MEAT'S GONNA BE ON THE BONE!
DID YOU SEE THAT?
THEY DIDN'T EVEN GET A CHANCE TO TOUCH HIM!
THEY'VE CALLED IN A RINGER!
HIS CLAWS-- CUT RIGHT THROUGH US!
THEY'RE RATTLED!
DON'T GIVE THEM A CHANCE TO RECOVER!
I DON'T KNOW WHO YOU ARE, SON.
BUT OUR FIGHT'S NOT WITH YOU.
YOU THINK THAT MATTERS TO ME?

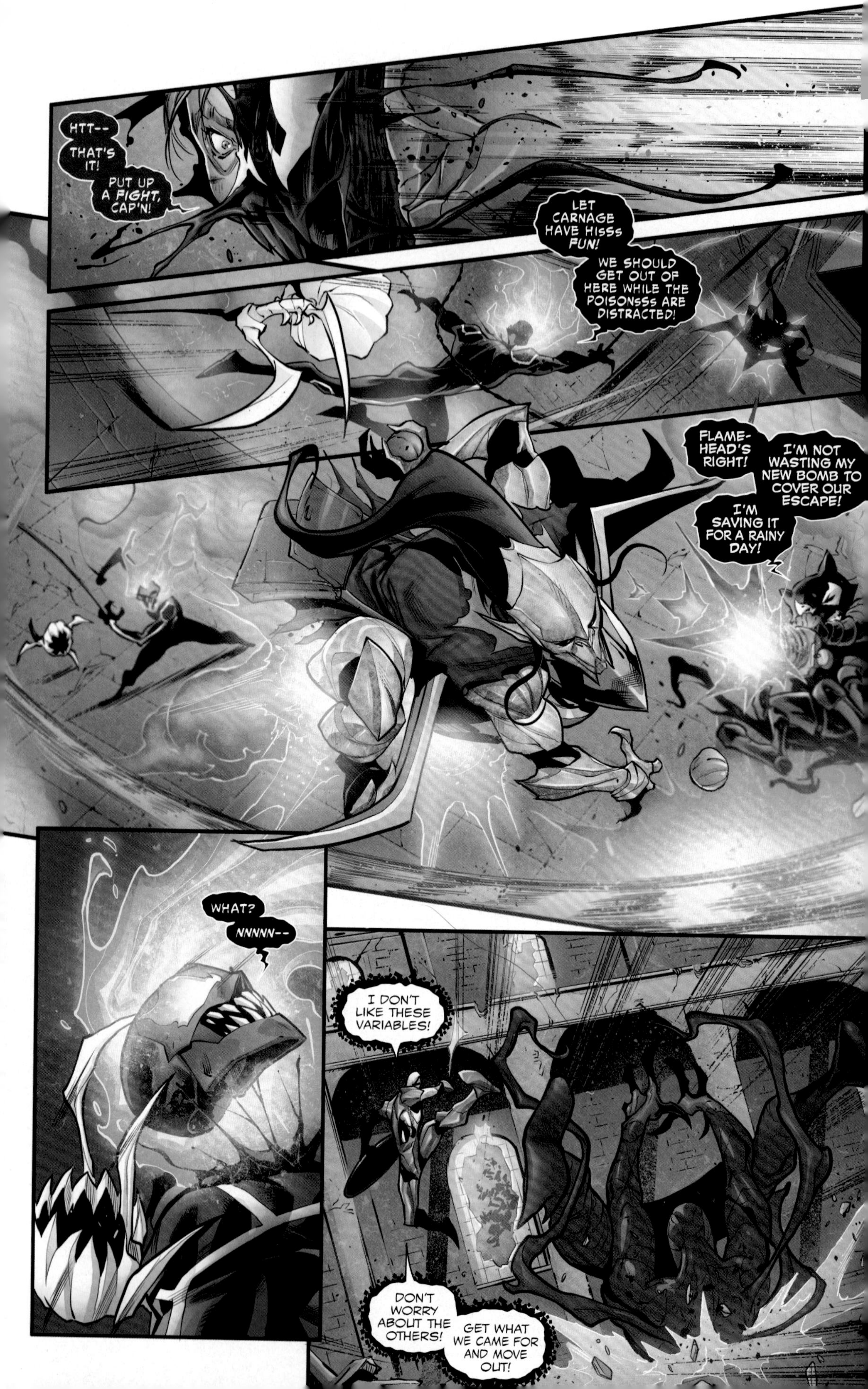
HTT--
THAT'S IT!
PUT UP A FIGHT, CAP'N!
LET CARNAGE HAVE HISSS FUN!
WE SHOULD GET OUT OF HERE WHILE THE POISONSSS ARE DISTRACTED!
FLAME-HEAD'S RIGHT!
I'M NOT WASTING MY NEW BOMB TO COVER OUR ESCAPE!
I'M SAVING IT FOR A RAINY DAY!
WHAT?
NNNNN--
I DON'T LIKE THESE VARIABLES!
DON'T WORRY ABOUT THE OTHERS!
GET WHAT WE CAME FOR AND MOVE OUT!

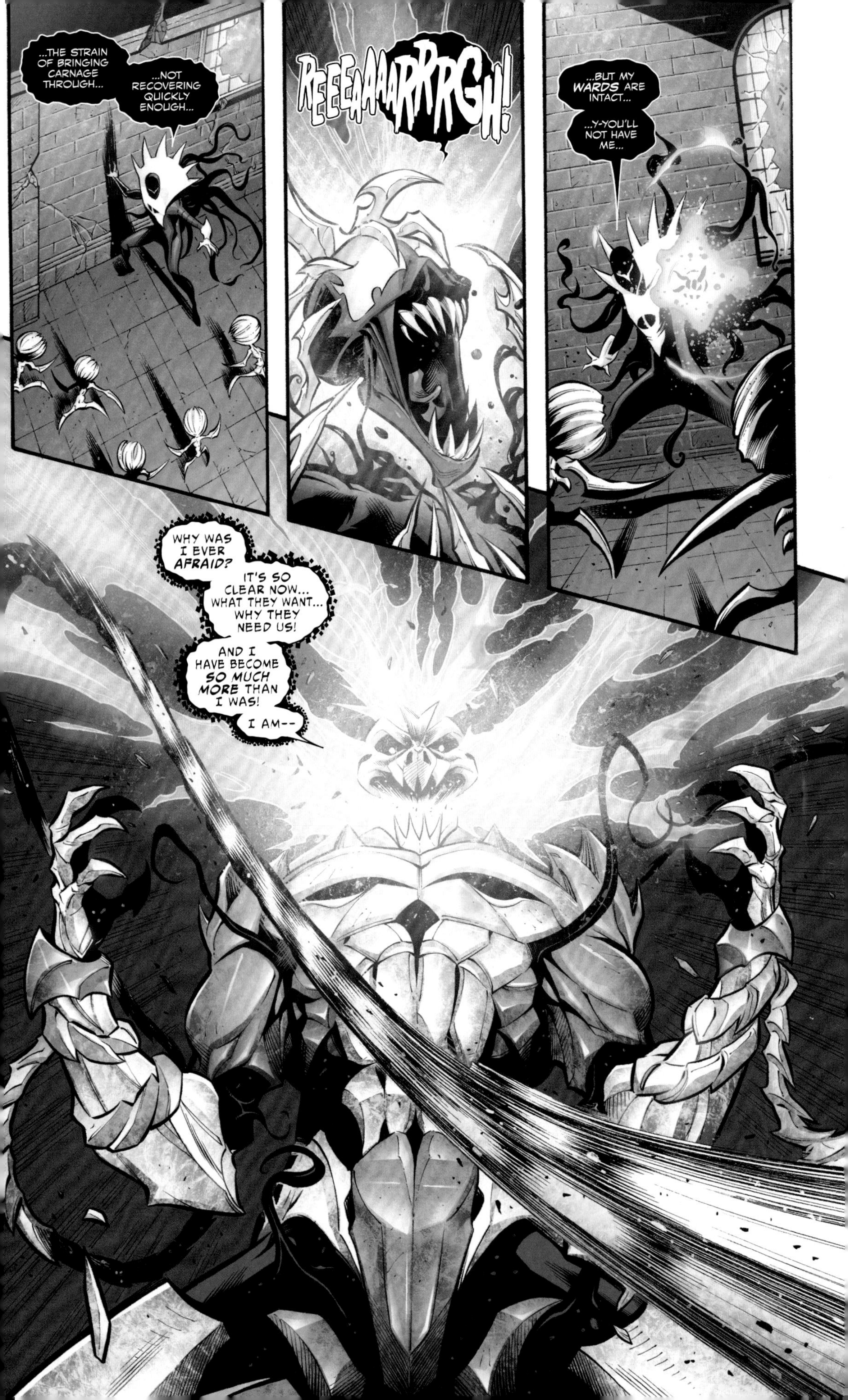
...THE STRAIN OF BRINGING CARNAGE THROUGH...
...NOT RECOVERING QUICKLY ENOUGH...
REEEAAAARRRGH!
...BUT MY WARDS ARE INTACT...
...Y-YOU'LL NOT HAVE ME...
WHY WAS I EVER AFRAID?
IT'S SO CLEAR NOW... WHAT THEY WANT... WHY THEY NEED US!
AND I HAVE BECOME SO MUCH MORE THAN I WAS!
I AM--

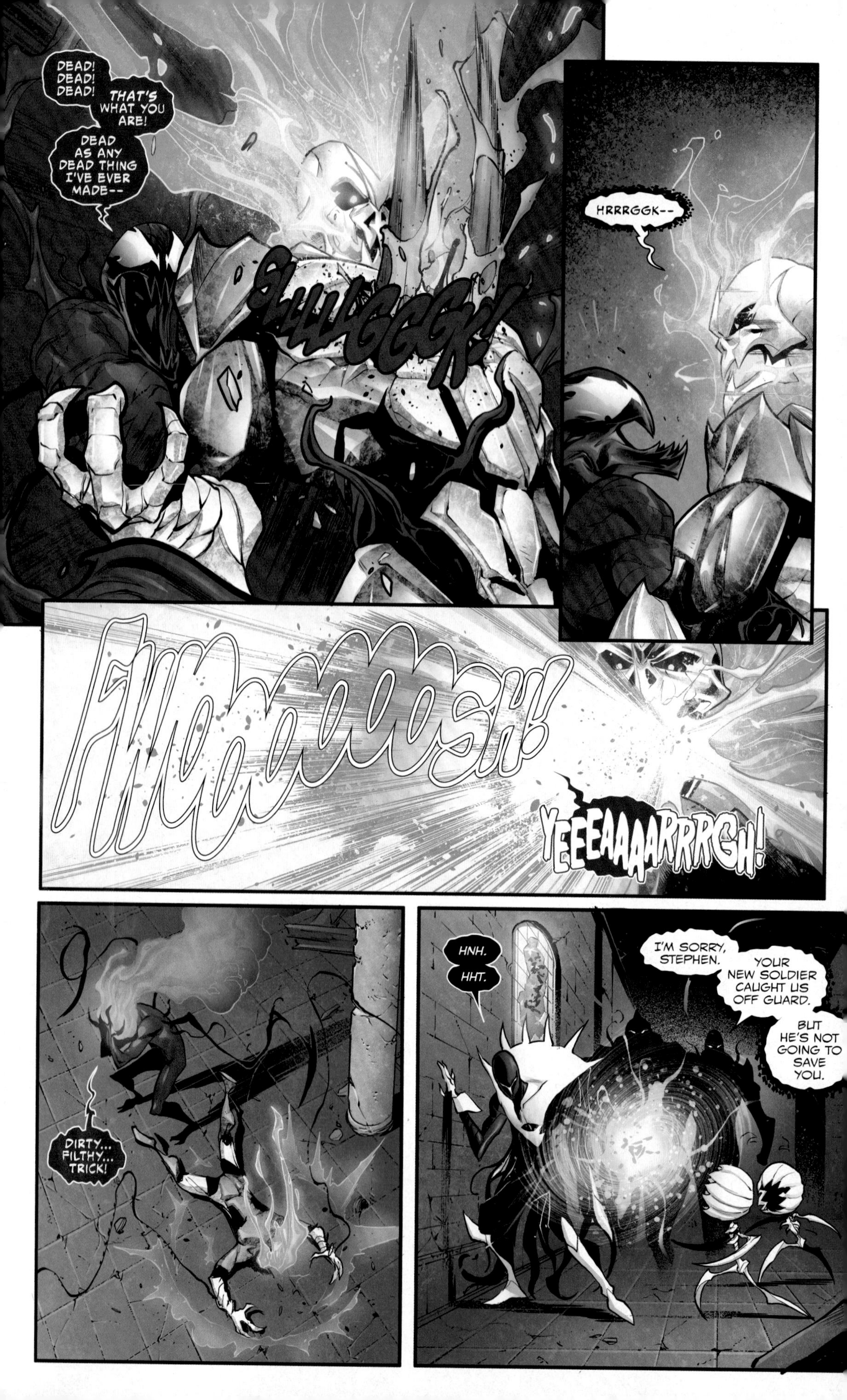
DEAD! DEAD! DEAD!
THAT'S WHAT YOU ARE!
DEAD AS ANY DEAD THING I'VE EVER MADE--
SHLUUGGGK!
HRRRGGK--
FWOOOOOSH!
YEEEAAAARRRGH!
DIRTY... FILTHY... TRICK!
HNH.
HHT.
I'M SORRY, STEPHEN.
YOUR NEW SOLDIER CAUGHT US OFF GUARD.
BUT HE'S NOT GOING TO SAVE YOU.

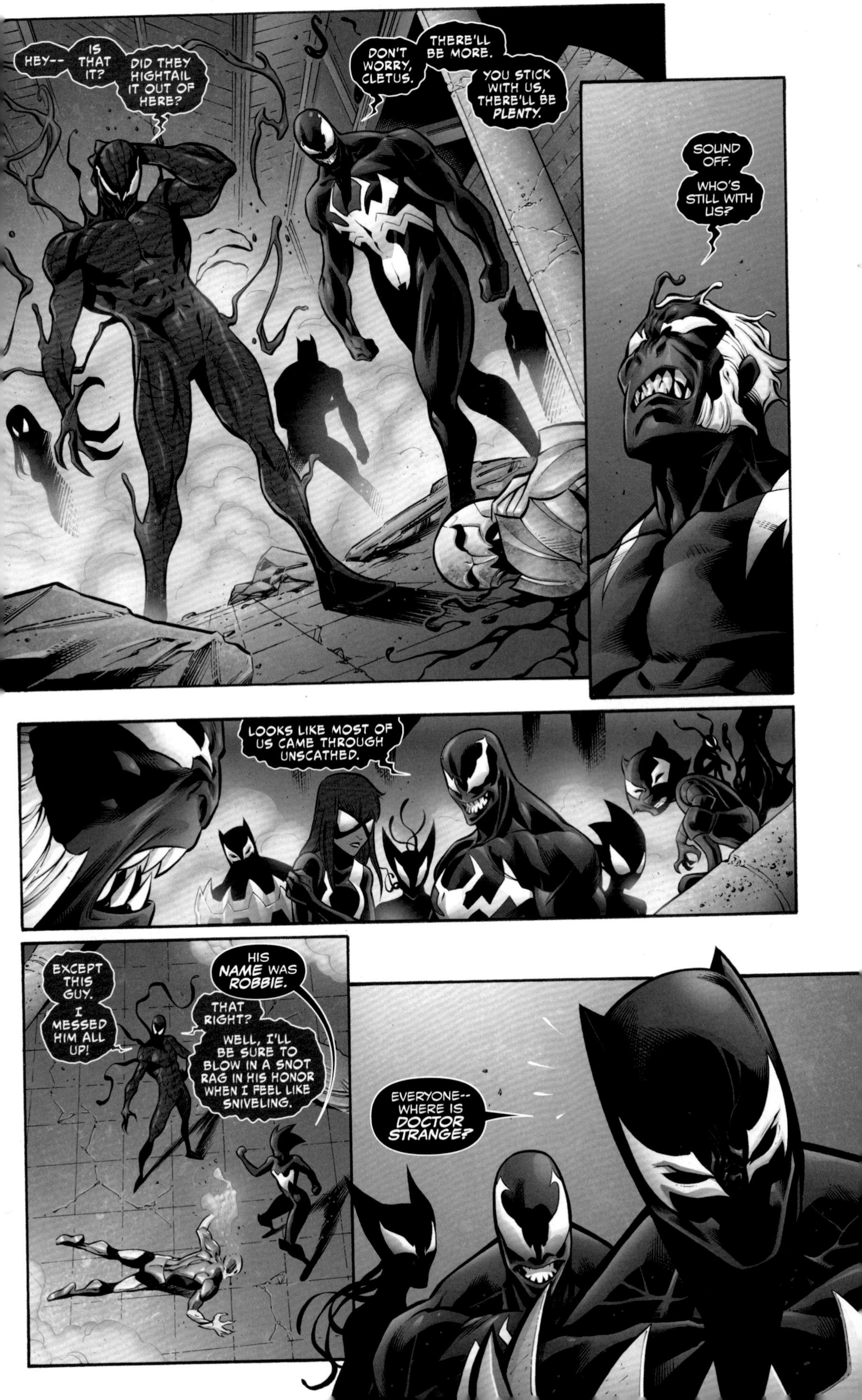
HEY--
IS THAT IT?
DID THEY HIGHTAIL IT OUT OF HERE?
DON'T WORRY, CLETUS.
THERE'LL BE MORE.
YOU STICK WITH US, THERE'LL BE PLENTY.
SOUND OFF.
WHO'S STILL WITH US?
LOOKS LIKE MOST OF US CAME THROUGH UNSCATHED.
EXCEPT THIS GUY.
I MESSED HIM ALL UP!
HIS NAME WAS ROBBIE.
THAT RIGHT?
WELL, I'LL BE SURE TO BLOW IN A SNOT RAG IN HIS HONOR WHEN I FEEL LIKE SNIVELING.
EVERYONE-- WHERE IS DOCTOR STRANGE?

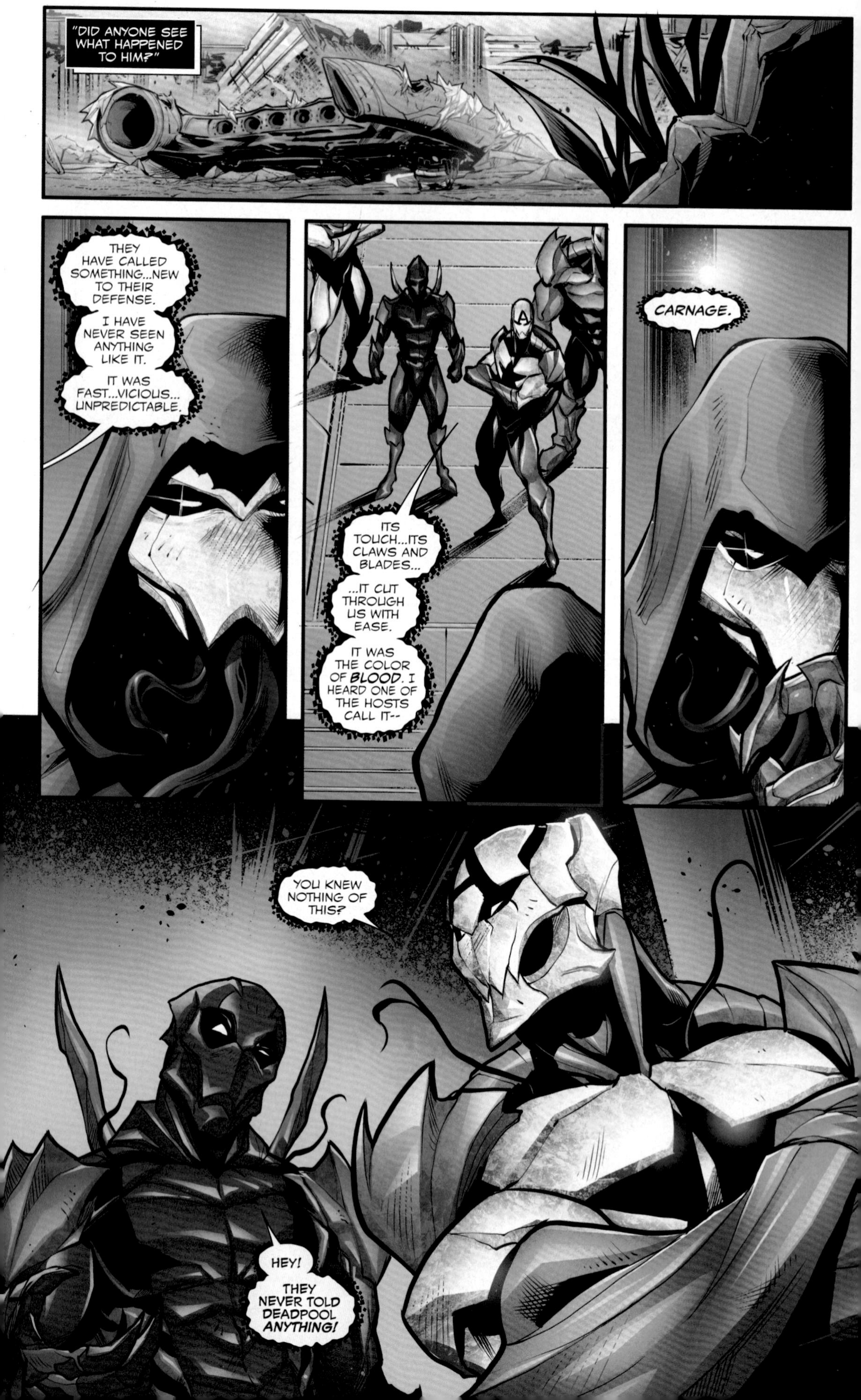
"DID ANYONE SEE WHAT HAPPENED TO HIM?"
THEY HAVE CALLED SOMETHING...NEW TO THEIR DEFENSE.
I HAVE NEVER SEEN ANYTHING LIKE IT.
IT WAS FAST...VICIOUS... UNPREDICTABLE.
ITS TOUCH...ITS CLAWS AND BLADES...
...IT CUT THROUGH US WITH EASE.
IT WAS THE COLOR OF BLOOD. I HEARD ONE OF THE HOSTS CALL IT--
CARNAGE.
YOU KNEW NOTHING OF THIS?
HEY!
THEY NEVER TOLD DEADPOOL ANYTHING!

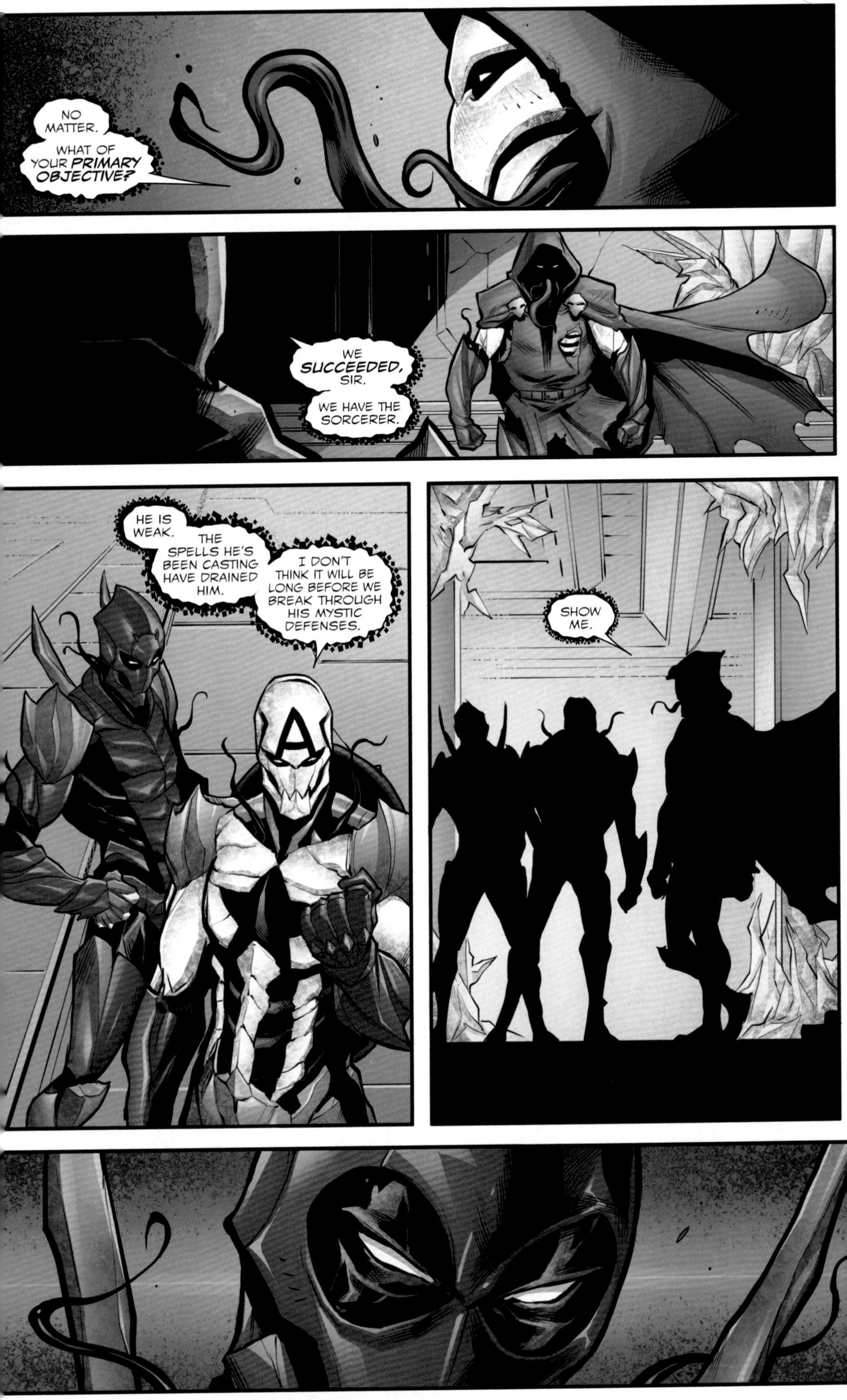
NO MATTER.
WHAT OF YOUR PRIMARY OBJECTIVE?
WE SUCCEEDED, SIR.
WE HAVE THE SORCERER.
HE IS WEAK.
THE SPELLS HE'S BEEN CASTING HAVE DRAINED HIM.
I DON'T THINK IT WILL BE LONG BEFORE WE BREAK THROUGH HIS MYSTIC DEFENSES.
SHOW ME.

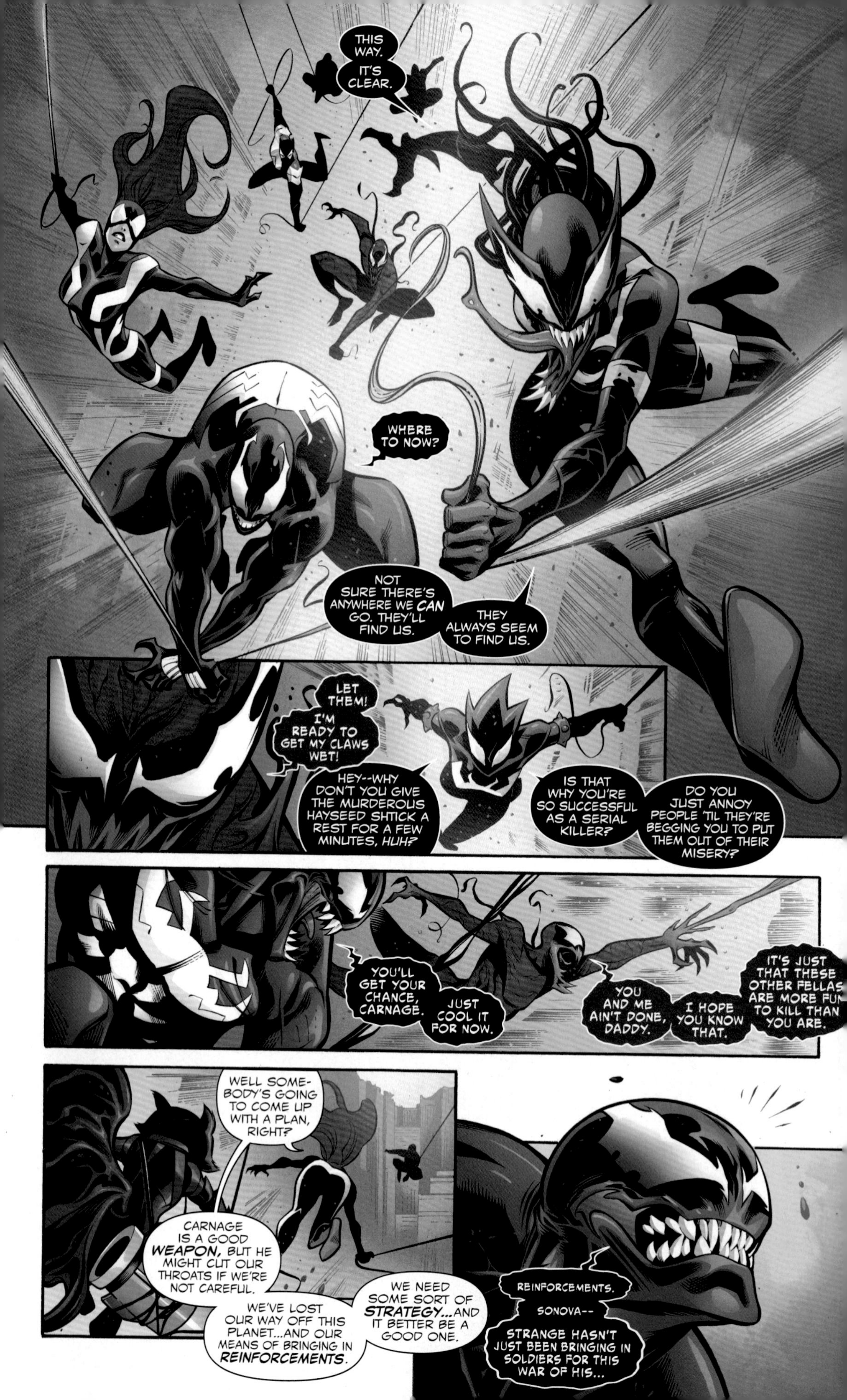
THIS WAY.
IT'S CLEAR.
WHERE TO NOW?
NOT SURE THERE'S ANYWHERE WE CAN GO. THEY'LL FIND US.
THEY ALWAYS SEEM TO FIND US.
LET THEM!
I'M READY TO GET MY CLAWS WET!
HEY--WHY DON'T YOU GIVE THE MURDEROUS HAYSEED SHTICK A REST FOR A FEW MINUTES, HUH?
IS THAT WHY YOU'RE SO SUCCESSFUL AS A SERIAL KILLER?
DO YOU JUST ANNOY PEOPLE 'TIL THEY'RE BEGGING YOU TO PUT THEM OUT OF THEIR MISERY?
YOU'LL GET YOUR CHANCE, CARNAGE.
JUST COOL IT FOR NOW.
YOU AND ME AIN'T DONE, DADDY.
I HOPE YOU KNOW THAT.
IT'S JUST THAT THESE OTHER FELLAS ARE MORE FUN TO KILL THAN YOU ARE.
WELL SOMEBODY'S GOING TO COME UP WITH A PLAN, RIGHT?
CARNAGE IS A GOOD WEAPON, BUT HE MIGHT CUT OUR THROATS IF WE'RE NOT CAREFUL.
WE'VE LOST OUR WAY OFF THIS PLANET...AND OUR MEANS OF BRINGING IN REINFORCEMENTS.
WE NEED SOME SORT OF STRATEGY...AND IT BETTER BE A GOOD ONE.
REINFORCEMENTS.
SONOVA--
STRANGE HASN'T JUST BEEN BRINGING IN SOLDIERS FOR THIS WAR OF HIS...

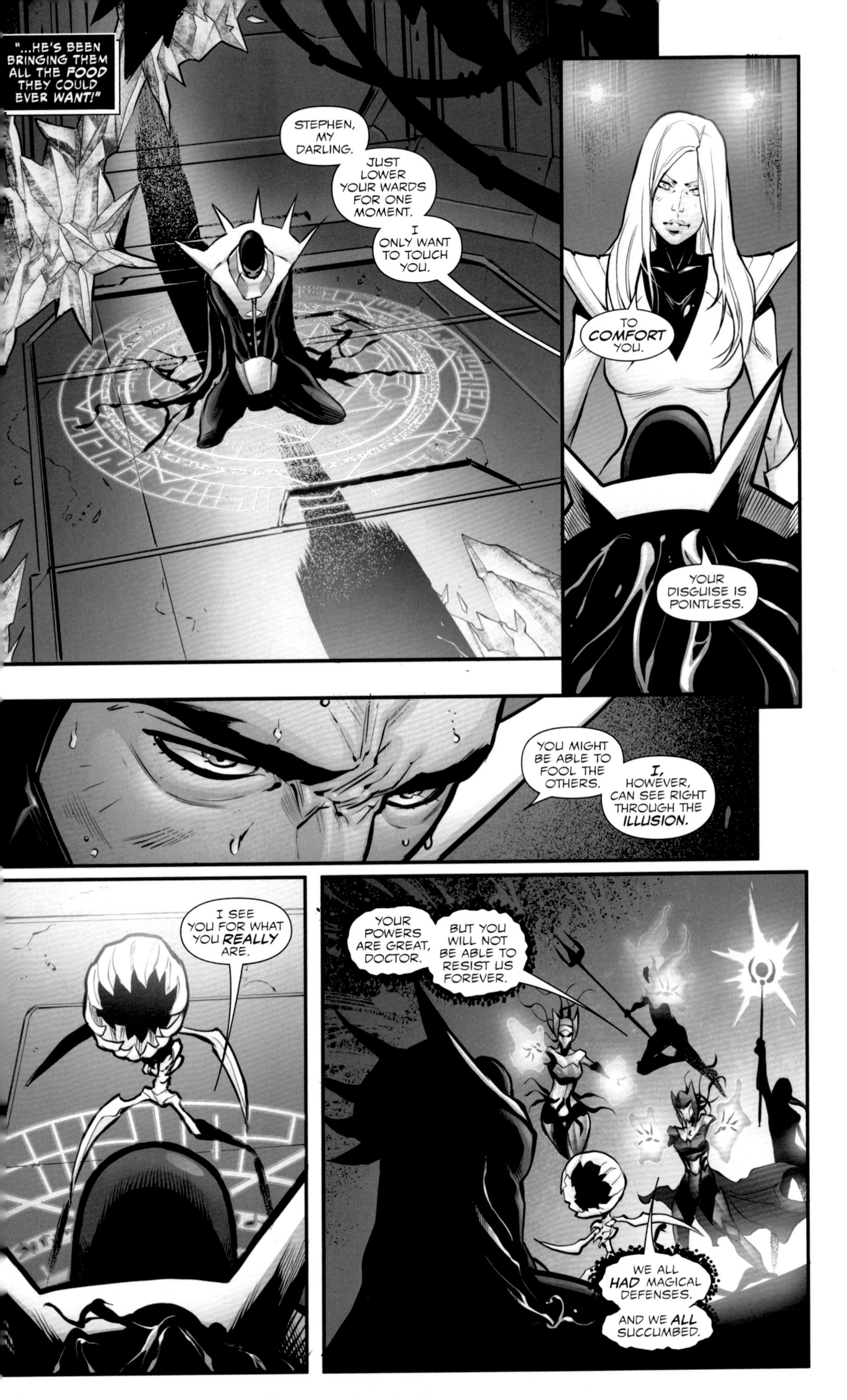
"...HE'S BEEN BRINGING THEM ALL THE FOOD THEY COULD EVER WANT!"
STEPHEN, MY DARLING.
JUST LOWER YOUR WARDS FOR ONE MOMENT.
I ONLY WANT TO TOUCH YOU.
TO COMFORT YOU.
YOUR DISGUISE IS POINTLESS.
YOU MIGHT BE ABLE TO FOOL THE OTHERS.
I, HOWEVER, CAN SEE RIGHT THROUGH THE ILLUSION.
I SEE YOU FOR WHAT YOU REALLY ARE.
YOUR POWERS ARE GREAT, DOCTOR.
BUT YOU WILL NOT BE ABLE TO RESIST US FOREVER.
WE ALL HAD MAGICAL DEFENSES.
AND WE ALL SUCCUMBED.

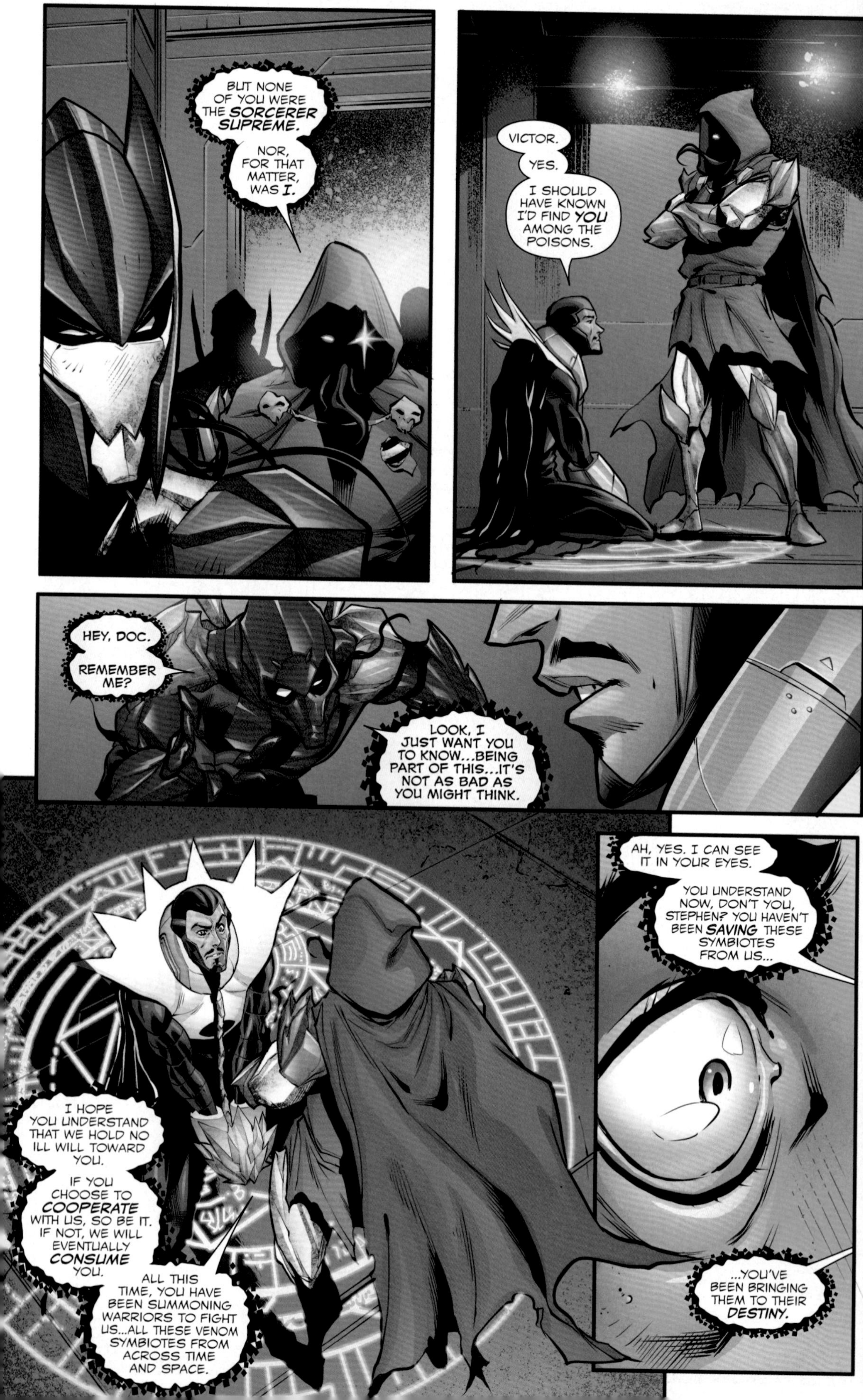
BUT NONE OF YOU WERE THE SORCERER SUPREME.
NOR, FOR THAT MATTER, WAS I.
VICTOR.
YES.
I SHOULD HAVE KNOWN I'D FIND YOU AMONG THE POISONS.
HEY, DOC.
REMEMBER ME?
LOOK, I JUST WANT YOU TO KNOW...BEING PART OF THIS...IT'S NOT AS BAD AS YOU MIGHT THINK.
I HOPE YOU UNDERSTAND THAT WE HOLD NO ILL WILL TOWARD YOU.
IF YOU CHOOSE TO COOPERATE WITH US, SO BE IT. IF NOT, WE WILL EVENTUALLY CONSUME YOU.
ALL THIS TIME, YOU HAVE BEEN SUMMONING WARRIORS TO FIGHT US...ALL THESE VENOM SYMBIOTES FROM ACROSS TIME AND SPACE.
AH, YES. I CAN SEE IT IN YOUR EYES.
YOU UNDERSTAND NOW, DON'T YOU, STEPHEN? YOU HAVEN'T BEEN SAVING THESE SYMBIOTES FROM US...
...YOU'VE BEEN BRINGING THEM TO THEIR DESTINY.

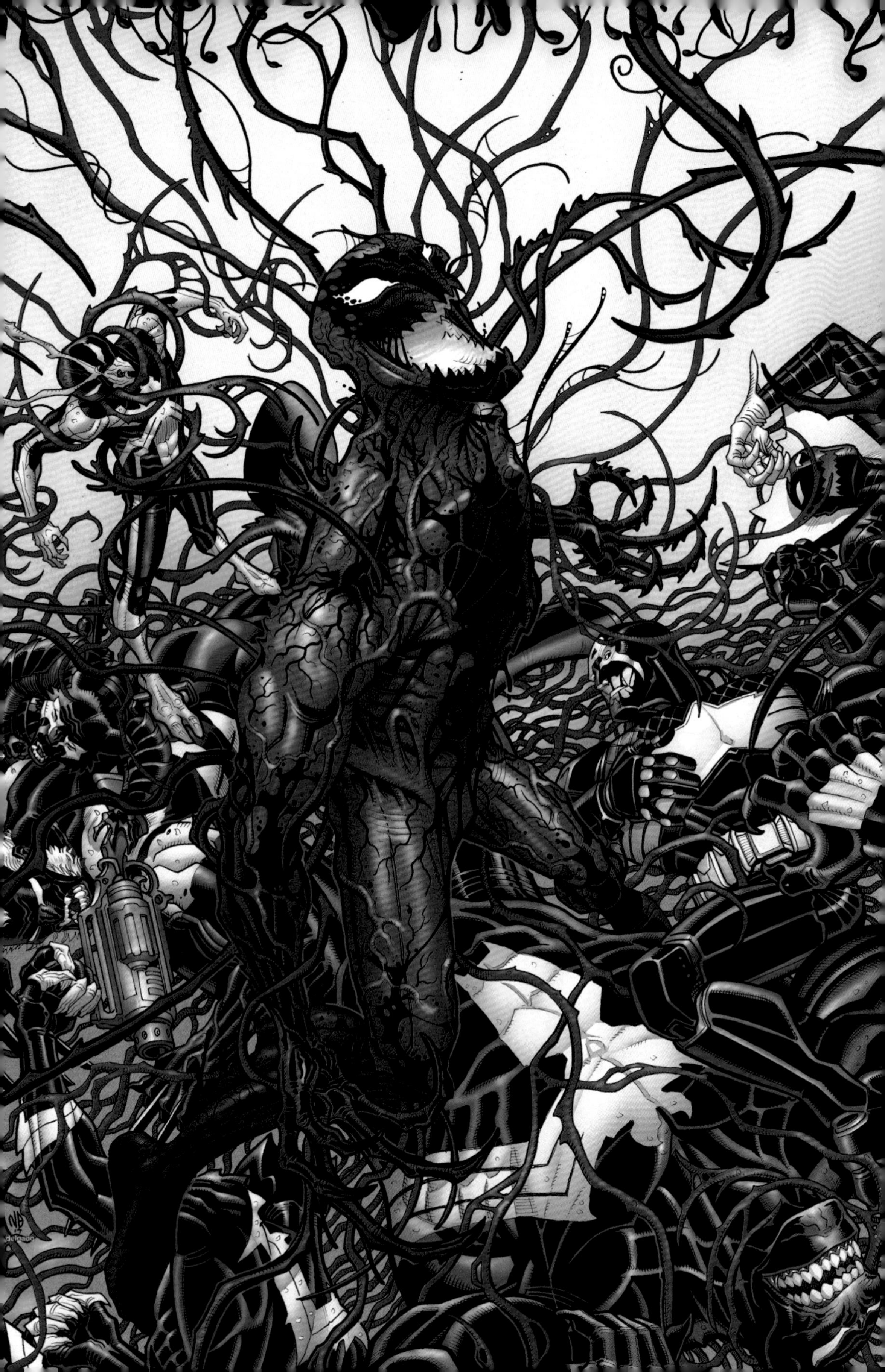

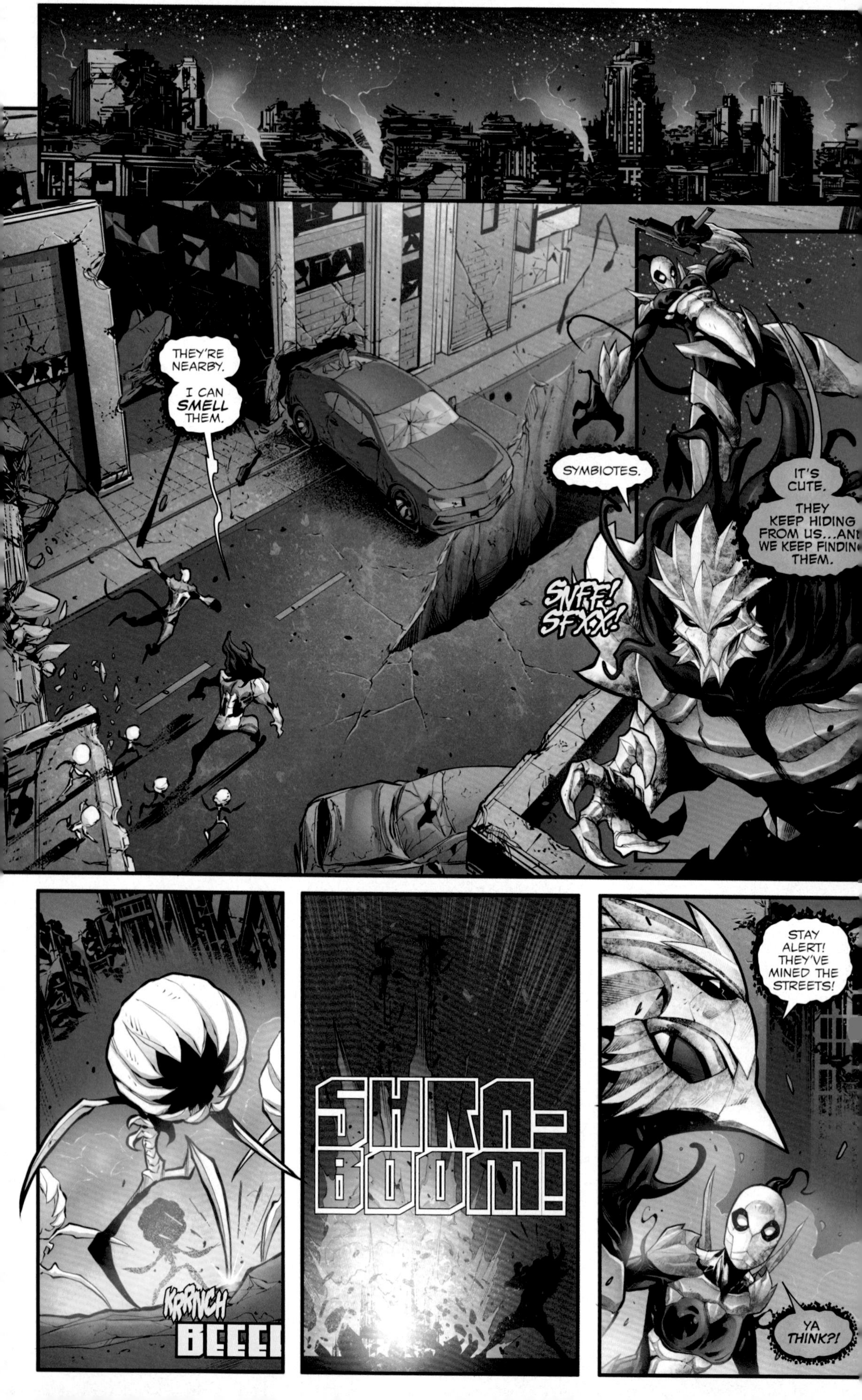
THEY'RE NEARBY.
I CAN SMELL THEM.
SYMBIOTES.
IT'S CUTE.
THEY KEEP HIDING FROM US...AND WE KEEP FINDING THEM.
SNFF! SFXOX!
KRRNCH
BEEEE
SHRA-BOOM!
STAY ALERT! THEY'VE MINED THE STREETS!
YA THINK?!

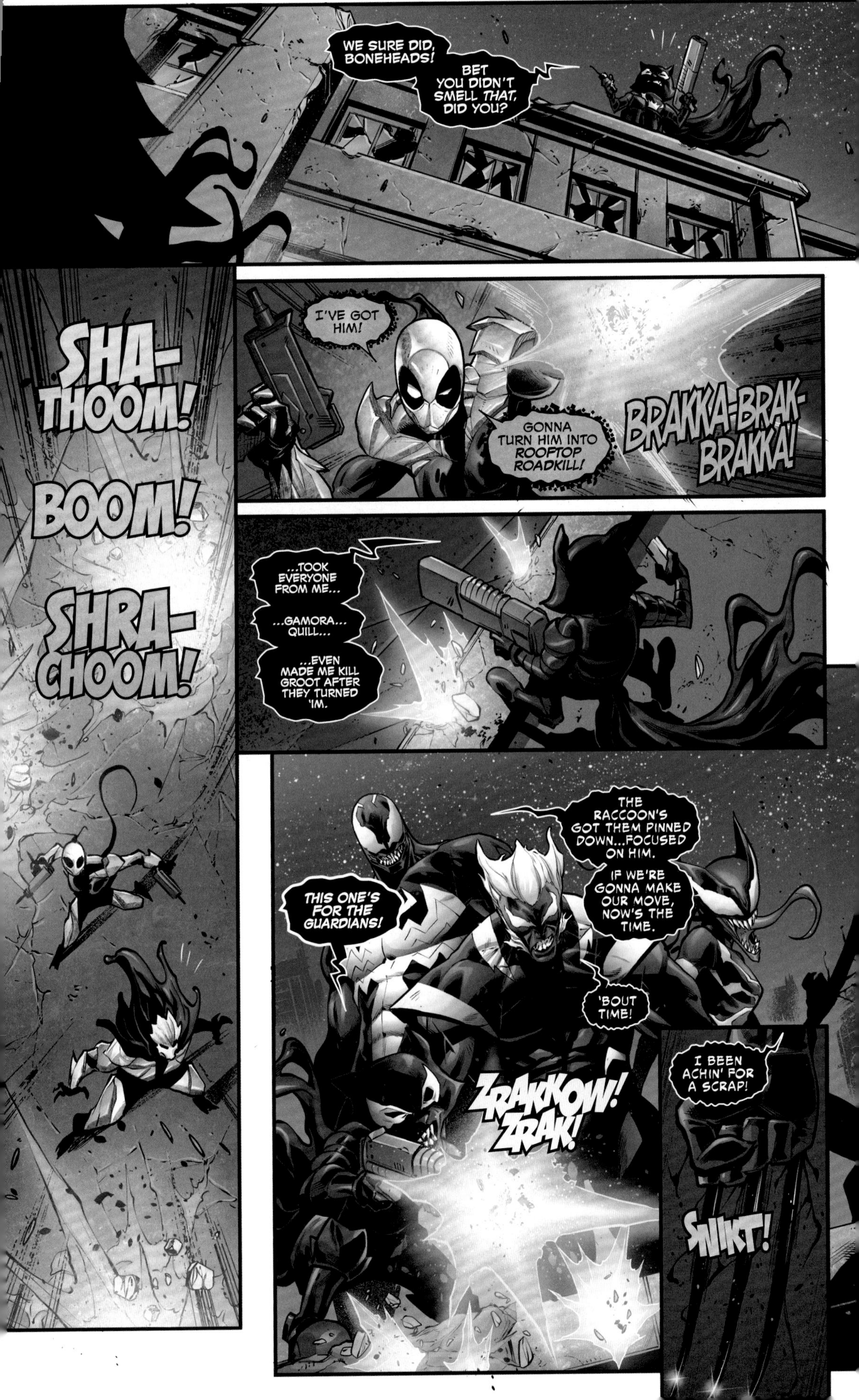
WE SURE DID, BONEHEADS!
BET YOU DIDN'T SMELL THAT, DID YOU?
SHA-THOOM!
BOOM!
SHRA-CHOOM!
I'VE GOT HIM!
GONNA TURN HIM INTO ROOFTOP ROADKILL!
BRAKKA-BRAK-BRAKKA!
...TOOK EVERYONE FROM ME...
...GAMORA... QUILL...
...EVEN MADE ME KILL GROOT AFTER THEY TURNED 'IM.
THE RACCOON'S GOT THEM PINNED DOWN...FOCUSED ON HIM.
IF WE'RE GONNA MAKE OUR MOVE, NOW'S THE TIME.
THIS ONE'S FOR THE GUARDIANS!
'BOUT TIME!
ZRAKKOW! ZRAK!
I BEEN ACHIN' FOR A SCRAP!
SNIKT!

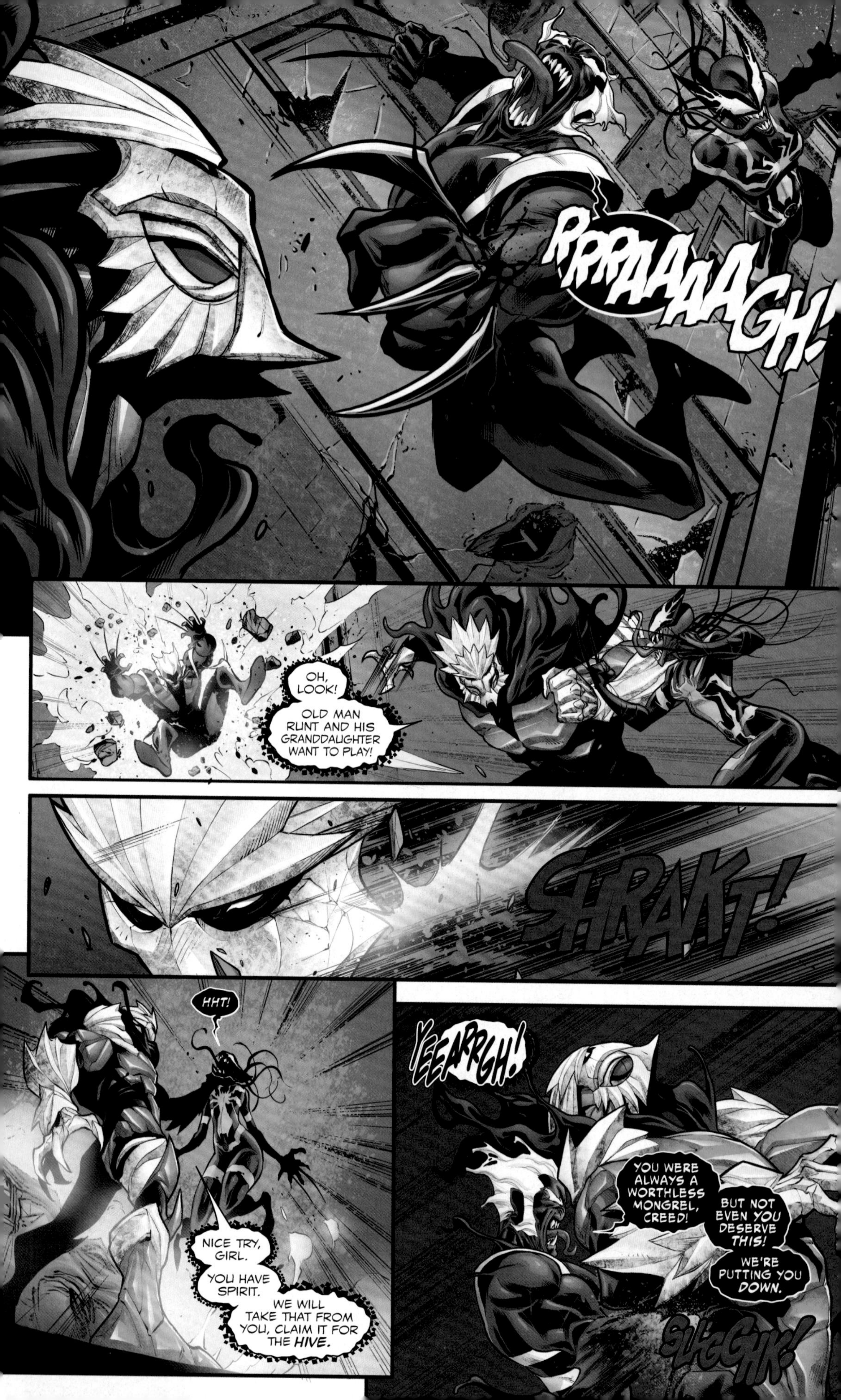
RRRAAAAAGH!
OH, LOOK!
OLD MAN RUNT AND HIS GRANDDAUGHTER WANT TO PLAY!
SHRAAKT!
HHT!
NICE TRY, GIRL.
YOU HAVE SPIRIT.
WE WILL TAKE THAT FROM YOU, CLAIM IT FOR THE HIVE.
YEEARRGH!
YOU WERE ALWAYS A WORTHLESS MONGREL, CREED!
BUT NOT EVEN YOU DESERVE THIS!
WE'RE PUTTING YOU DOWN.
SLUGGHK!

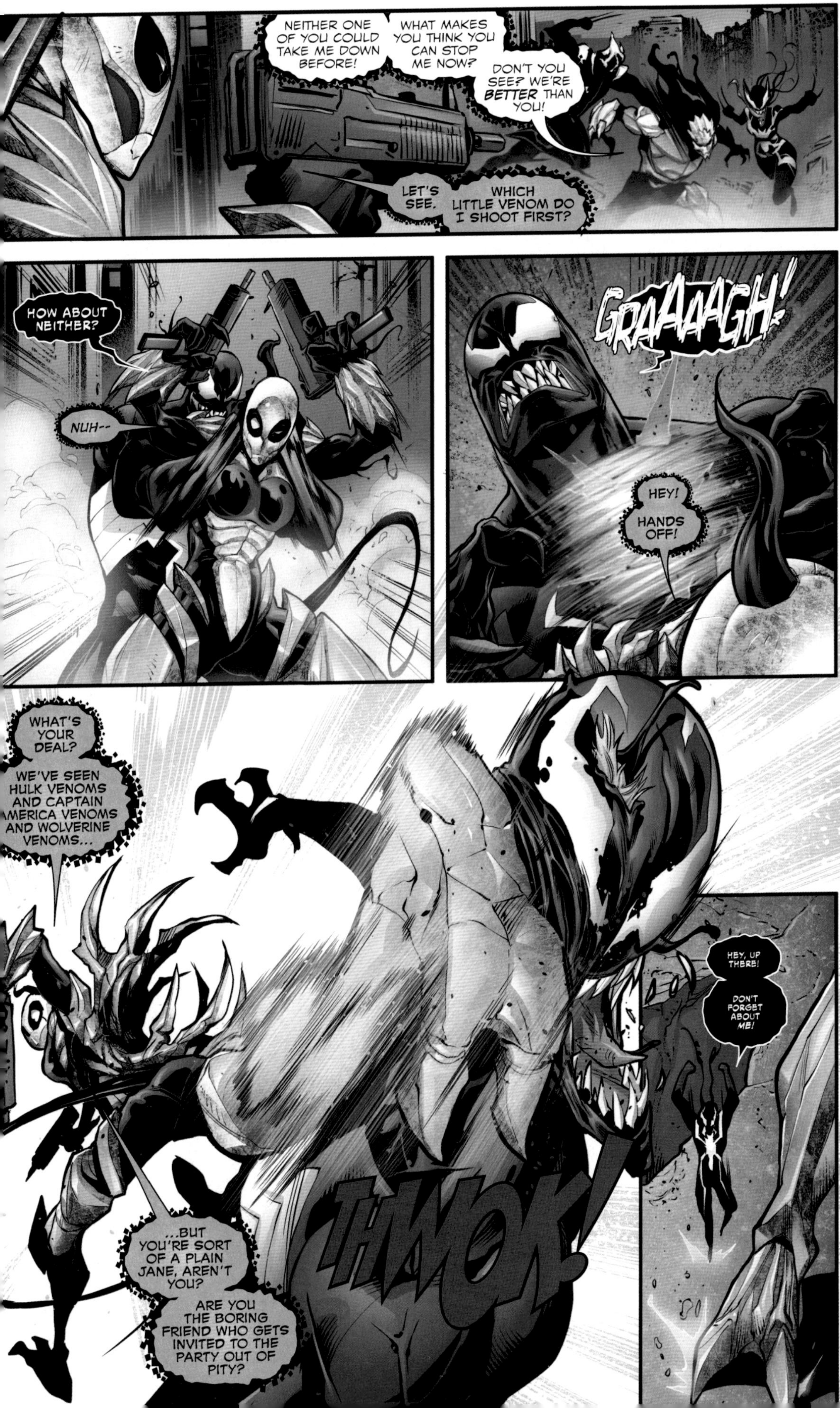
NEITHER ONE OF YOU COULD TAKE ME DOWN BEFORE!
WHAT MAKES YOU THINK YOU CAN STOP ME NOW?
DON'T YOU SEE? WE'RE **BETTER** THAN YOU!
LET'S SEE.
WHICH LITTLE VENOM DO I SHOOT FIRST?
HOW ABOUT NEITHER?
NUH--
GRAAAAGH!
HEY!
HANDS OFF!
WHAT'S YOUR DEAL?
WE'VE SEEN HULK VENOMS AND CAPTAIN AMERICA VENOMS AND WOLVERINE VENOMS...
...BUT YOU'RE SORT OF A PLAIN JANE, AREN'T YOU?
ARE YOU THE BORING FRIEND WHO GETS INVITED TO THE PARTY OUT OF PITY?
THWOK!
HEY, UP THERE!
DON'T FORGET ABOUT **ME**!

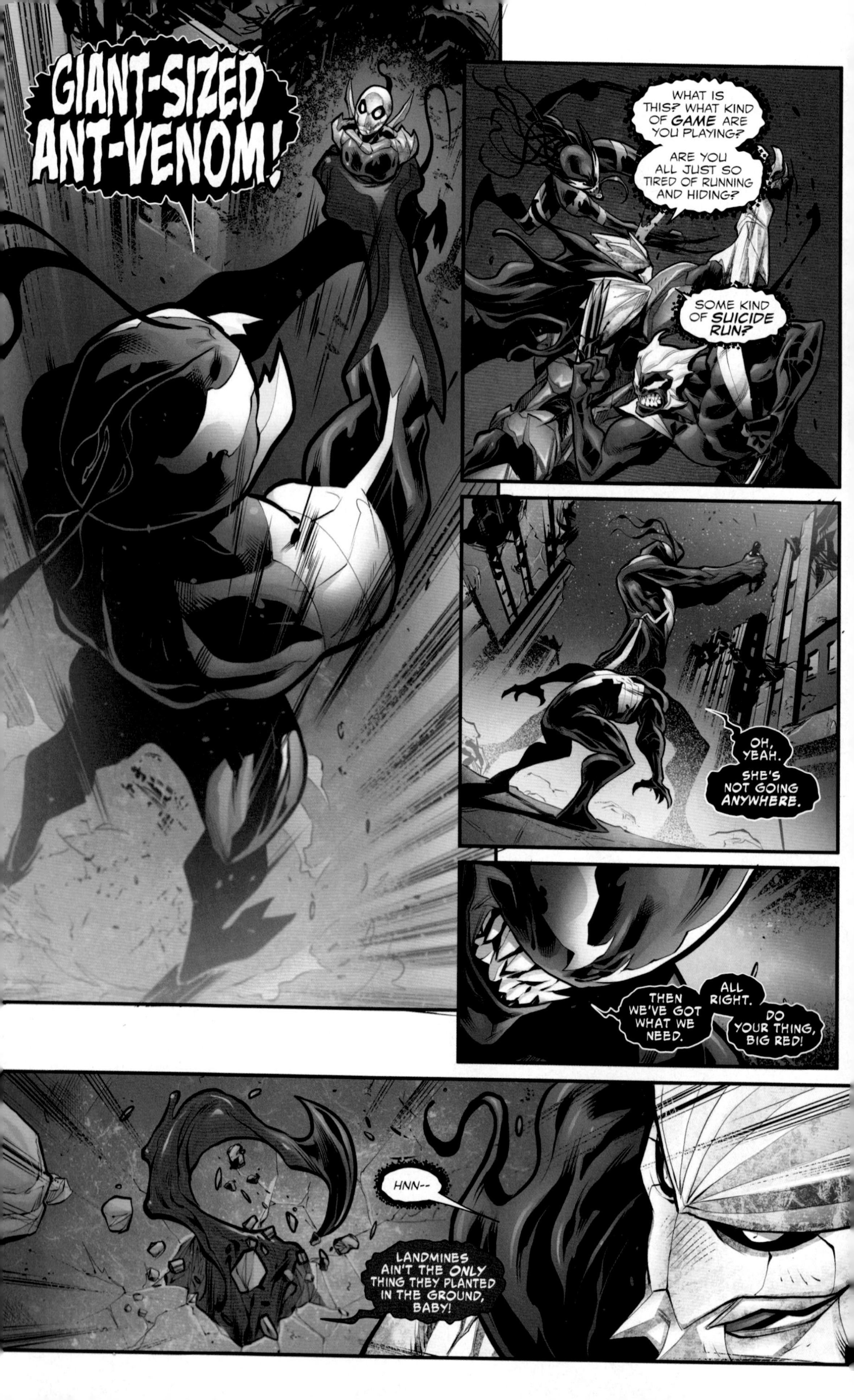
GIANT-SIZED ANT-VENOM!
WHAT IS THIS? WHAT KIND OF GAME ARE YOU PLAYING?
ARE YOU ALL JUST SO TIRED OF RUNNING AND HIDING?
SOME KIND OF SUICIDE RUN?
OH, YEAH.
SHE'S NOT GOING ANYWHERE.
THEN WE'VE GOT WHAT WE NEED.
ALL RIGHT.
DO YOUR THING, BIG RED!
HNN--
LANDMINES AIN'T THE ONLY THING THEY PLANTED IN THE GROUND, BABY!

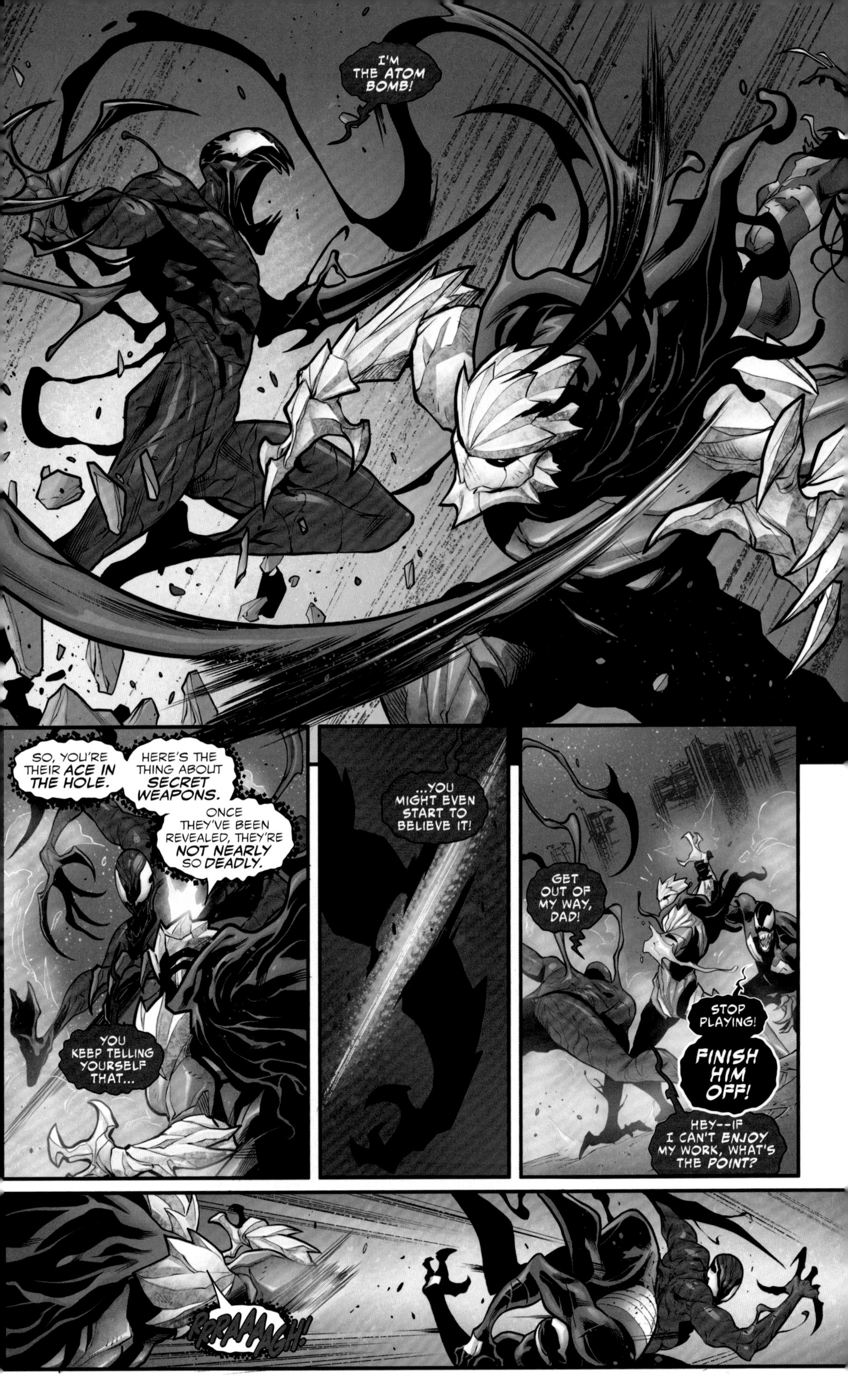
I'M THE ATOM BOMB!
SO, YOU'RE THEIR ACE IN THE HOLE.
HERE'S THE THING ABOUT SECRET WEAPONS.
ONCE THEY'VE BEEN REVEALED, THEY'RE NOT NEARLY SO DEADLY.
YOU KEEP TELLING YOURSELF THAT...
...YOU MIGHT EVEN START TO BELIEVE IT!
GET OUT OF MY WAY, DAD!
STOP PLAYING!
FINISH HIM OFF!
HEY--IF I CAN'T ENJOY MY WORK, WHAT'S THE POINT?
RRRAAAAGH!

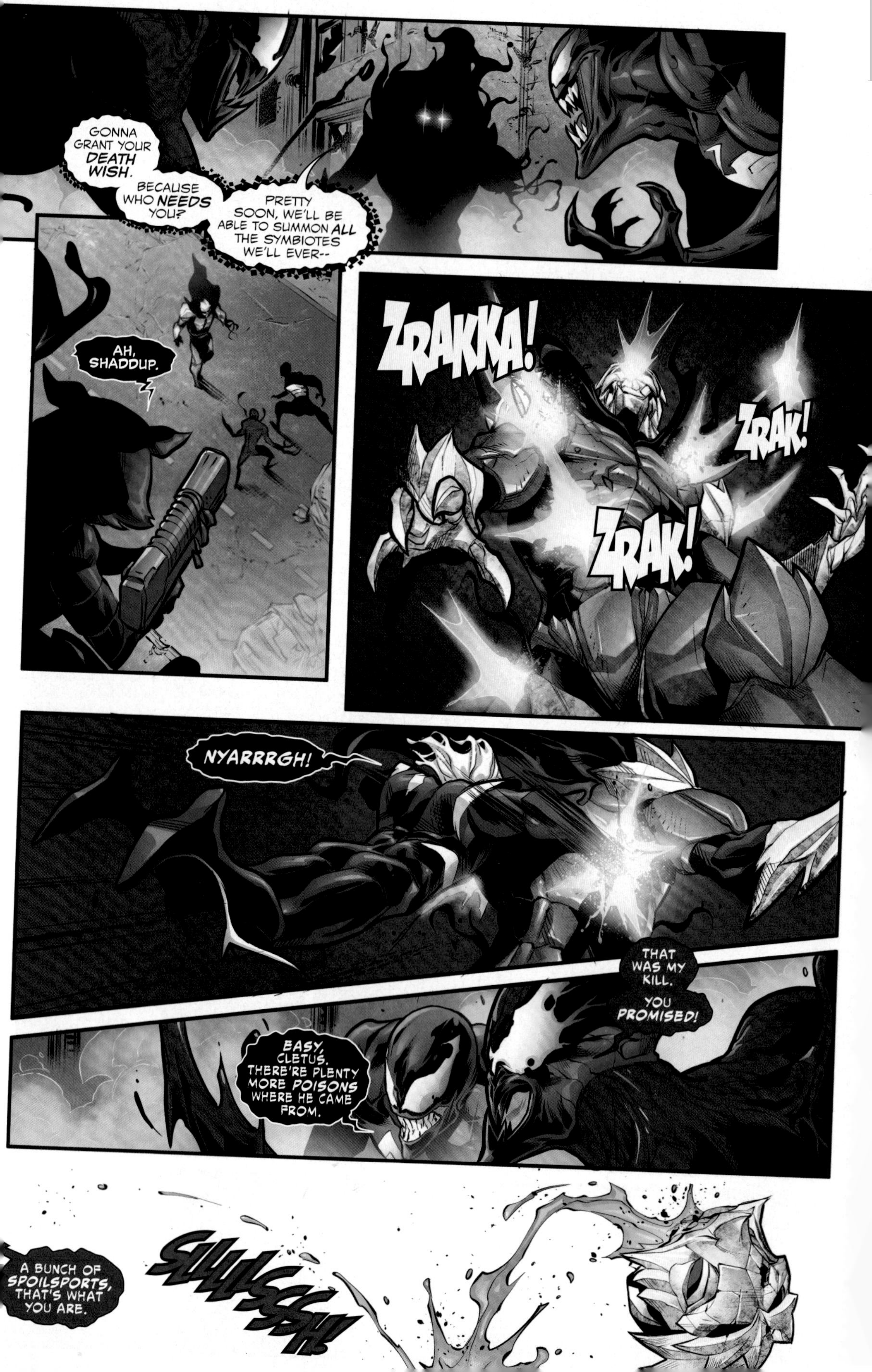

GONNA GRANT YOUR DEATH WISH.
BECAUSE WHO NEEDS YOU?
PRETTY SOON, WE'LL BE ABLE TO SUMMON ALL THE SYMBIOTES WE'LL EVER--
AH, SHADDUP.
ZRAKKA!
ZRAK!
ZRAK!
NYARRRGH!
THAT WAS MY KILL.
YOU PROMISED!
EASY, CLETUS. THERE'RE PLENTY MORE POISONS WHERE HE CAME FROM.
A BUNCH OF SPOILSPORTS, THAT'S WHAT YOU ARE.
SHLUSSSH!

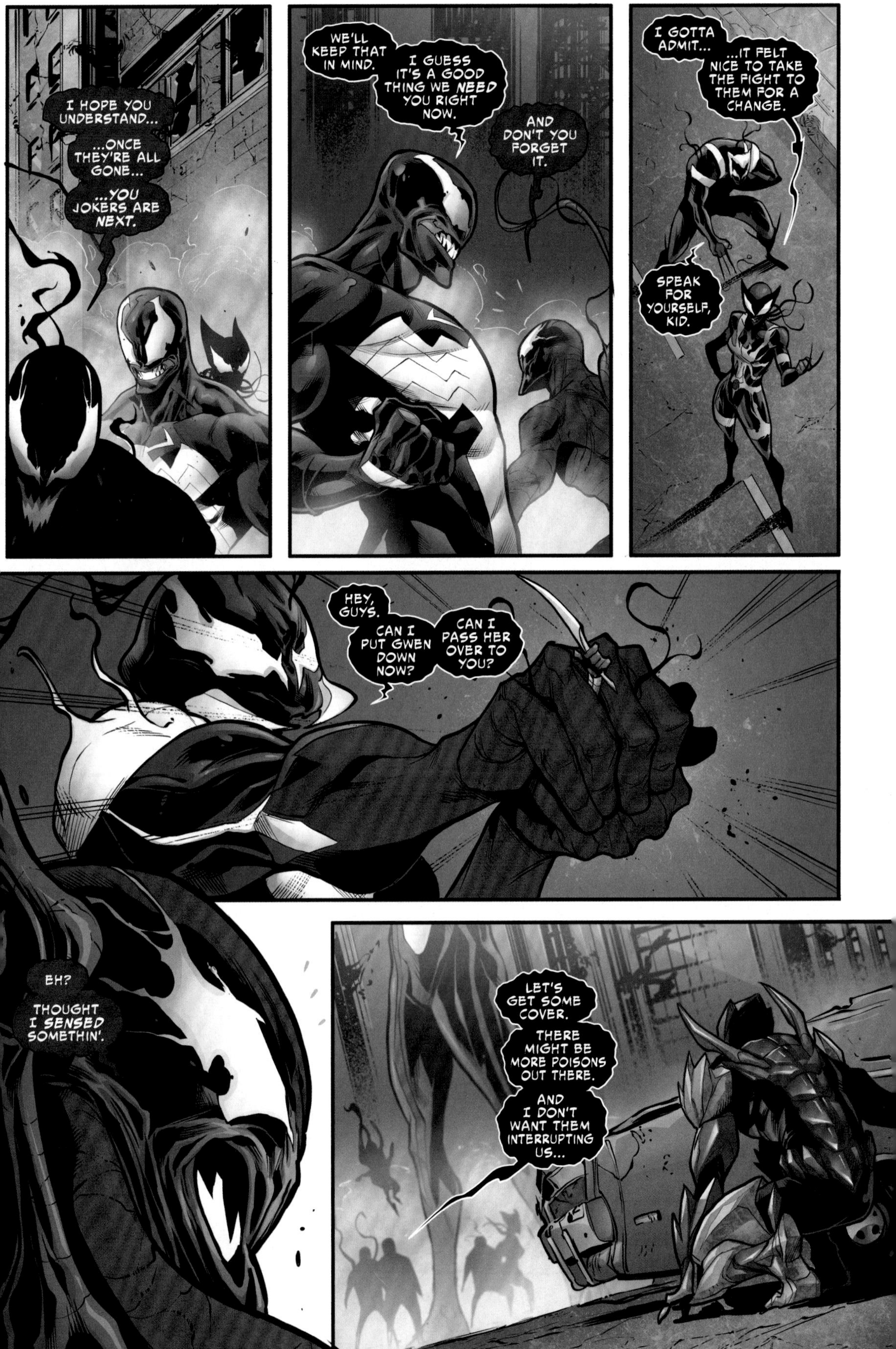
I HOPE YOU UNDERSTAND...
...ONCE THEY'RE ALL GONE...
...YOU JOKERS ARE NEXT.
WE'LL KEEP THAT IN MIND.
I GUESS IT'S A GOOD THING WE NEED YOU RIGHT NOW.
AND DON'T YOU FORGET IT.
I GOTTA ADMIT...
...IT FELT NICE TO TAKE THE FIGHT TO THEM FOR A CHANGE.
SPEAK FOR YOURSELF, KID.
HEY, GUYS.
CAN I PUT GWEN DOWN NOW?
CAN I PASS HER OVER TO YOU?
EH?
THOUGHT I SENSED SOMETHIN'.
LET'S GET SOME COVER.
THERE MIGHT BE MORE POISONS OUT THERE.
AND I DON'T WANT THEM INTERRUPTING US...

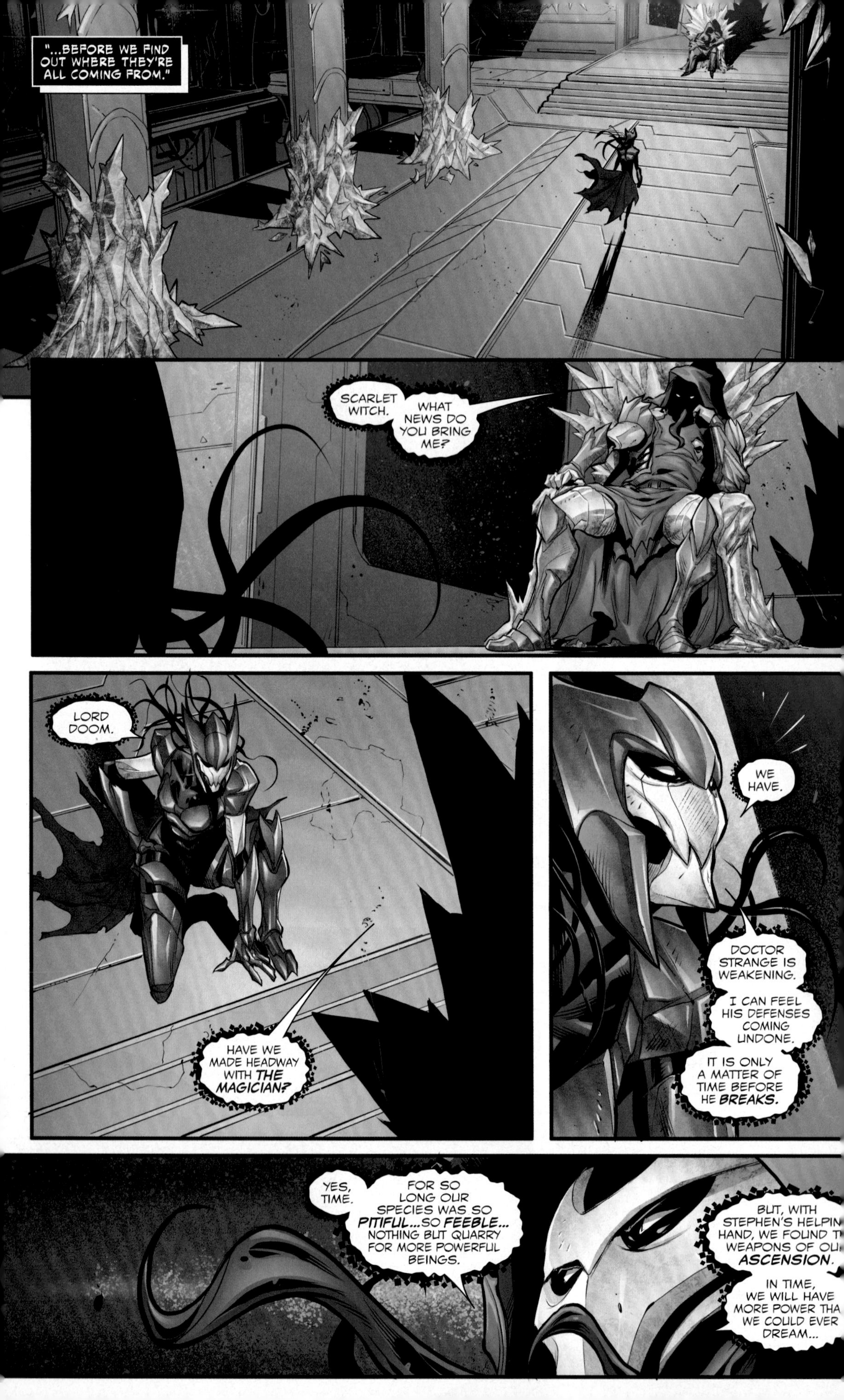

"...BEFORE WE FIND OUT WHERE THEY'RE ALL COMING FROM."
SCARLET WITCH.
WHAT NEWS DO YOU BRING ME?
LORD DOOM.
HAVE WE MADE HEADWAY WITH **THE MAGICIAN?**
WE HAVE.
DOCTOR STRANGE IS WEAKENING.
I CAN FEEL HIS DEFENSES COMING UNDONE.
IT IS ONLY A MATTER OF TIME BEFORE HE **BREAKS.**
YES, TIME.
FOR SO LONG OUR SPECIES WAS SO **PITIFUL**...SO **FEEBLE**... NOTHING BUT QUARRY FOR MORE POWERFUL BEINGS.
BUT, WITH STEPHEN'S HELPIN HAND, WE FOUND T WEAPONS OF OU **ASCENSION**.
IN TIME, WE WILL HAVE MORE POWER THA WE COULD EVER DREAM...

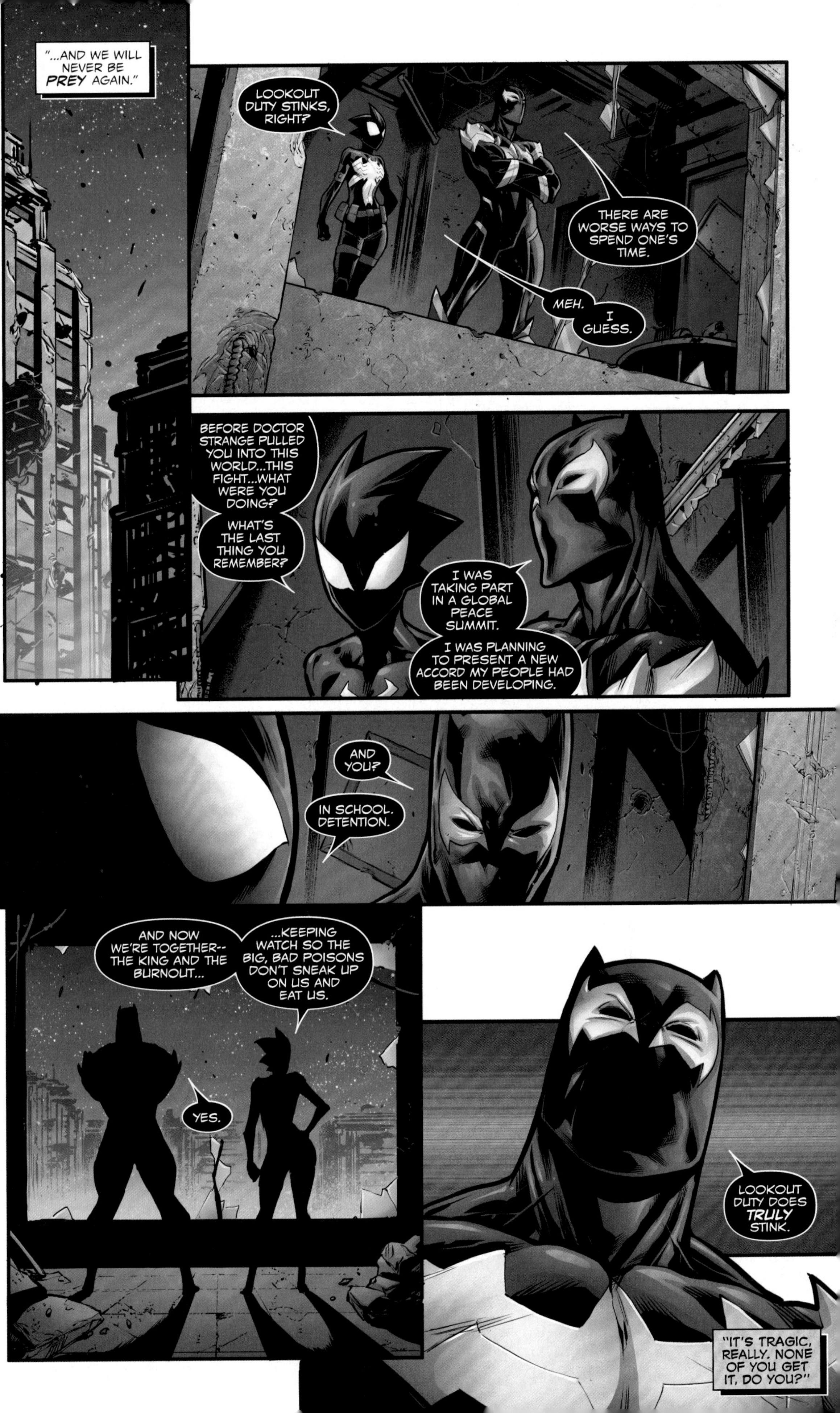
"...AND WE WILL NEVER BE PREY AGAIN."
LOOKOUT DUTY STINKS, RIGHT?
THERE ARE WORSE WAYS TO SPEND ONE'S TIME.
MEH. I GUESS.
BEFORE DOCTOR STRANGE PULLED YOU INTO THIS WORLD...THIS FIGHT...WHAT WERE YOU DOING?
WHAT'S THE LAST THING YOU REMEMBER?
I WAS TAKING PART IN A GLOBAL PEACE SUMMIT.
I WAS PLANNING TO PRESENT A NEW ACCORD MY PEOPLE HAD BEEN DEVELOPING.
AND YOU?
IN SCHOOL. DETENTION.
AND NOW WE'RE TOGETHER-- THE KING AND THE BURNOUT...
...KEEPING WATCH SO THE BIG, BAD POISONS DON'T SNEAK UP ON US AND EAT US.
YES.
LOOKOUT DUTY DOES TRULY STINK.
"IT'S TRAGIC, REALLY. NONE OF YOU GET IT, DO YOU?"

WHAT YOU'RE FIGHTING AGAINST IS *BEAUTIFUL.*

THREE BEINGS BECOMING ONE.

THE WEAKNESSES OF *FLESH...*OF *CONSCIENCE...* ARE TORN AWAY...

...AND WE ALL BECOME STRONG IN THE *HIVE.*

YOU, TOO, CAN KNOW THIS *SERENITY.*

YOU ONLY NEED TO STOP FIGHTING.

THERE'S NO REASON TO BE AFRAID.

NOT FOR *US,* THERE AIN'T.

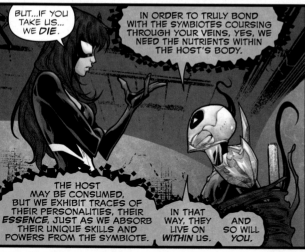

BUT...IF YOU TAKE US... WE *DIE.*

IN ORDER TO TRULY BOND WITH THE SYMBIOTES COURSING THROUGH YOUR VEINS, YES, WE NEED THE NUTRIENTS WITHIN THE HOST'S BODY.

THE HOST MAY BE CONSUMED, BUT WE EXHIBIT TRACES OF THEIR PERSONALITIES, THEIR *ESSENCE,* JUST AS WE ABSORB THEIR UNIQUE SKILLS AND POWERS FROM THE SYMBIOTE.

IN THAT WAY, THEY LIVE ON *WITHIN* US.

AND SO WILL *YOU.*

YOU CALL US *POISONS.* BUT THAT IS A NAME THAT COMES FROM *FEAR.*

WE ARE THE *PERFECT HOSTS* FOR THE KLYNTAR. THROUGH CONSUMING YOUR PHYSICAL BODIES AND BONDING WITH THE SYMBIOTES, WE *SILENCE* THEM. QUELL THE CHAOS OF YOUR TWO MINDS VYING FOR CONTROL.

TRUE SYMBIOSIS. *UNION.*

WHEN THEY BOND WITH US, THEY BECOME *APEX PREDATORS.*

AND DEEP DOWN, THAT IS WHAT EVERY VENOM WANTS...

...WHETHER YOU ADMIT IT OR NOT.

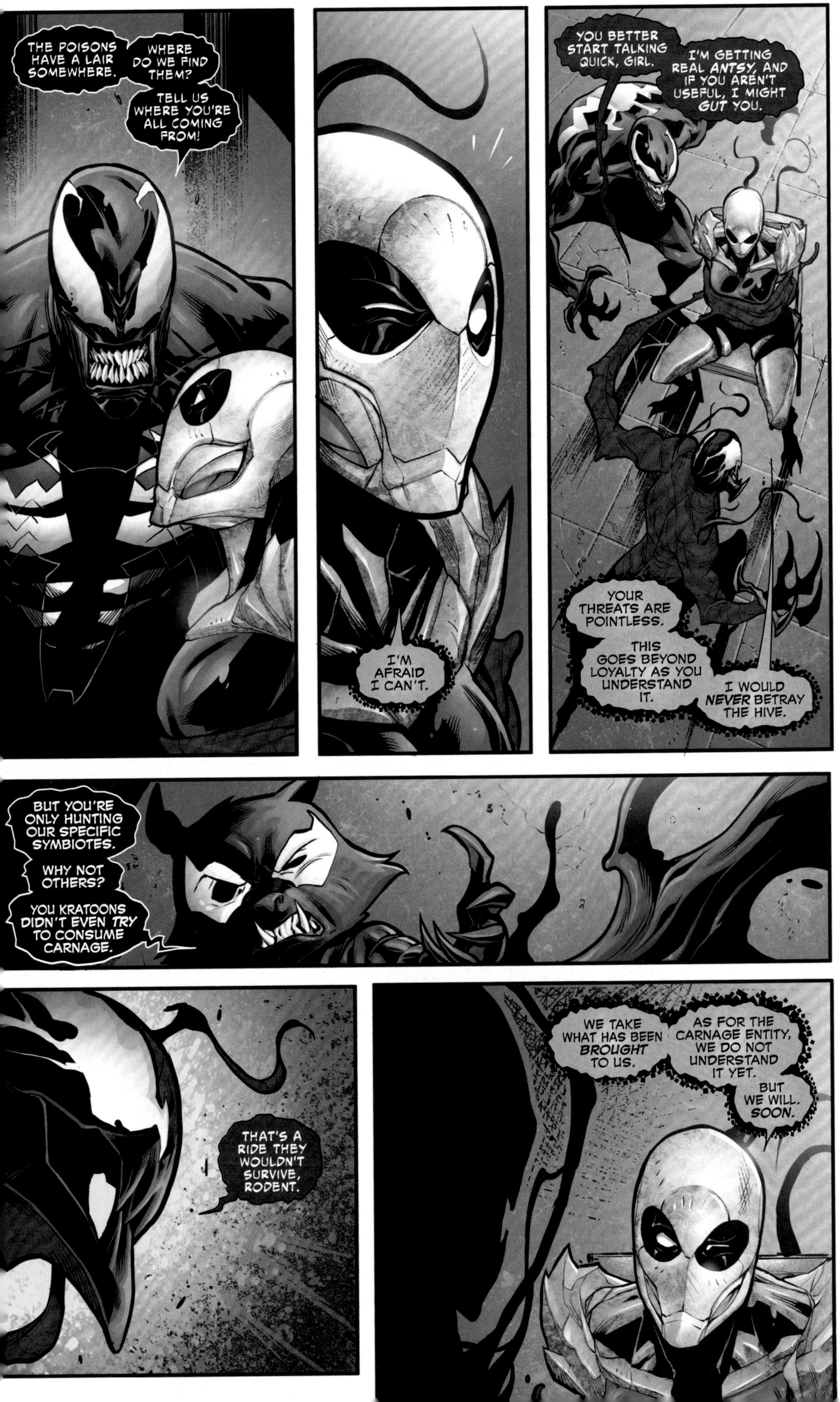
THE POISONS HAVE A LAIR SOMEWHERE.
WHERE DO WE FIND THEM?
TELL US WHERE YOU'RE ALL COMING FROM!
I'M AFRAID I CAN'T.
YOU BETTER START TALKING QUICK, GIRL.
I'M GETTING REAL ANTSY, AND IF YOU AREN'T USEFUL, I MIGHT GUT YOU.
YOUR THREATS ARE POINTLESS.
THIS GOES BEYOND LOYALTY AS YOU UNDERSTAND IT.
I WOULD NEVER BETRAY THE HIVE.
BUT YOU'RE ONLY HUNTING OUR SPECIFIC SYMBIOTES.
WHY NOT OTHERS?
YOU KRATOONS DIDN'T EVEN TRY TO CONSUME CARNAGE.
WE TAKE WHAT HAS BEEN BROUGHT TO US.
AS FOR THE CARNAGE ENTITY, WE DO NOT UNDERSTAND IT YET.
BUT WE WILL. SOON.
THAT'S A RIDE THEY WOULDN'T SURVIVE, RODENT.

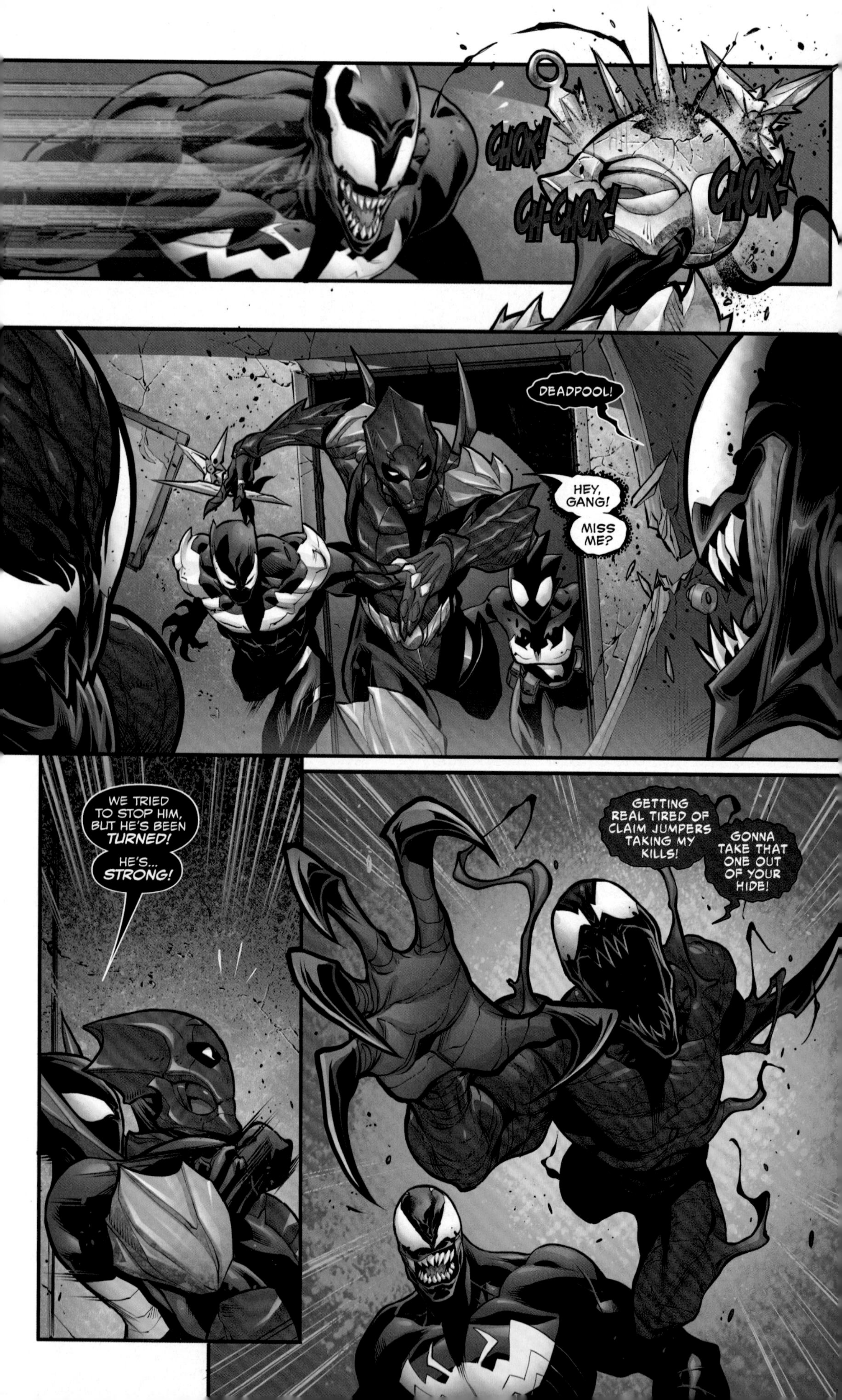

CHOK!
CH-CHOK!
CHOK!
DEADPOOL!
HEY, GANG!
MISS ME?
WE TRIED TO STOP HIM, BUT HE'S BEEN TURNED!
HE'S... STRONG!
GETTING REAL TIRED OF CLAIM JUMPERS TAKING MY KILLS!
GONNA TAKE THAT ONE OUT OF YOUR HIDE!

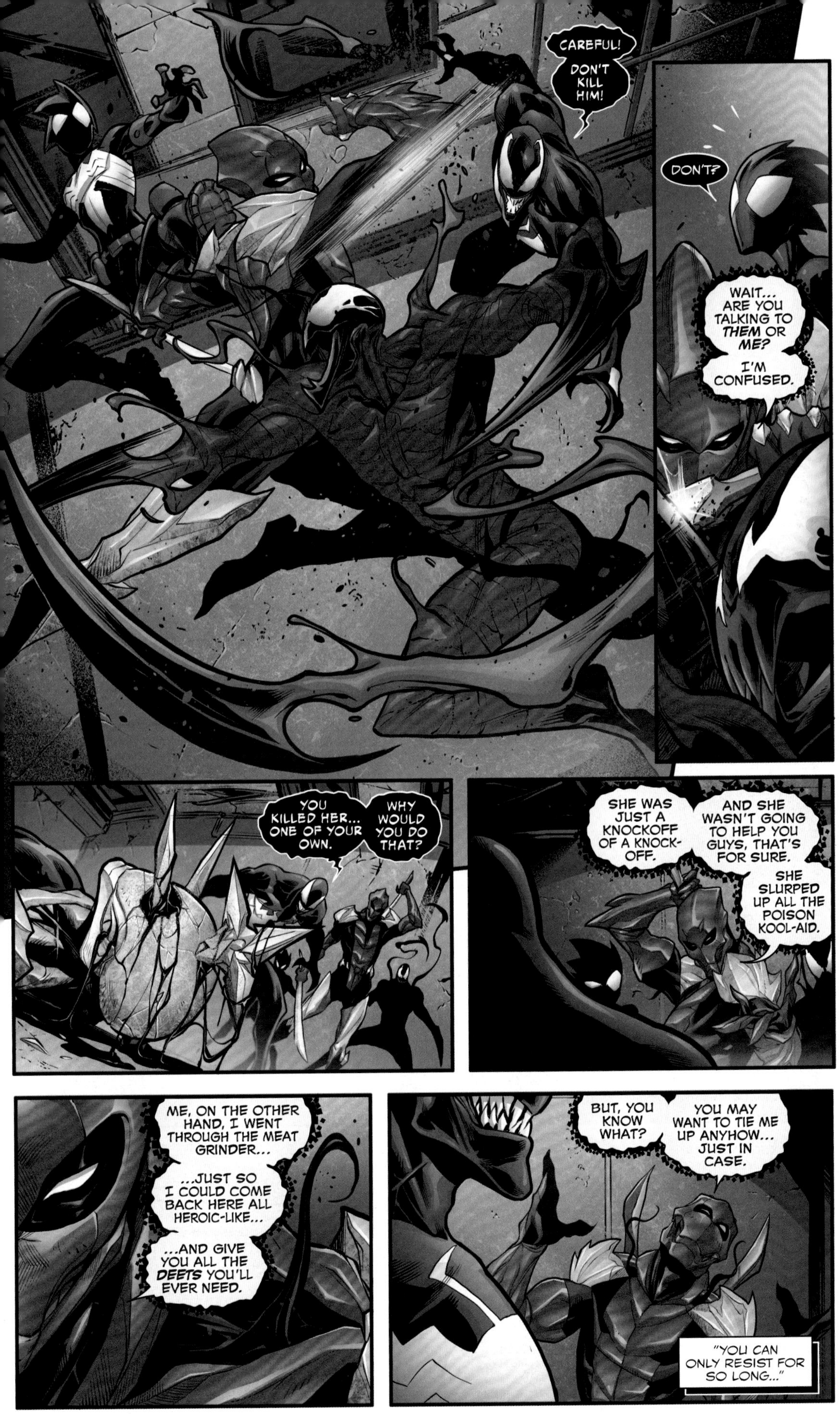
CAREFUL!
DON'T KILL HIM!
DON'T?
WAIT... ARE YOU TALKING TO *THEM* OR *ME?*
I'M CONFUSED.
YOU KILLED HER... ONE OF YOUR OWN.
WHY WOULD YOU DO THAT?
SHE WAS JUST A KNOCKOFF OF A KNOCK-OFF.
AND SHE WASN'T GOING TO HELP YOU GUYS, THAT'S FOR SURE.
SHE SLURPED UP ALL THE POISON KOOL-AID.
ME, ON THE OTHER HAND, I WENT THROUGH THE MEAT GRINDER...
...JUST SO I COULD COME BACK HERE ALL HEROIC-LIKE...
...AND GIVE YOU ALL THE *DEETS* YOU'LL EVER NEED.
BUT, YOU KNOW WHAT?
YOU MAY WANT TO TIE ME UP ANYHOW... JUST IN CASE.
"YOU CAN ONLY RESIST FOR SO LONG..."

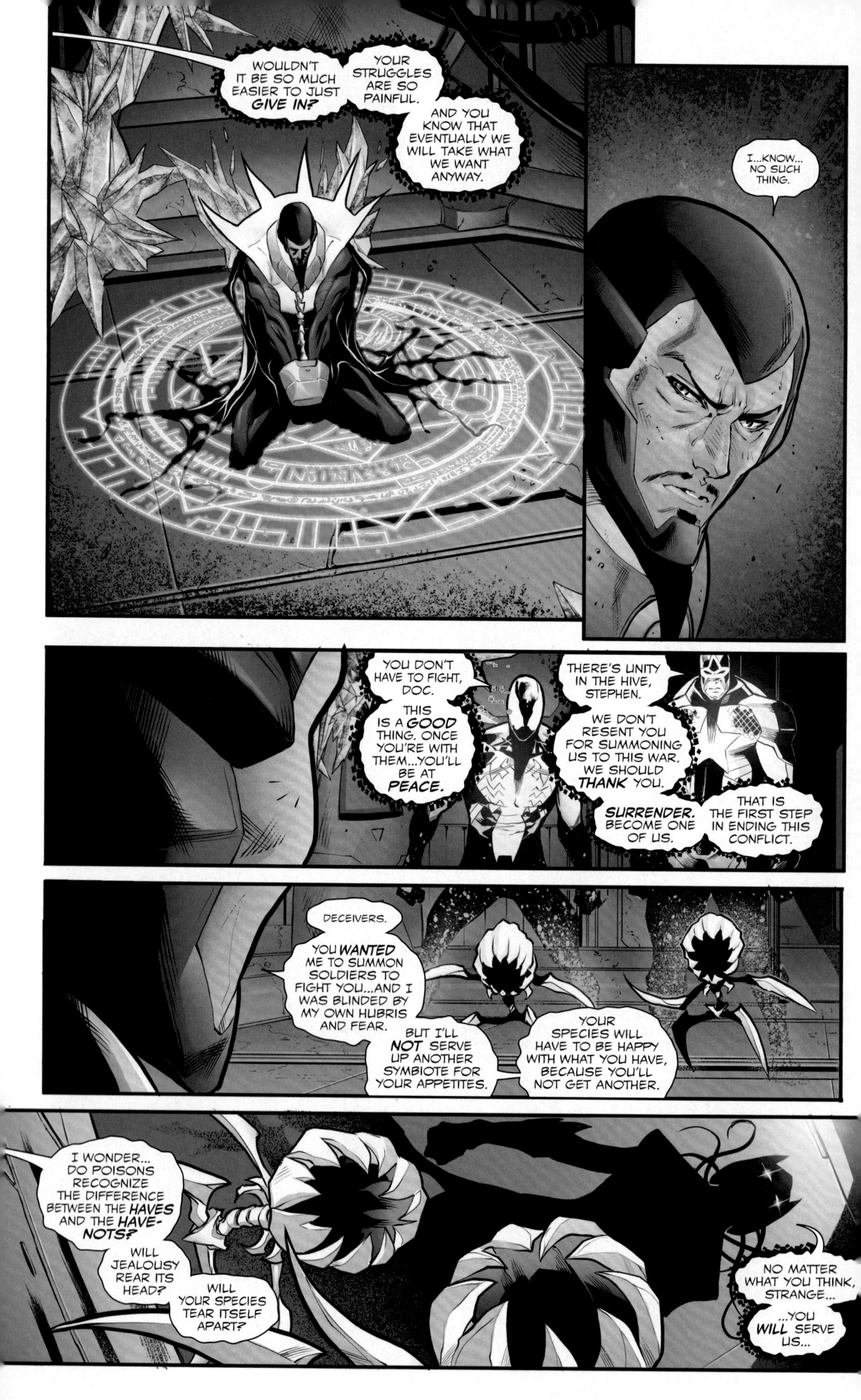
WOULDN'T IT BE SO MUCH EASIER TO JUST GIVE IN?
YOUR STRUGGLES ARE SO PAINFUL.
AND YOU KNOW THAT EVENTUALLY WE WILL TAKE WHAT WE WANT ANYWAY.
I...KNOW... NO SUCH THING.
YOU DON'T HAVE TO FIGHT, DOC.
THIS IS A GOOD THING. ONCE YOU'RE WITH THEM...YOU'LL BE AT PEACE.
THERE'S UNITY IN THE HIVE, STEPHEN.
WE DON'T RESENT YOU FOR SUMMONING US TO THIS WAR. WE SHOULD THANK YOU.
SURRENDER. BECOME ONE OF US.
THAT IS THE FIRST STEP IN ENDING THIS CONFLICT.
DECEIVERS.
YOU WANTED ME TO SUMMON SOLDIERS TO FIGHT YOU...AND I WAS BLINDED BY MY OWN HUBRIS AND FEAR.
BUT I'LL NOT SERVE UP ANOTHER SYMBIOTE FOR YOUR APPETITES.
YOUR SPECIES WILL HAVE TO BE HAPPY WITH WHAT YOU HAVE, BECAUSE YOU'LL NOT GET ANOTHER.
I WONDER... DO POISONS RECOGNIZE THE DIFFERENCE BETWEEN THE HAVES AND THE HAVE-NOTS?
WILL JEALOUSY REAR ITS HEAD?
WILL YOUR SPECIES TEAR ITSELF APART?
NO MATTER WHAT YOU THINK, STRANGE...
...YOU WILL SERVE US...

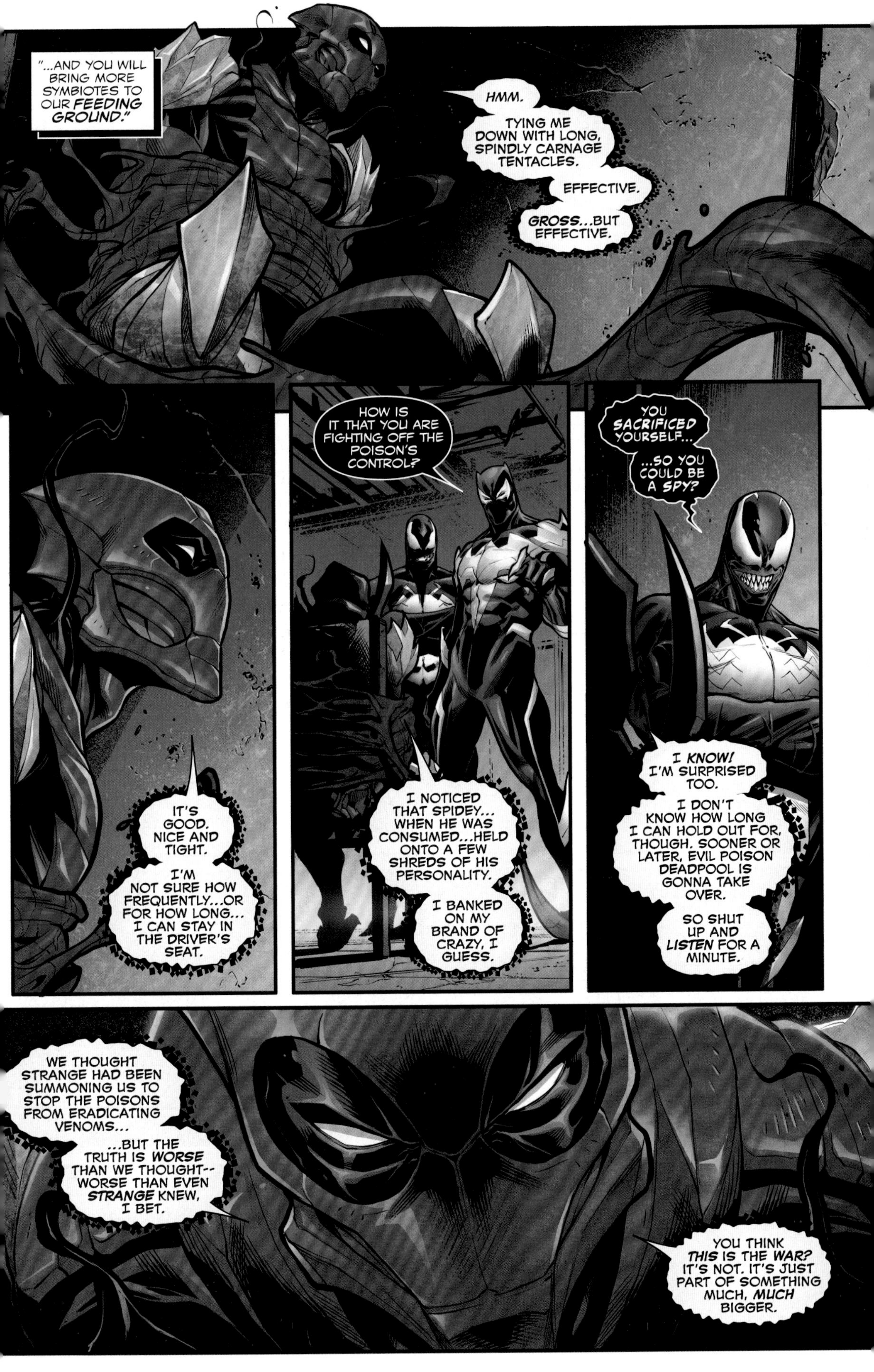
"...AND YOU WILL BRING MORE SYMBIOTES TO OUR FEEDING GROUND."
HMM.
TYING ME DOWN WITH LONG, SPINDLY CARNAGE TENTACLES.
EFFECTIVE.
GROSS...BUT EFFECTIVE.
IT'S GOOD. NICE AND TIGHT.
I'M NOT SURE HOW FREQUENTLY...OR FOR HOW LONG... I CAN STAY IN THE DRIVER'S SEAT.
HOW IS IT THAT YOU ARE FIGHTING OFF THE POISON'S CONTROL?
I NOTICED THAT SPIDEY... WHEN HE WAS CONSUMED...HELD ONTO A FEW SHREDS OF HIS PERSONALITY.
I BANKED ON MY BRAND OF CRAZY, I GUESS.
YOU SACRIFICED YOURSELF...
...SO YOU COULD BE A SPY?
I KNOW! I'M SURPRISED TOO.
I DON'T KNOW HOW LONG I CAN HOLD OUT FOR, THOUGH. SOONER OR LATER, EVIL POISON DEADPOOL IS GONNA TAKE OVER.
SO SHUT UP AND LISTEN FOR A MINUTE.
WE THOUGHT STRANGE HAD BEEN SUMMONING US TO STOP THE POISONS FROM ERADICATING VENOMS...
...BUT THE TRUTH IS WORSE THAN WE THOUGHT--WORSE THAN EVEN STRANGE KNEW, I BET.
YOU THINK THIS IS THE WAR? IT'S NOT. IT'S JUST PART OF SOMETHING MUCH, MUCH BIGGER.

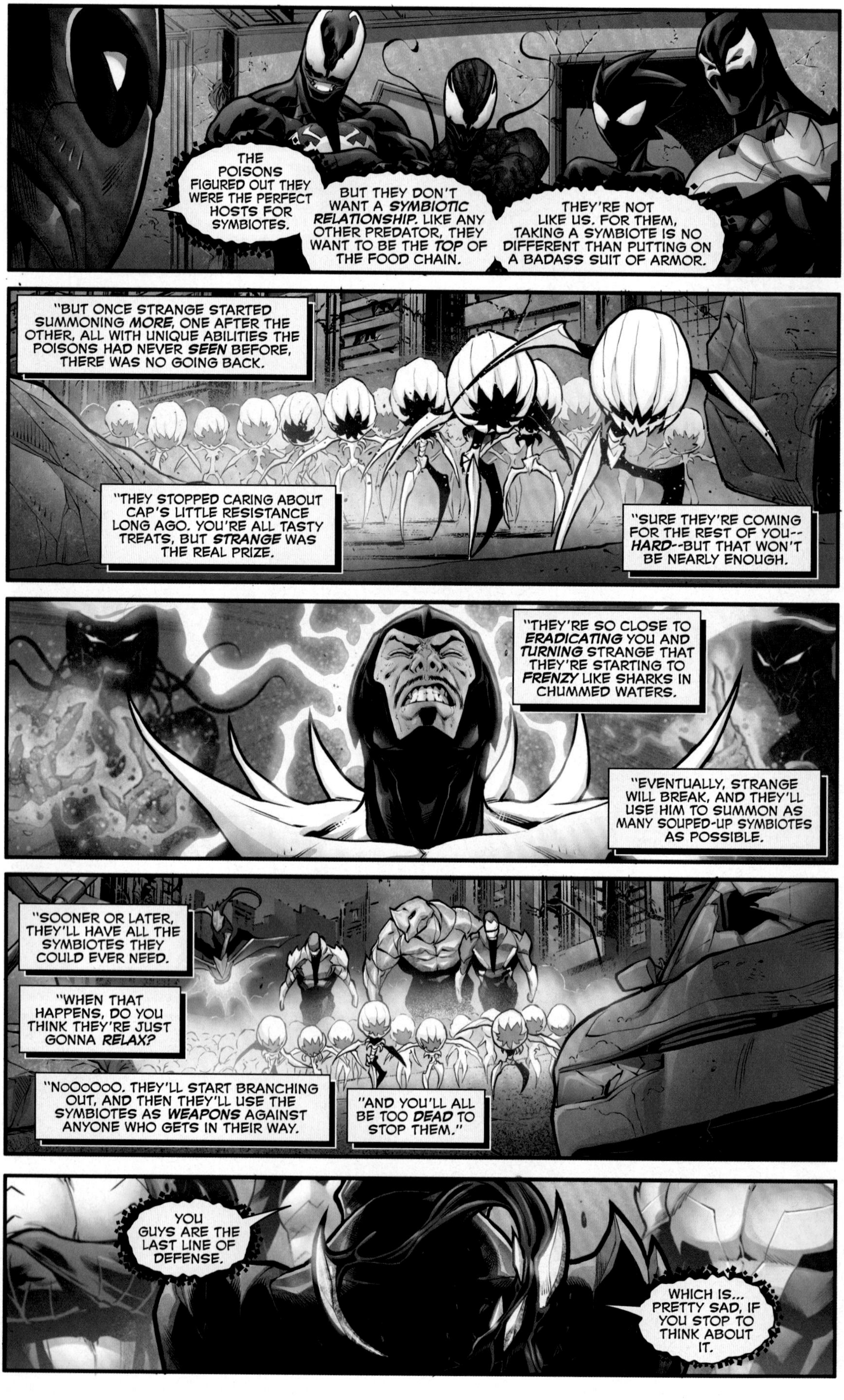
THE POISONS FIGURED OUT THEY WERE THE PERFECT HOSTS FOR SYMBIOTES.
BUT THEY DON'T WANT A SYMBIOTIC RELATIONSHIP. LIKE ANY OTHER PREDATOR, THEY WANT TO BE THE TOP OF THE FOOD CHAIN.
THEY'RE NOT LIKE US. FOR THEM, TAKING A SYMBIOTE IS NO DIFFERENT THAN PUTTING ON A BADASS SUIT OF ARMOR.
"BUT ONCE STRANGE STARTED SUMMONING MORE, ONE AFTER THE OTHER, ALL WITH UNIQUE ABILITIES THE POISONS HAD NEVER SEEN BEFORE, THERE WAS NO GOING BACK.
"THEY STOPPED CARING ABOUT CAP'S LITTLE RESISTANCE LONG AGO. YOU'RE ALL TASTY TREATS, BUT STRANGE WAS THE REAL PRIZE.
"SURE THEY'RE COMING FOR THE REST OF YOU--HARD--BUT THAT WON'T BE NEARLY ENOUGH.
"THEY'RE SO CLOSE TO ERADICATING YOU AND TURNING STRANGE THAT THEY'RE STARTING TO FRENZY LIKE SHARKS IN CHUMMED WATERS.
"EVENTUALLY, STRANGE WILL BREAK, AND THEY'LL USE HIM TO SUMMON AS MANY SOUPED-UP SYMBIOTES AS POSSIBLE.
"SOONER OR LATER, THEY'LL HAVE ALL THE SYMBIOTES THEY COULD EVER NEED.
"WHEN THAT HAPPENS, DO YOU THINK THEY'RE JUST GONNA RELAX?
"NOOOOOO. THEY'LL START BRANCHING OUT, AND THEN THEY'LL USE THE SYMBIOTES AS WEAPONS AGAINST ANYONE WHO GETS IN THEIR WAY.
"AND YOU'LL ALL BE TOO DEAD TO STOP THEM."
YOU GUYS ARE THE LAST LINE OF DEFENSE.
WHICH IS... PRETTY SAD, IF YOU STOP TO THINK ABOUT IT.

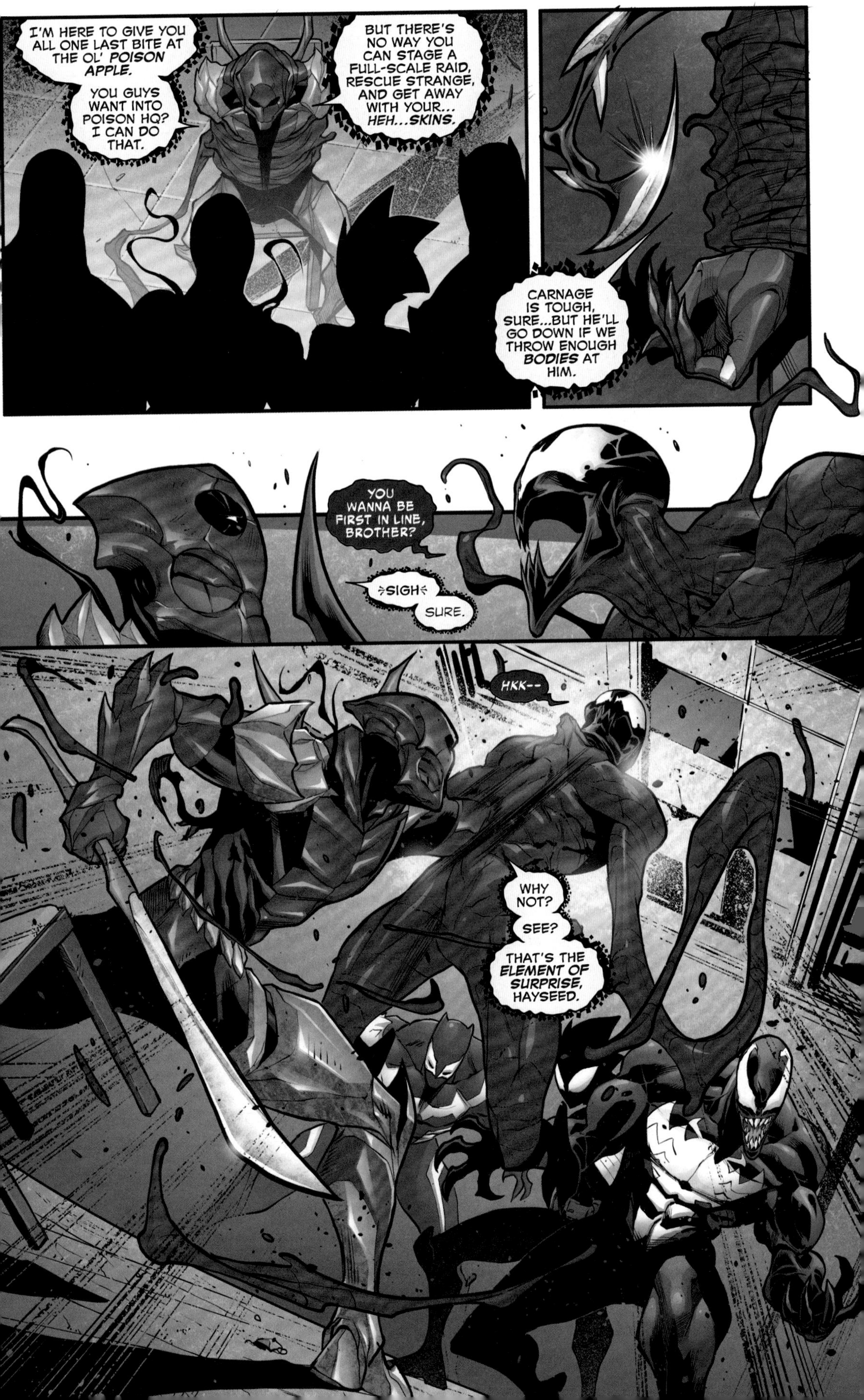
I'M HERE TO GIVE YOU ALL ONE LAST BITE AT THE OL' POISON APPLE.
YOU GUYS WANT INTO POISON HQ? I CAN DO THAT.
BUT THERE'S NO WAY YOU CAN STAGE A FULL-SCALE RAID, RESCUE STRANGE, AND GET AWAY WITH YOUR... HEH...SKINS.
CARNAGE IS TOUGH, SURE...BUT HE'LL GO DOWN IF WE THROW ENOUGH BODIES AT HIM.
YOU WANNA BE FIRST IN LINE, BROTHER?
SIGH
SURE.
HKK--
WHY NOT?
SEE?
THAT'S THE ELEMENT OF SURPRISE, HAYSEED.

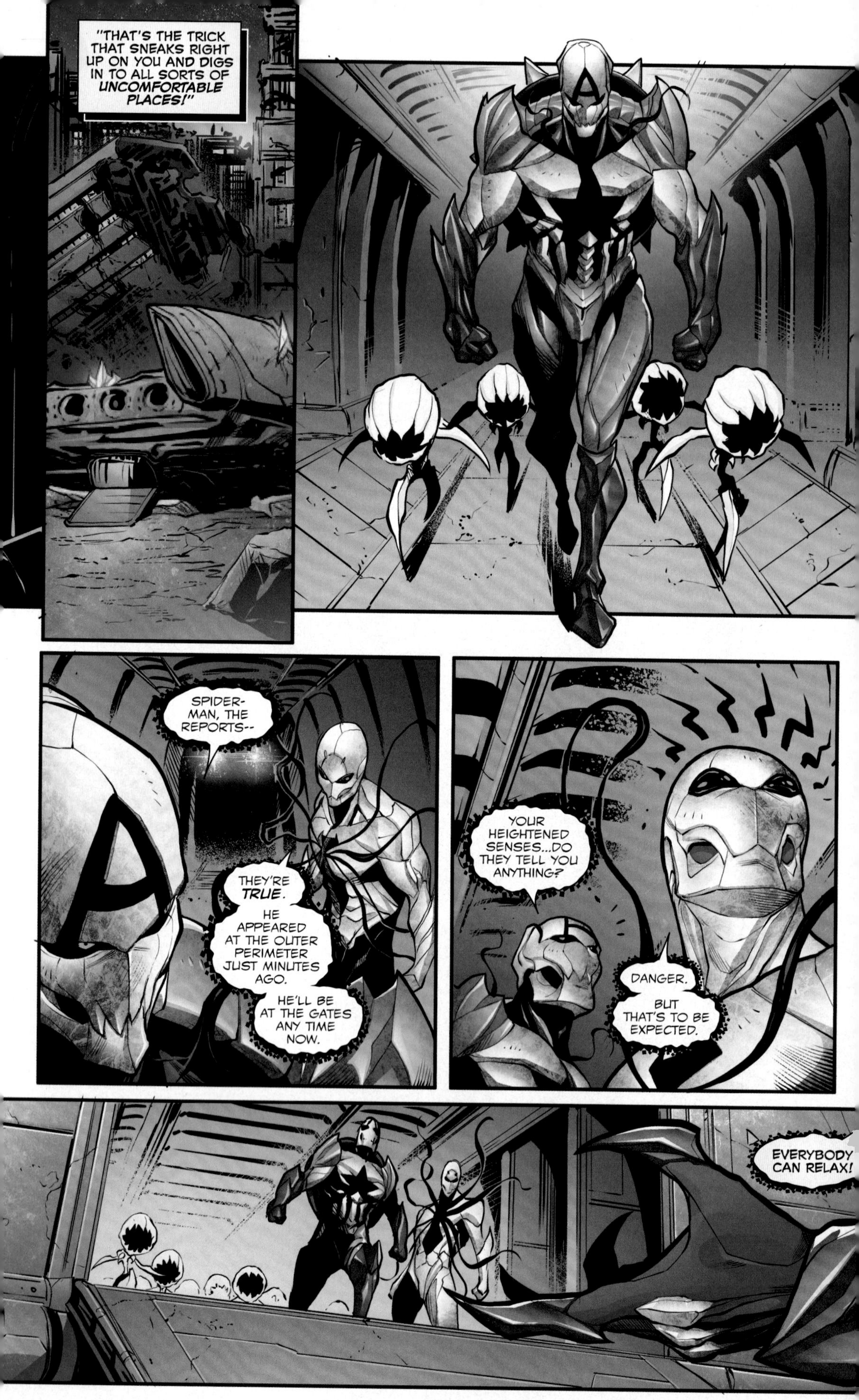
"THAT'S THE TRICK THAT SNEAKS RIGHT UP ON YOU AND DIGS IN TO ALL SORTS OF UNCOMFORTABLE PLACES!"
SPIDER-MAN, THE REPORTS--
THEY'RE TRUE.
HE APPEARED AT THE OUTER PERIMETER JUST MINUTES AGO.
HE'LL BE AT THE GATES ANY TIME NOW.
YOUR HEIGHTENED SENSES...DO THEY TELL YOU ANYTHING?
DANGER.
BUT THAT'S TO BE EXPECTED.
EVERYBODY CAN RELAX!

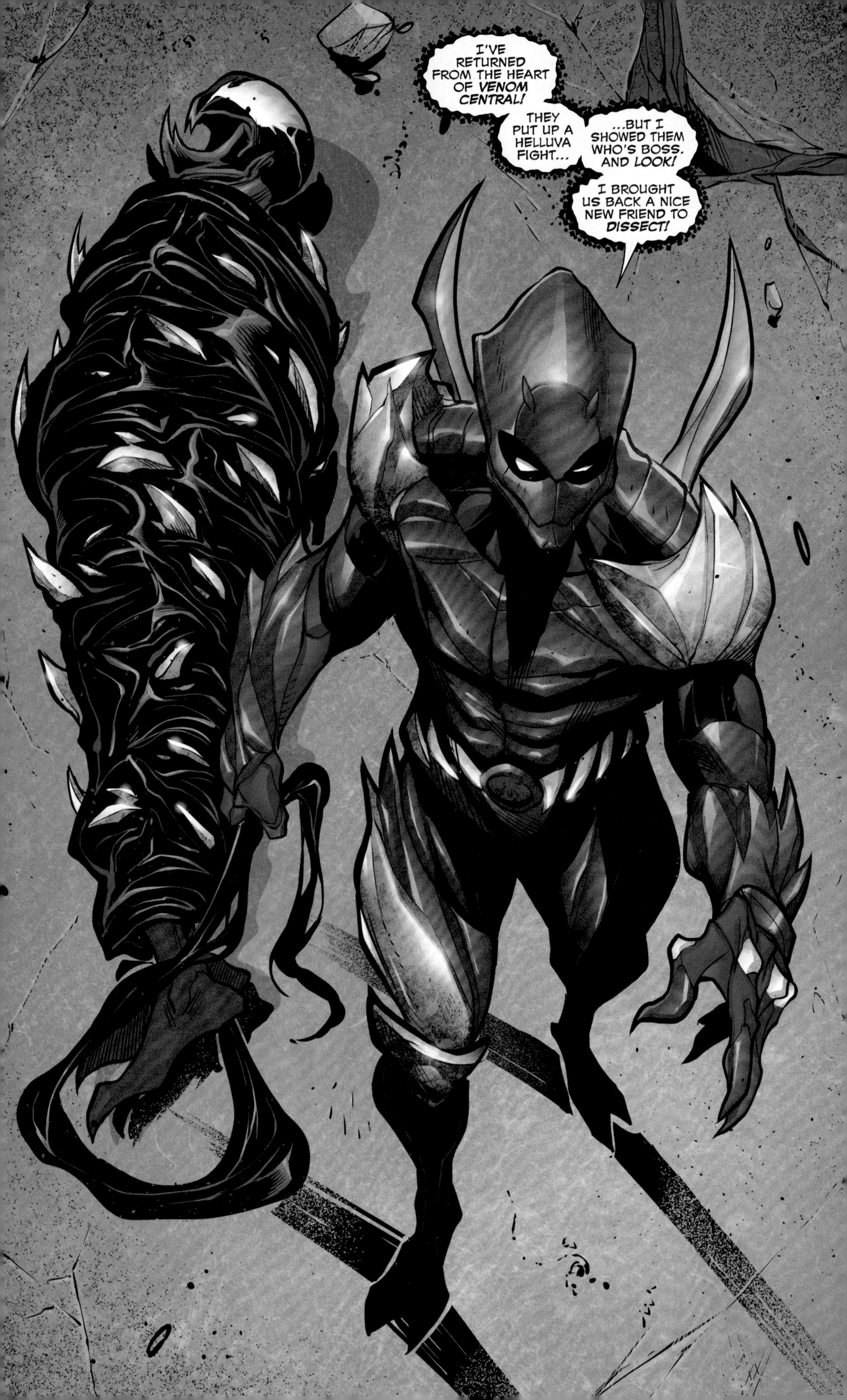
I'VE RETURNED FROM THE HEART OF *VENOM CENTRAL!*
THEY PUT UP A HELLUVA FIGHT...
...BUT I SHOWED THEM WHO'S BOSS. AND *LOOK!*
I BROUGHT US BACK A NICE NEW FRIEND TO *DISSECT!*

5

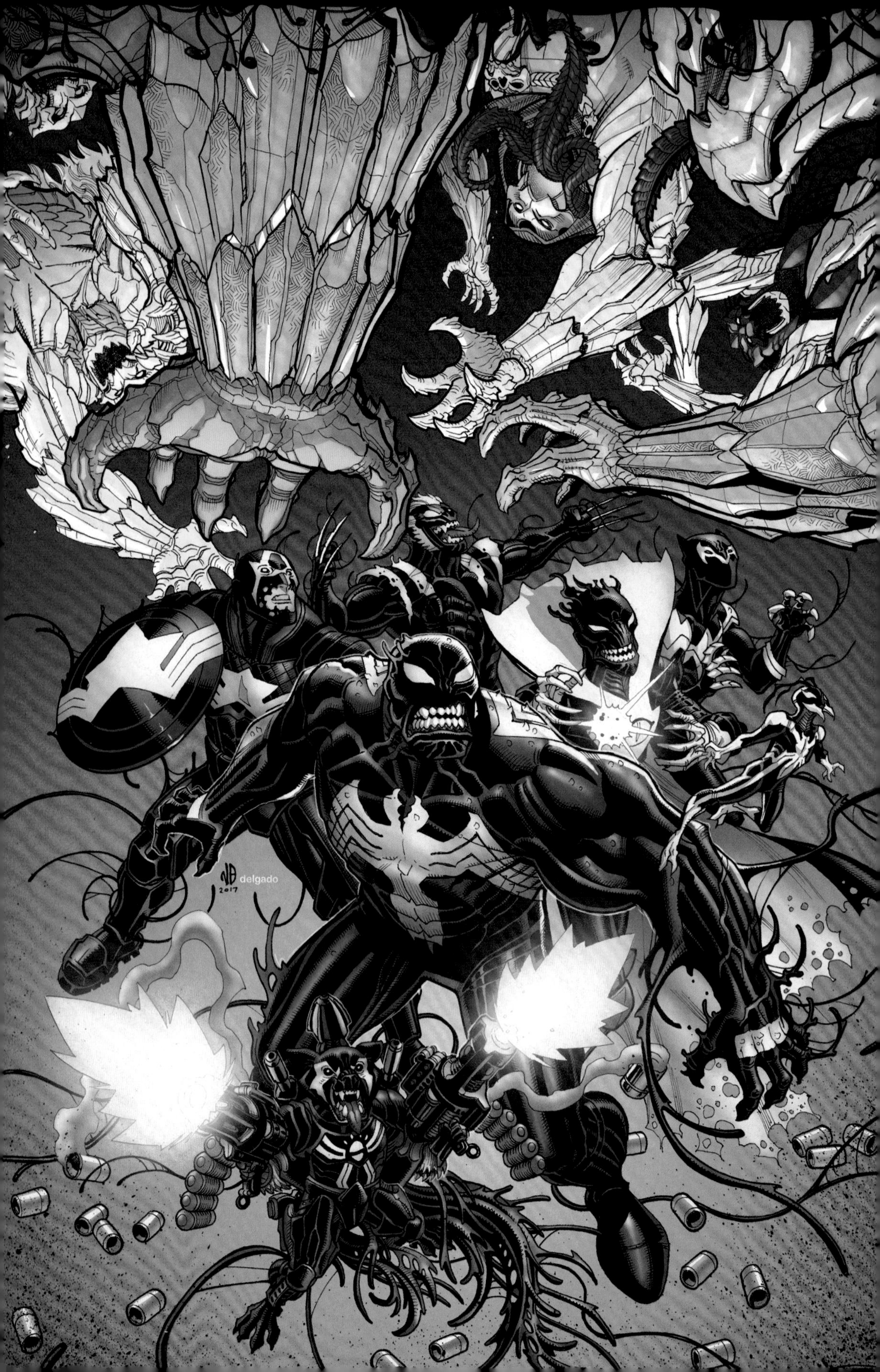
delgado
2017

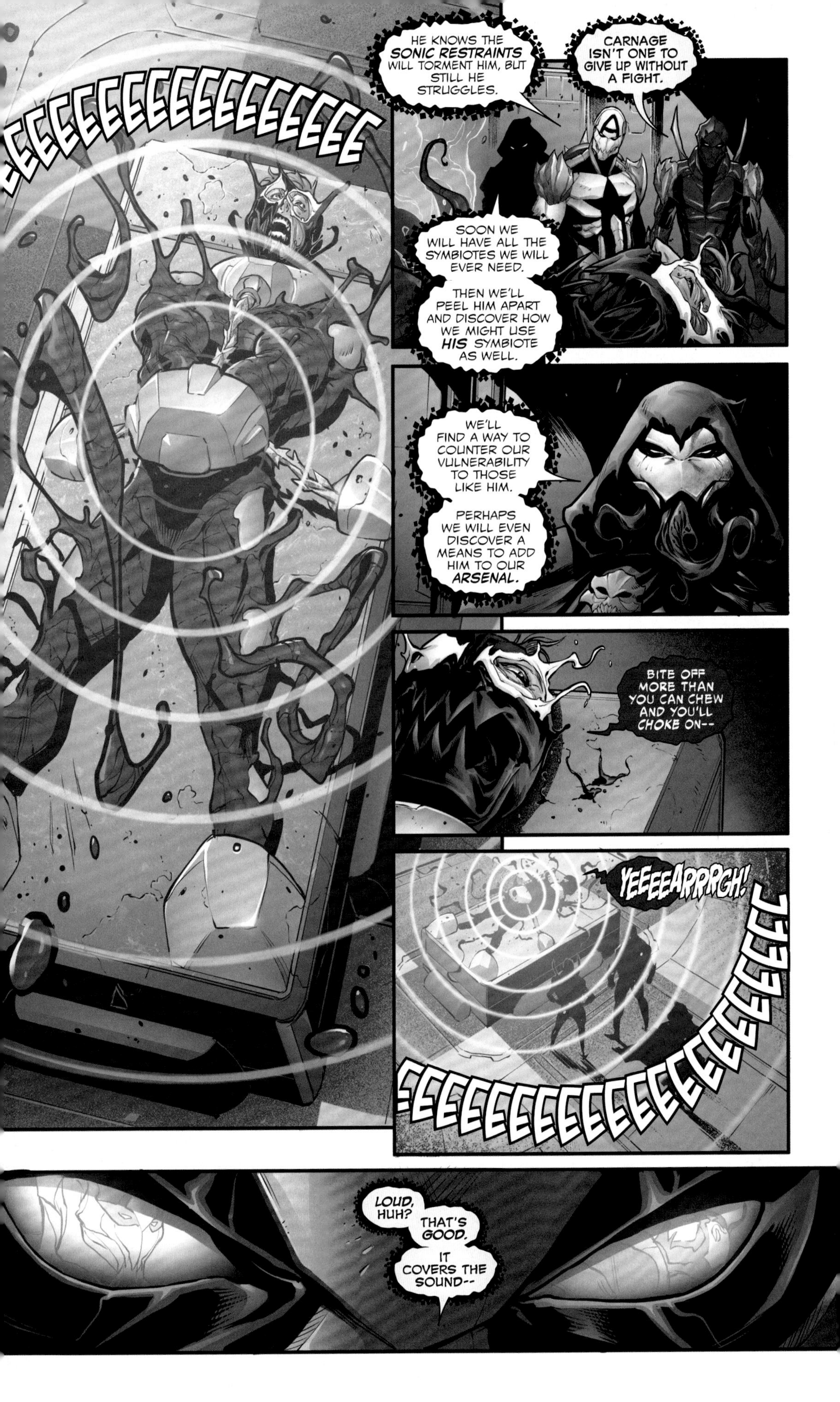

EEEEEEEEEEEEEEEEEE
HE KNOWS THE SONIC RESTRAINTS WILL TORMENT HIM, BUT STILL HE STRUGGLES.
CARNAGE ISN'T ONE TO GIVE UP WITHOUT A FIGHT.
SOON WE WILL HAVE ALL THE SYMBIOTES WE WILL EVER NEED.
THEN WE'LL PEEL HIM APART AND DISCOVER HOW WE MIGHT USE HIS SYMBIOTE AS WELL.
WE'LL FIND A WAY TO COUNTER OUR VULNERABILITY TO THOSE LIKE HIM.
PERHAPS WE WILL EVEN DISCOVER A MEANS TO ADD HIM TO OUR ARSENAL.
BITE OFF MORE THAN YOU CAN CHEW AND YOU'LL CHOKE ON--
YEEEEARRRGH!
EEEEEEEEEEEEEEEEEEEEEEEE
LOUD, HUH?
THAT'S GOOD.
IT COVERS THE SOUND--

EEEEEEEEEEEEEEEEEEEEEEEEEEEEEEEEEEEEEEEEEEE

--OF ME GUTTING YOU!

NICE JOB SETTING OFF THOSE RESTRAINTS TO GIVE US A LITTLE COVER.

WASN'T ON PURPOSE.

WELL... NICE JOB BEING AN IDIOT.

ON YER FEET, CARNAGE.

WE'VE STILL GOT A JOB TO DO.

IT'S GONNA BE A BLOODY RIDE!

YEAH, YEAH.

CAUSE A DISTRACTION SO THE REST OF YOUR LITTLE BUDDIES CAN MAKE THEIR MOVE.

WELL, STRAP IN.

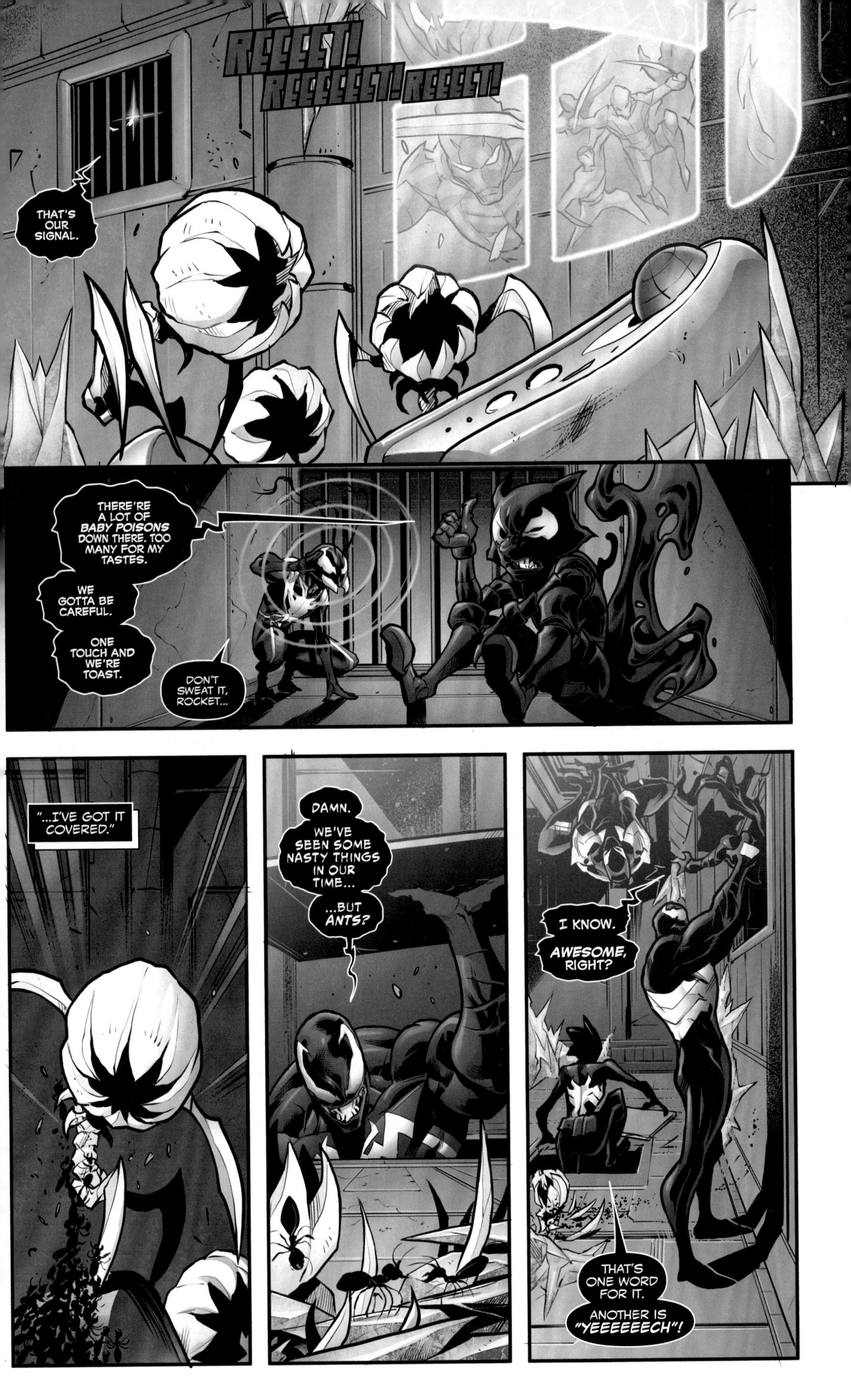
REEEET! REEEEEET! REEEET!
THAT'S OUR SIGNAL.
THERE'RE A LOT OF BABY POISONS DOWN THERE. TOO MANY FOR MY TASTES.
WE GOTTA BE CAREFUL.
ONE TOUCH AND WE'RE TOAST.
DON'T SWEAT IT, ROCKET...
"...I'VE GOT IT COVERED."
DAMN.
WE'VE SEEN SOME NASTY THINGS IN OUR TIME...
...BUT ANTS?
I KNOW.
AWESOME, RIGHT?
THAT'S ONE WORD FOR IT.
ANOTHER IS "YEEEEEECH"!

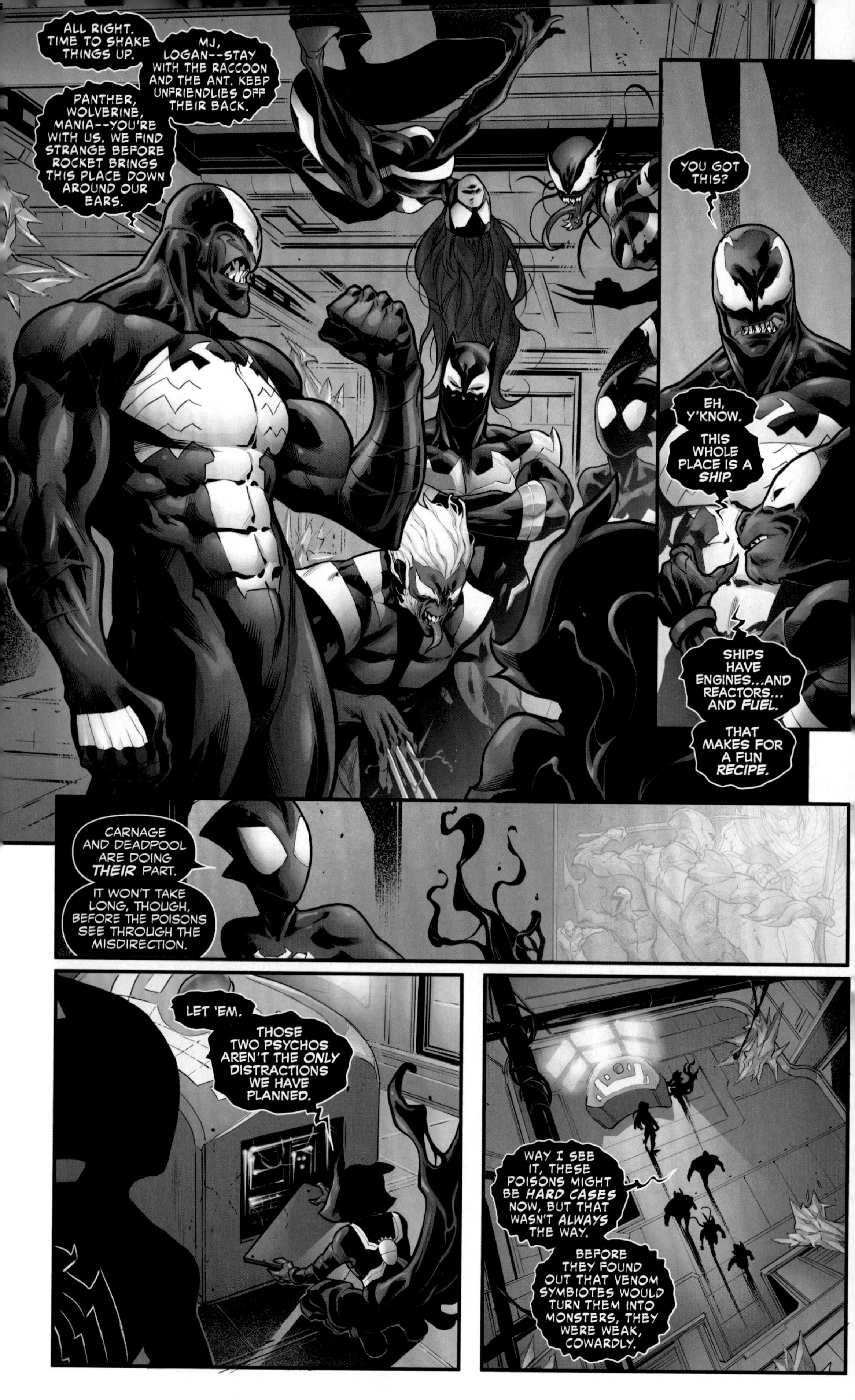
ALL RIGHT. TIME TO SHAKE THINGS UP.
MJ, LOGAN--STAY WITH THE RACCOON AND THE ANT. KEEP UNFRIENDLIES OFF THEIR BACK.
PANTHER, WOLVERINE, MANIA--YOU'RE WITH US. WE FIND STRANGE BEFORE ROCKET BRINGS THIS PLACE DOWN AROUND OUR EARS.
YOU GOT THIS?
EH, Y'KNOW.
THIS WHOLE PLACE IS A SHIP.
SHIPS HAVE ENGINES...AND REACTORS... AND FUEL.
THAT MAKES FOR A FUN RECIPE.
CARNAGE AND DEADPOOL ARE DOING THEIR PART.
IT WON'T TAKE LONG, THOUGH, BEFORE THE POISONS SEE THROUGH THE MISDIRECTION.
LET 'EM.
THOSE TWO PSYCHOS AREN'T THE ONLY DISTRACTIONS WE HAVE PLANNED.
WAY I SEE IT, THESE POISONS MIGHT BE HARD CASES NOW, BUT THAT WASN'T ALWAYS THE WAY.
BEFORE THEY FOUND OUT THAT VENOM SYMBIOTES WOULD TURN THEM INTO MONSTERS, THEY WERE WEAK, COWARDLY.

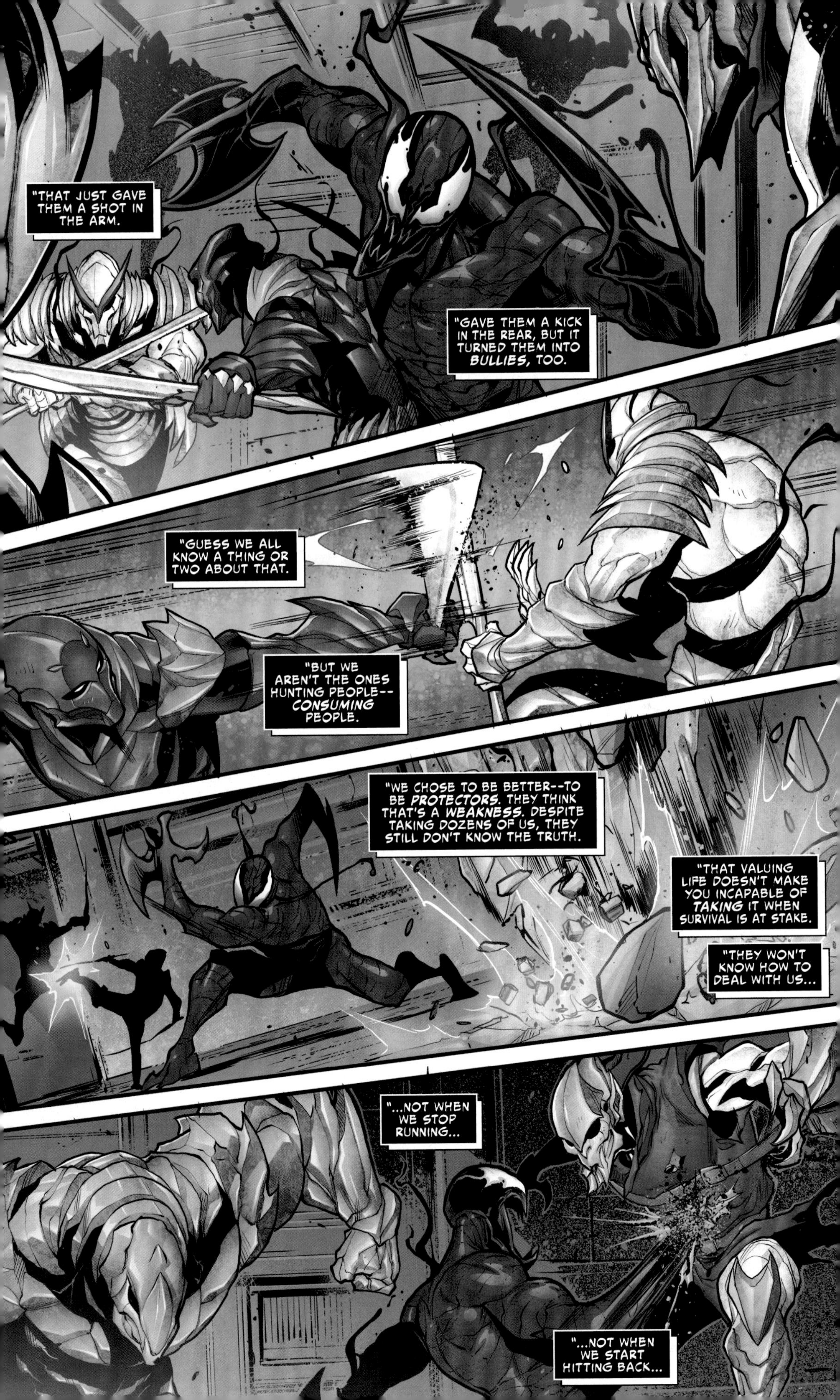
"THAT JUST GAVE THEM A SHOT IN THE ARM.
"GAVE THEM A KICK IN THE REAR, BUT IT TURNED THEM INTO *BULLIES*, TOO.
"GUESS WE ALL KNOW A THING OR TWO ABOUT THAT.
"BUT WE AREN'T THE ONES HUNTING PEOPLE-- *CONSUMING* PEOPLE.
"WE CHOSE TO BE BETTER--TO BE *PROTECTORS*. THEY THINK THAT'S A *WEAKNESS*. DESPITE TAKING DOZENS OF US, THEY STILL DON'T KNOW THE TRUTH.
"THAT VALUING LIFE DOESN'T MAKE YOU INCAPABLE OF *TAKING* IT WHEN SURVIVAL IS AT STAKE.
"THEY WON'T KNOW HOW TO DEAL WITH US...
"...NOT WHEN WE STOP RUNNING...
"...NOT WHEN WE START HITTING BACK...

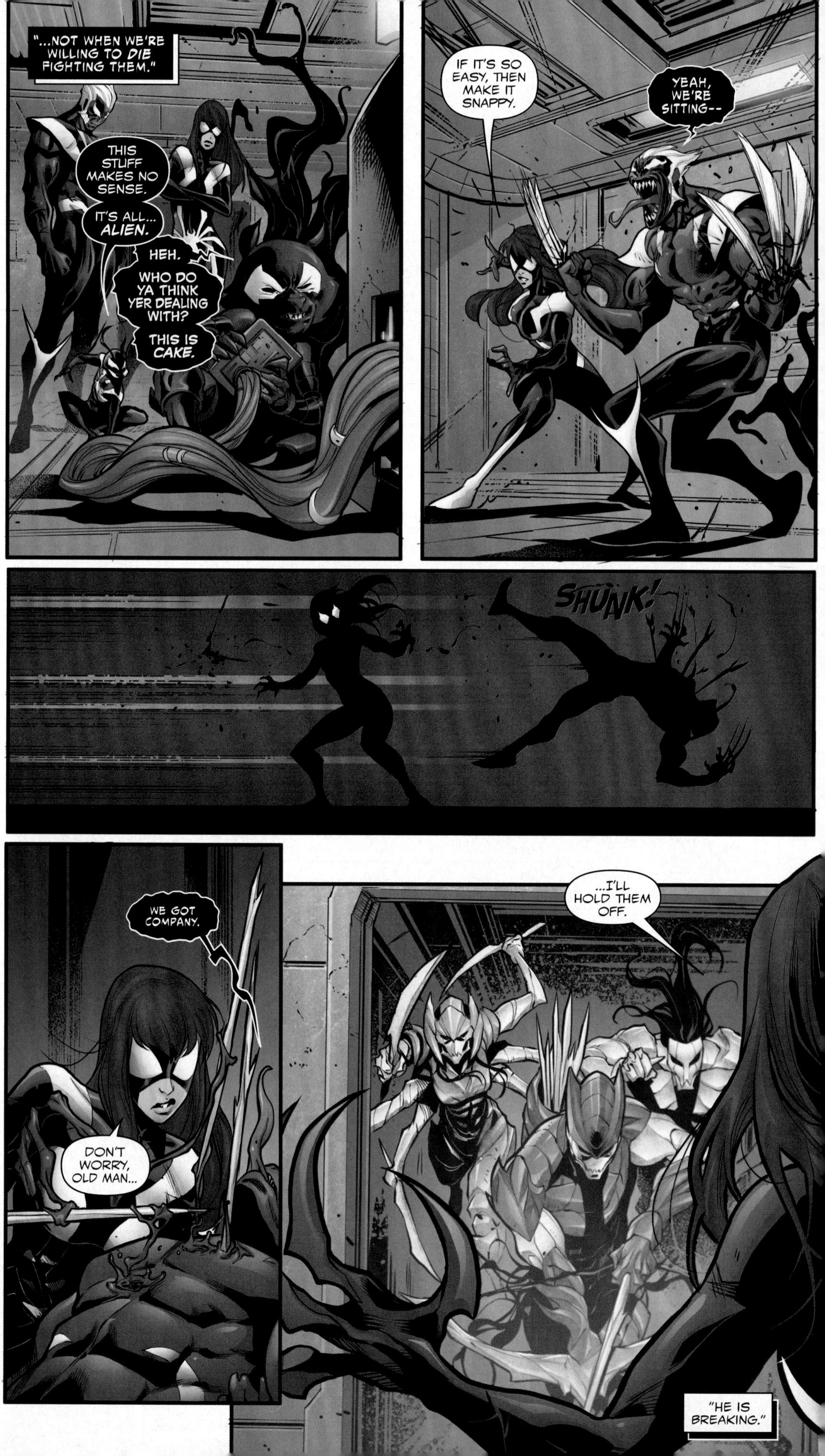

"...NOT WHEN WE'RE WILLING TO DIE FIGHTING THEM."
THIS STUFF MAKES NO SENSE.
IT'S ALL... ALIEN.
HEH.
WHO DO YA THINK YER DEALING WITH?
THIS IS CAKE.
IF IT'S SO EASY, THEN MAKE IT SNAPPY.
YEAH, WE'RE SITTING--
SHUNK!
WE GOT COMPANY.
DON'T WORRY, OLD MAN...
...I'LL HOLD THEM OFF.
"HE IS BREAKING."

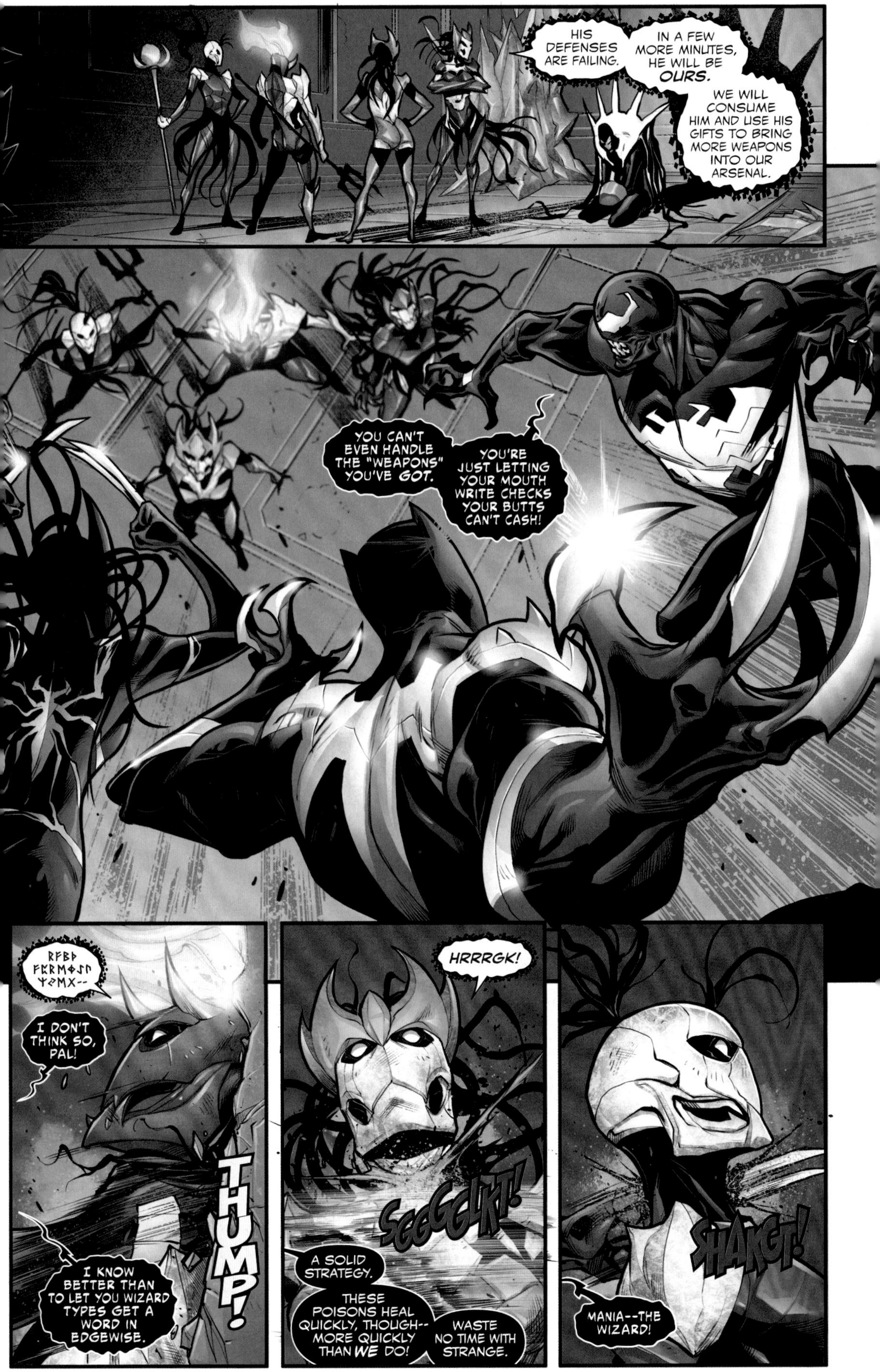
HIS DEFENSES ARE FAILING.
IN A FEW MORE MINUTES, HE WILL BE OURS.
WE WILL CONSUME HIM AND USE HIS GIFTS TO BRING MORE WEAPONS INTO OUR ARSENAL.
YOU CAN'T EVEN HANDLE THE "WEAPONS" YOU'VE GOT.
YOU'RE JUST LETTING YOUR MOUTH WRITE CHECKS YOUR BUTTS CAN'T CASH!
I DON'T THINK SO, PAL!
THUMP!
I KNOW BETTER THAN TO LET YOU WIZARD TYPES GET A WORD IN EDGEWISE.
HRRRGK!
SGGGGLKT!
A SOLID STRATEGY.
THESE POISONS HEAL QUICKLY, THOUGH-- MORE QUICKLY THAN WE DO!
WASTE NO TIME WITH STRANGE.
SHAKGT!
MANIA--THE WIZARD!

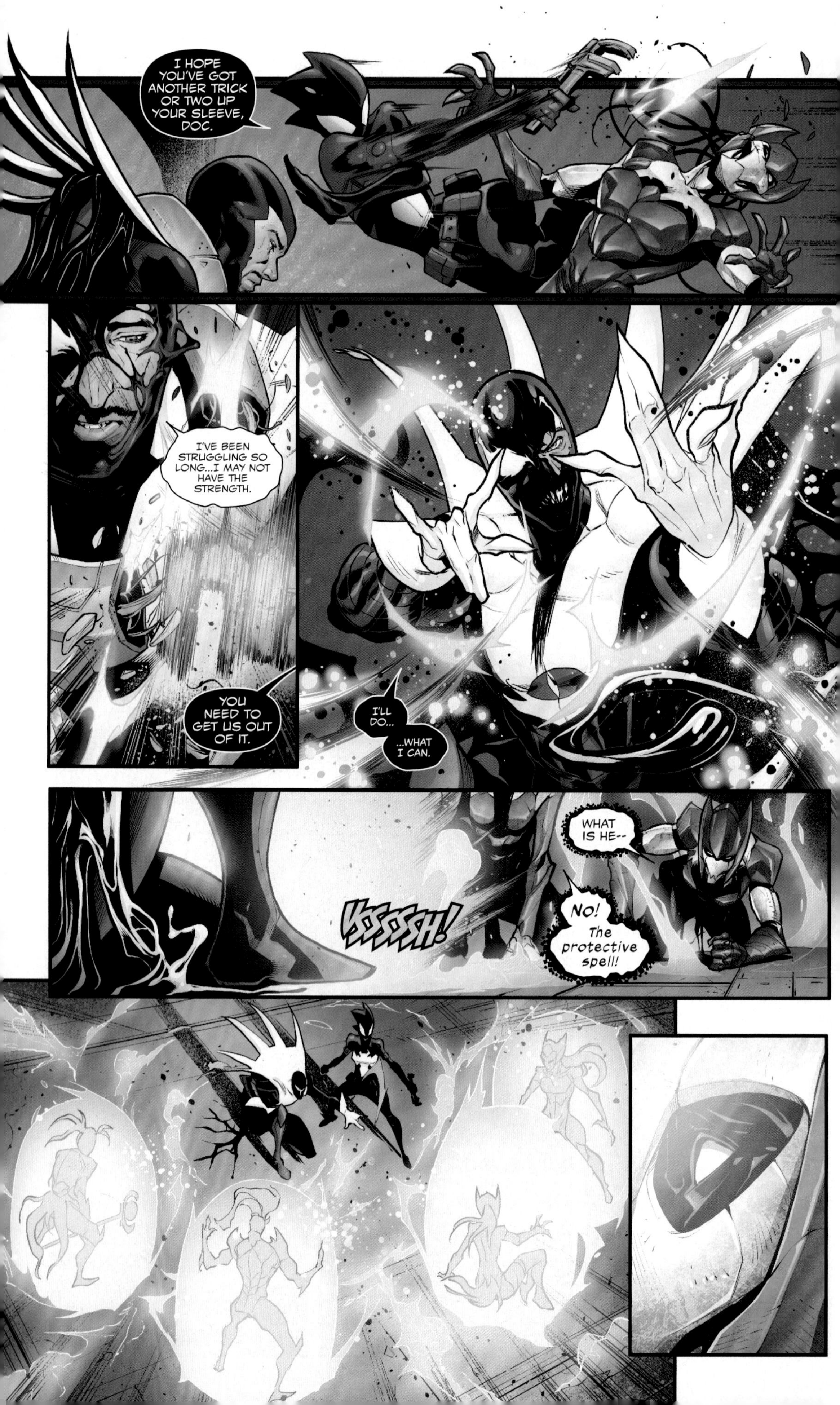

I HOPE YOU'VE GOT ANOTHER TRICK OR TWO UP YOUR SLEEVE, DOC.
I'VE BEEN STRUGGLING SO LONG...I MAY NOT HAVE THE STRENGTH.
YOU NEED TO GET US OUT OF IT.
I'LL DO...
...WHAT I CAN.
WHAT IS HE--
VSSSSH!
NO! The protective spell!

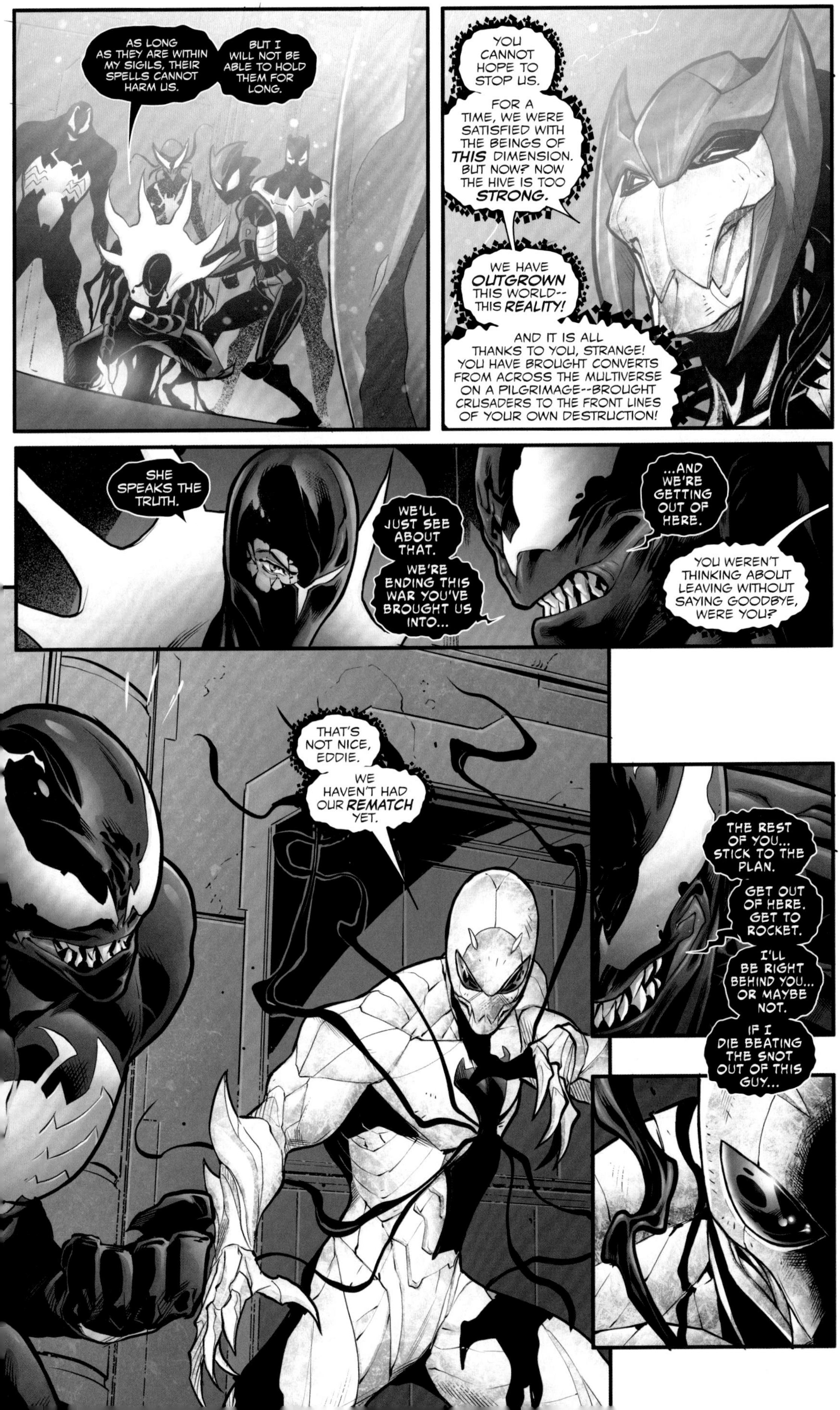
AS LONG AS THEY ARE WITHIN MY SIGILS, THEIR SPELLS CANNOT HARM US.
BUT I WILL NOT BE ABLE TO HOLD THEM FOR LONG.
YOU CANNOT HOPE TO STOP US.
FOR A TIME, WE WERE SATISFIED WITH THE BEINGS OF THIS DIMENSION. BUT NOW? NOW THE HIVE IS TOO STRONG.
WE HAVE OUTGROWN THIS WORLD-- THIS REALITY!
AND IT IS ALL THANKS TO YOU, STRANGE! YOU HAVE BROUGHT CONVERTS FROM ACROSS THE MULTIVERSE ON A PILGRIMAGE--BROUGHT CRUSADERS TO THE FRONT LINES OF YOUR OWN DESTRUCTION!
SHE SPEAKS THE TRUTH.
WE'LL JUST SEE ABOUT THAT.
WE'RE ENDING THIS WAR YOU'VE BROUGHT US INTO...
...AND WE'RE GETTING OUT OF HERE.
YOU WEREN'T THINKING ABOUT LEAVING WITHOUT SAYING GOODBYE, WERE YOU?
THAT'S NOT NICE, EDDIE.
WE HAVEN'T HAD OUR REMATCH YET.
THE REST OF YOU... STICK TO THE PLAN.
GET OUT OF HERE. GET TO ROCKET.
I'LL BE RIGHT BEHIND YOU... OR MAYBE NOT.
IF I DIE BEATING THE SNOT OUT OF THIS GUY...

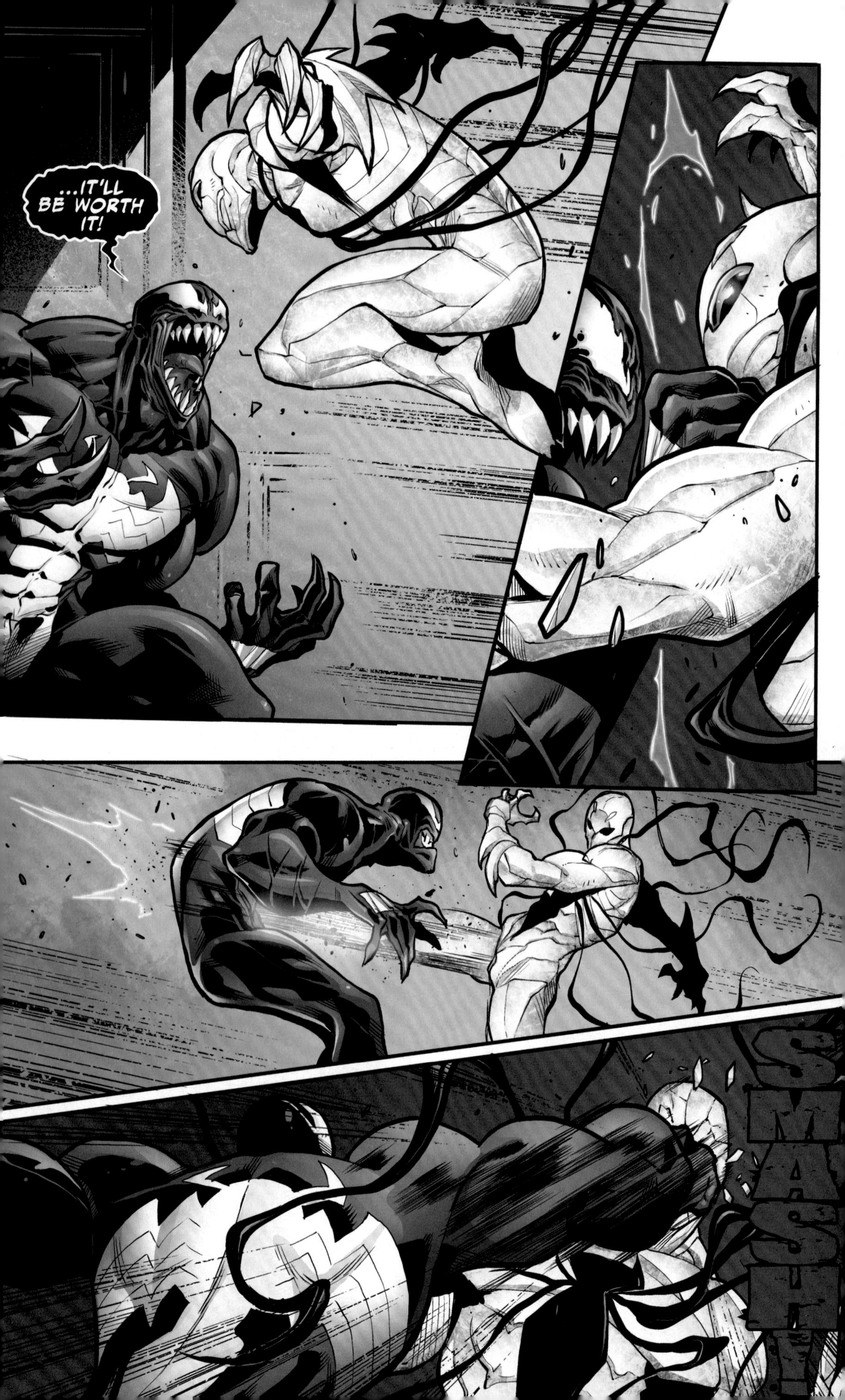
...IT'LL BE WORTH IT!
SMASH!

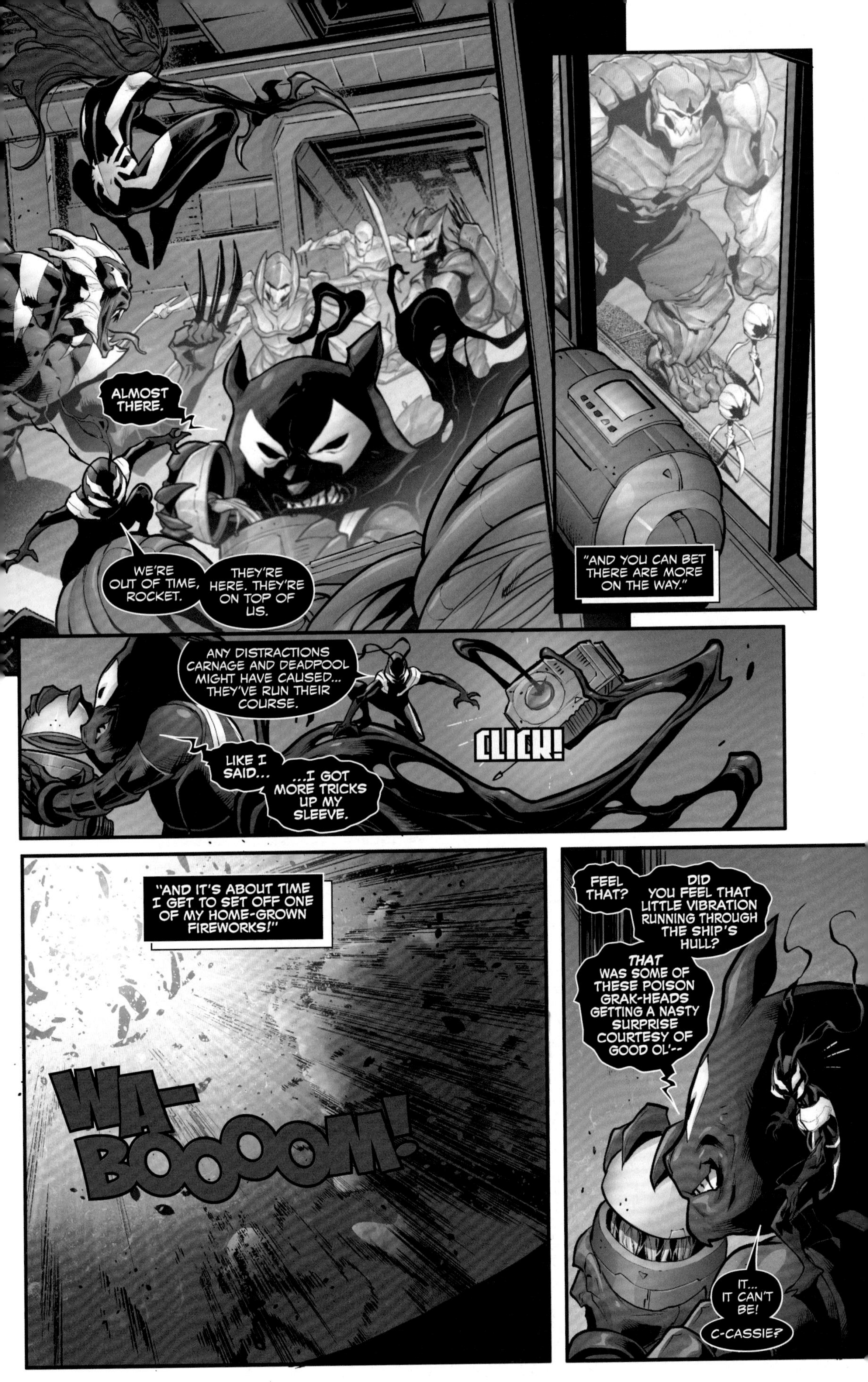
ALMOST THERE.
WE'RE OUT OF TIME, ROCKET.
THEY'RE HERE. THEY'RE ON TOP OF US.
"AND YOU CAN BET THERE ARE MORE ON THE WAY."
ANY DISTRACTIONS CARNAGE AND DEADPOOL MIGHT HAVE CAUSED... THEY'VE RUN THEIR COURSE.
LIKE I SAID...
...I GOT MORE TRICKS UP MY SLEEVE.
CLICK!
"AND IT'S ABOUT TIME I GET TO SET OFF ONE OF MY HOME-GROWN FIREWORKS!"
WA-BOOOOOM!
FEEL THAT?
DID YOU FEEL THAT LITTLE VIBRATION RUNNING THROUGH THE SHIP'S HULL?
THAT WAS SOME OF THESE POISON GRAK-HEADS GETTING A NASTY SURPRISE COURTESY OF GOOD OL'--
IT... IT CAN'T BE!
C-CASSIE?

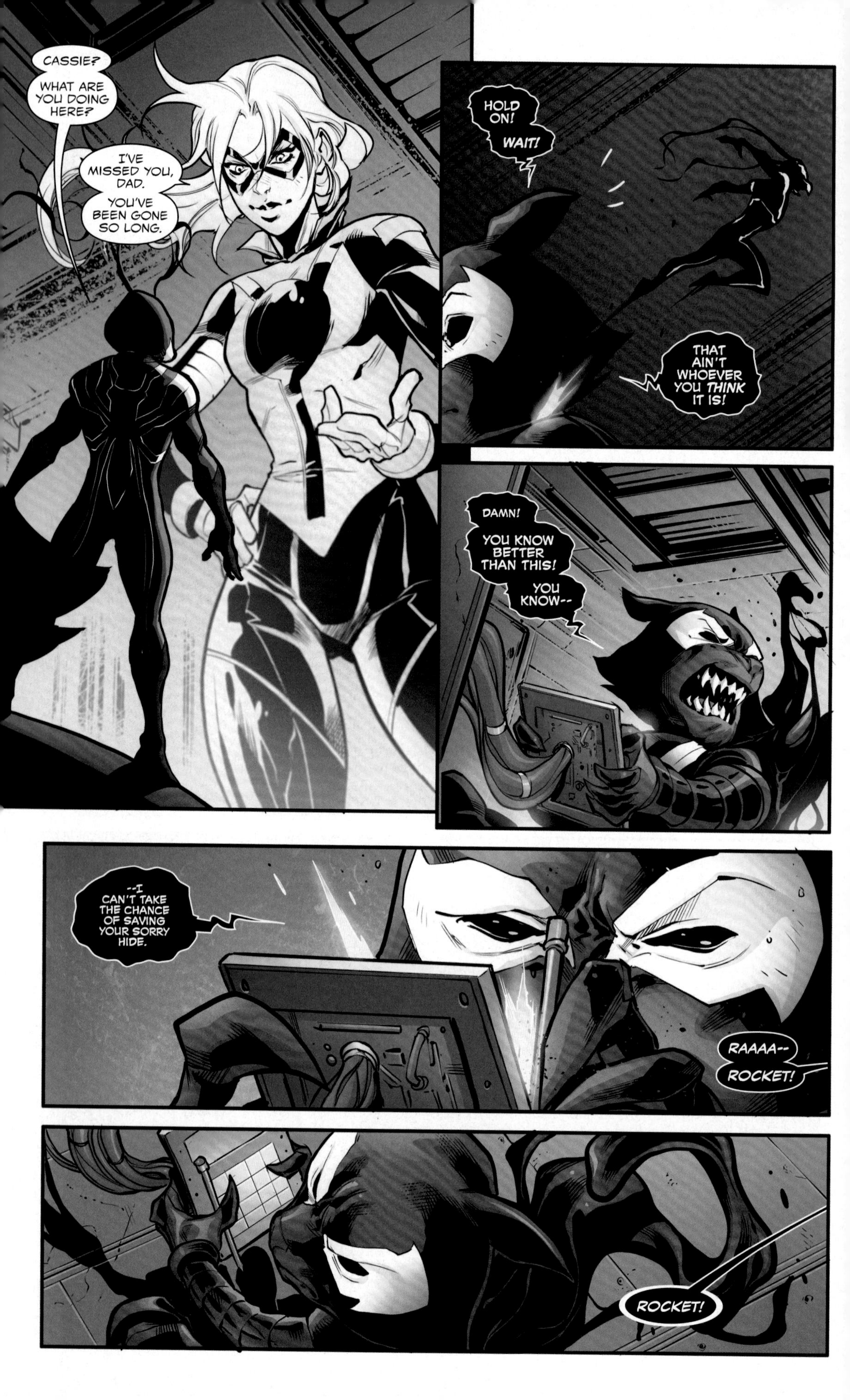
CASSIE?
WHAT ARE YOU DOING HERE?
I'VE MISSED YOU, DAD.
YOU'VE BEEN GONE SO LONG.
HOLD ON!
WAIT!
THAT AIN'T WHOEVER YOU THINK IT IS!
DAMN!
YOU KNOW BETTER THAN THIS!
YOU KNOW--
--I CAN'T TAKE THE CHANCE OF SAVING YOUR SORRY HIDE.
RAAAA--
ROCKET!
ROCKET!

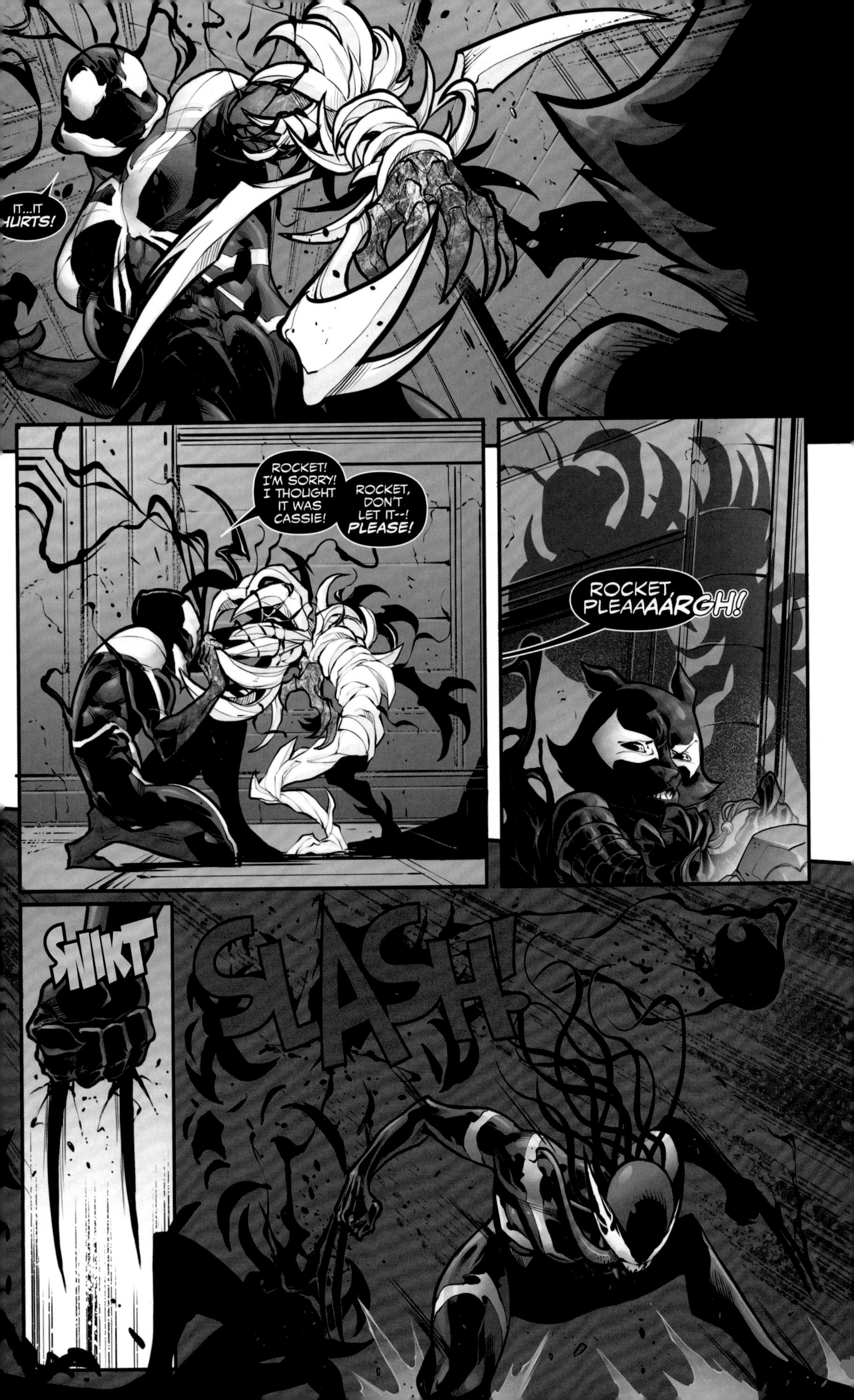
IT...IT HURTS!
ROCKET! I'M SORRY! I THOUGHT IT WAS CASSIE!
ROCKET, DON'T LET IT--! PLEASE!
ROCKET, PLEAAAARGH!
SNIKT
SLASH!

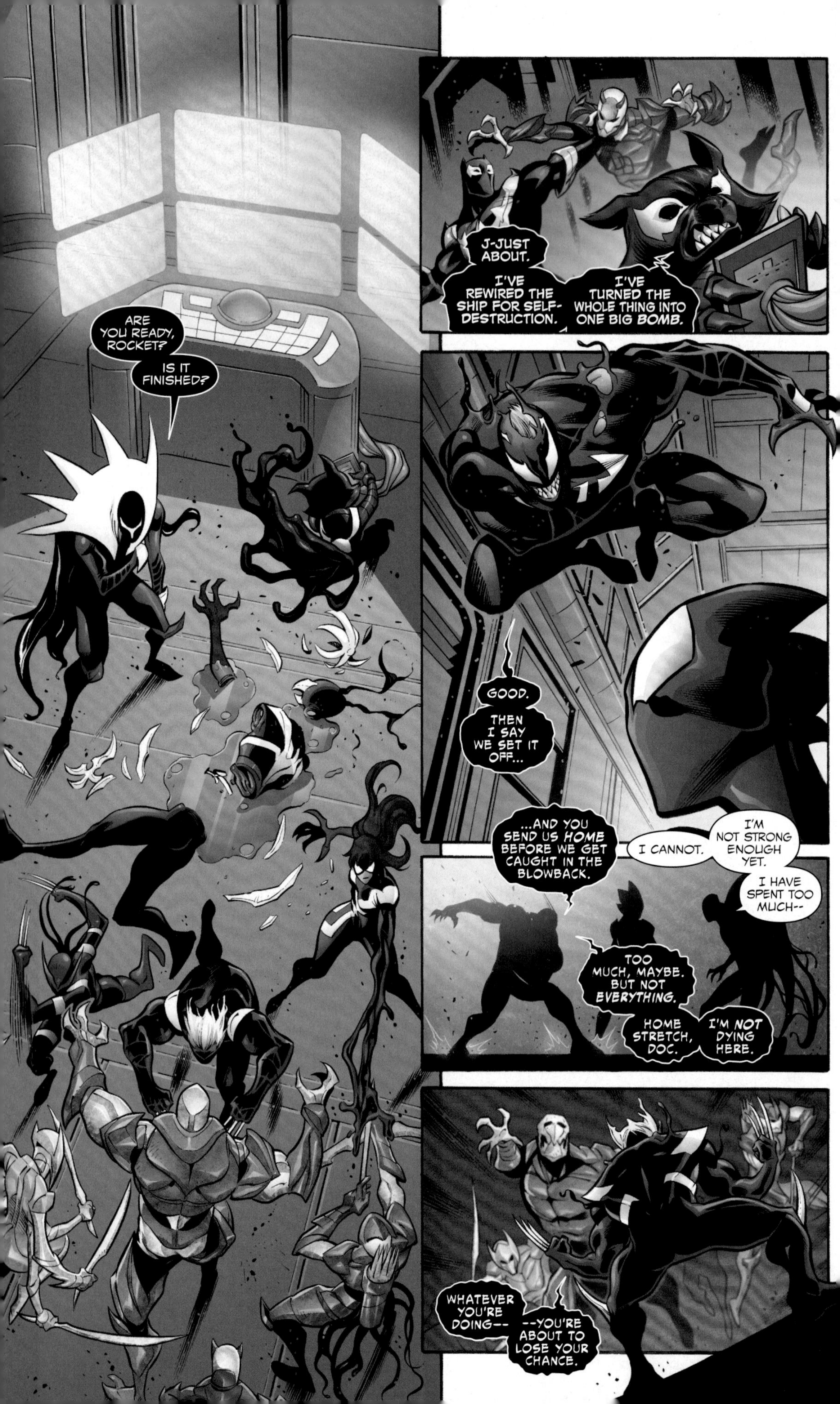

ARE YOU READY, ROCKET?
IS IT FINISHED?
J-JUST ABOUT.
I'VE REWIRED THE SHIP FOR SELF-DESTRUCTION.
I'VE TURNED THE WHOLE THING INTO ONE BIG BOMB.
GOOD.
THEN I SAY WE SET IT OFF...
...AND YOU SEND US HOME BEFORE WE GET CAUGHT IN THE BLOWBACK.
I CANNOT.
I'M NOT STRONG ENOUGH YET.
I HAVE SPENT TOO MUCH--
TOO MUCH, MAYBE. BUT NOT EVERYTHING.
HOME STRETCH, DOC.
I'M NOT DYING HERE.
WHATEVER YOU'RE DOING--
--YOU'RE ABOUT TO LOSE YOUR CHANCE.

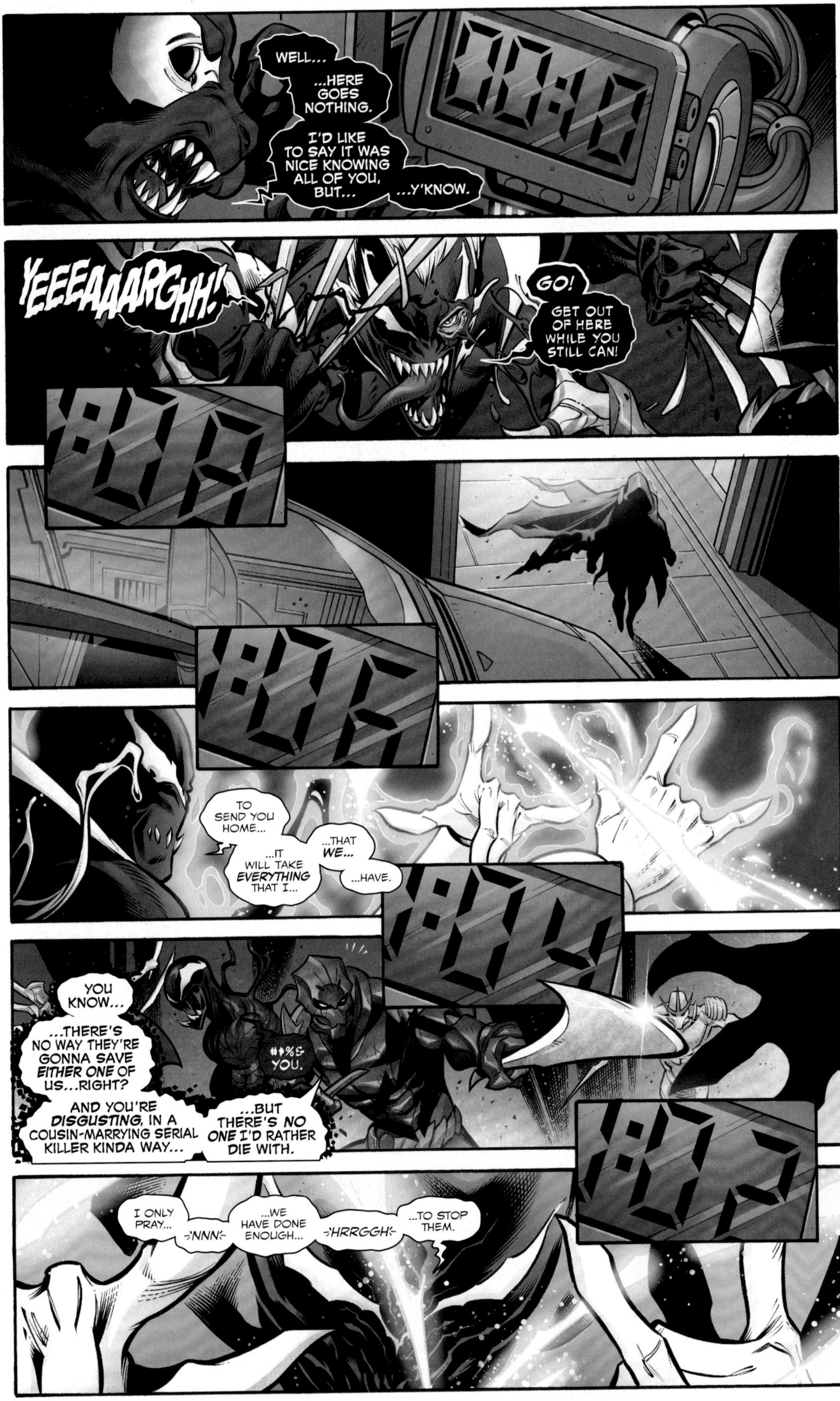

WELL...
...HERE GOES NOTHING.
I'D LIKE TO SAY IT WAS NICE KNOWING ALL OF YOU, BUT...
...Y'KNOW.
YEEEAAARGHH!
GO!
GET OUT OF HERE WHILE YOU STILL CAN!
TO SEND YOU HOME...
...IT WILL TAKE EVERYTHING THAT I...
...THAT WE...
...HAVE.
YOU KNOW...
...THERE'S NO WAY THEY'RE GONNA SAVE EITHER ONE OF US...RIGHT?
#$%& YOU.
AND YOU'RE DISGUSTING, IN A COUSIN-MARRYING SERIAL KILLER KINDA WAY...
...BUT THERE'S NO ONE I'D RATHER DIE WITH.
I ONLY PRAY...
NNN
...WE HAVE DONE ENOUGH...
HRRGGH
...TO STOP THEM.

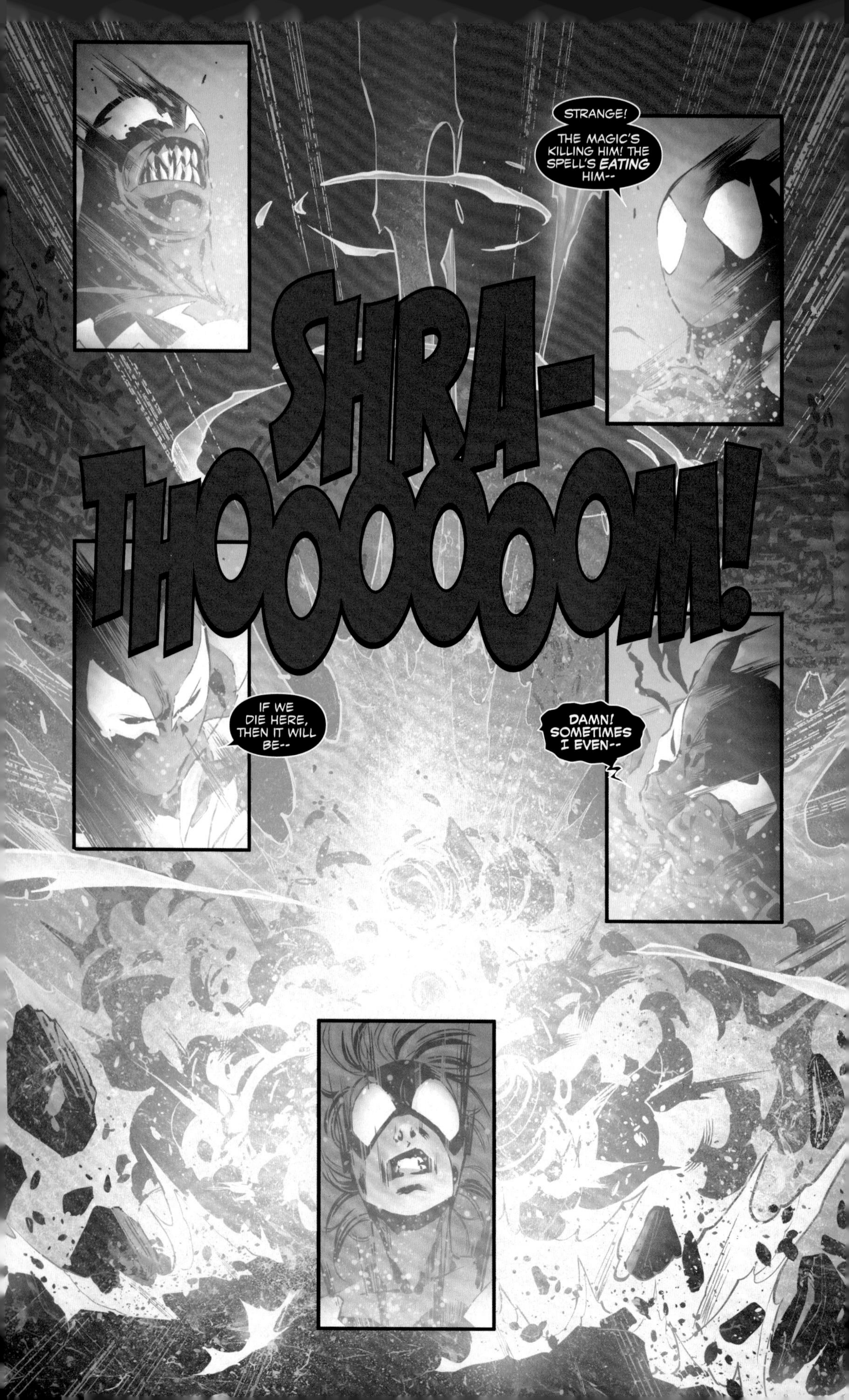
STRANGE!
THE MAGIC'S KILLING HIM! THE SPELL'S EATING HIM--
SHRA-THOOOOOOM!
IF WE DIE HERE, THEN IT WILL BE--
DAMN! SOMETIMES I EVEN--

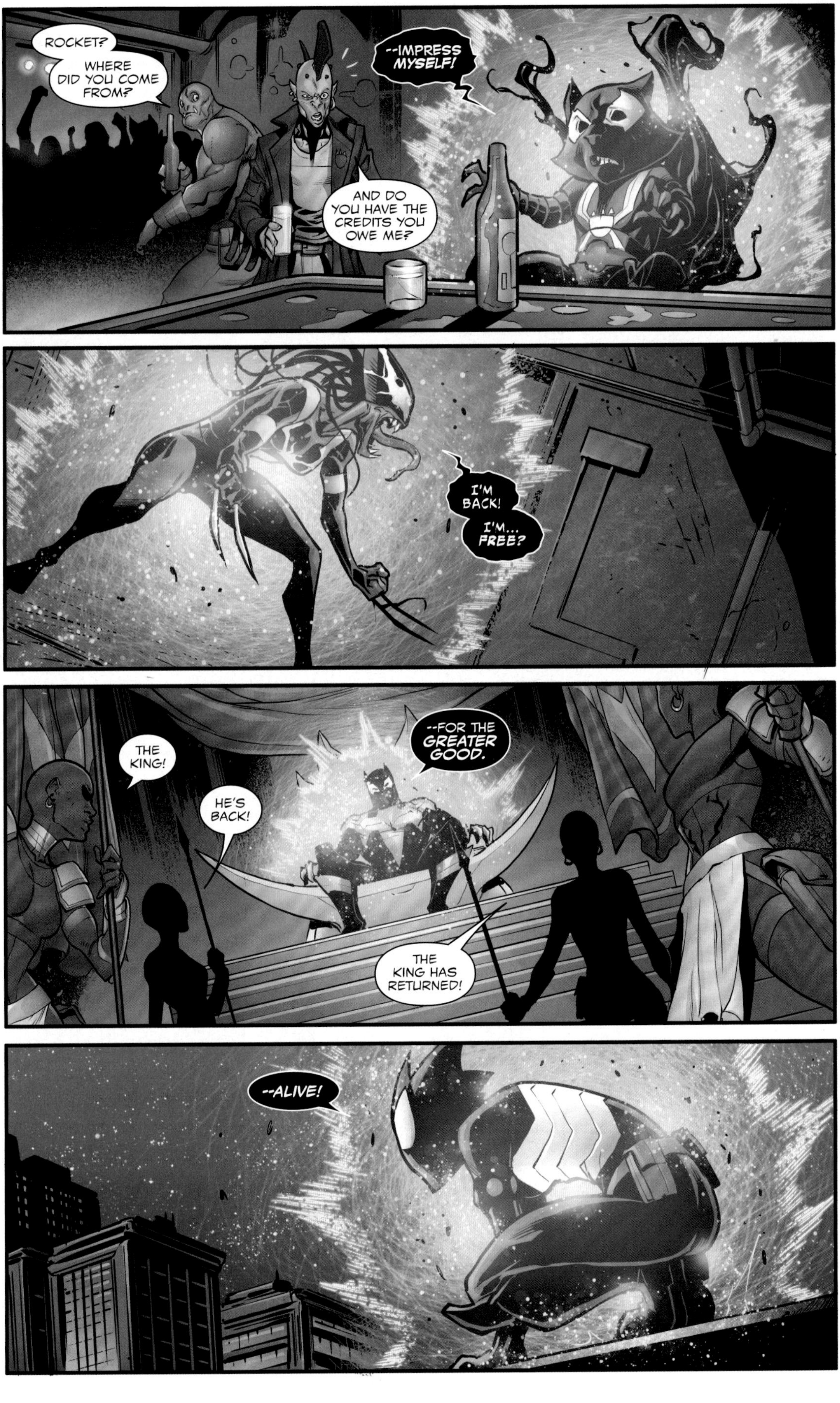
ROCKET? WHERE DID YOU COME FROM?
--IMPRESS MYSELF!
AND DO YOU HAVE THE CREDITS YOU OWE ME?
I'M BACK!
I'M... FREE?
THE KING!
HE'S BACK!
--FOR THE GREATER GOOD.
THE KING HAS RETURNED!
--ALIVE!

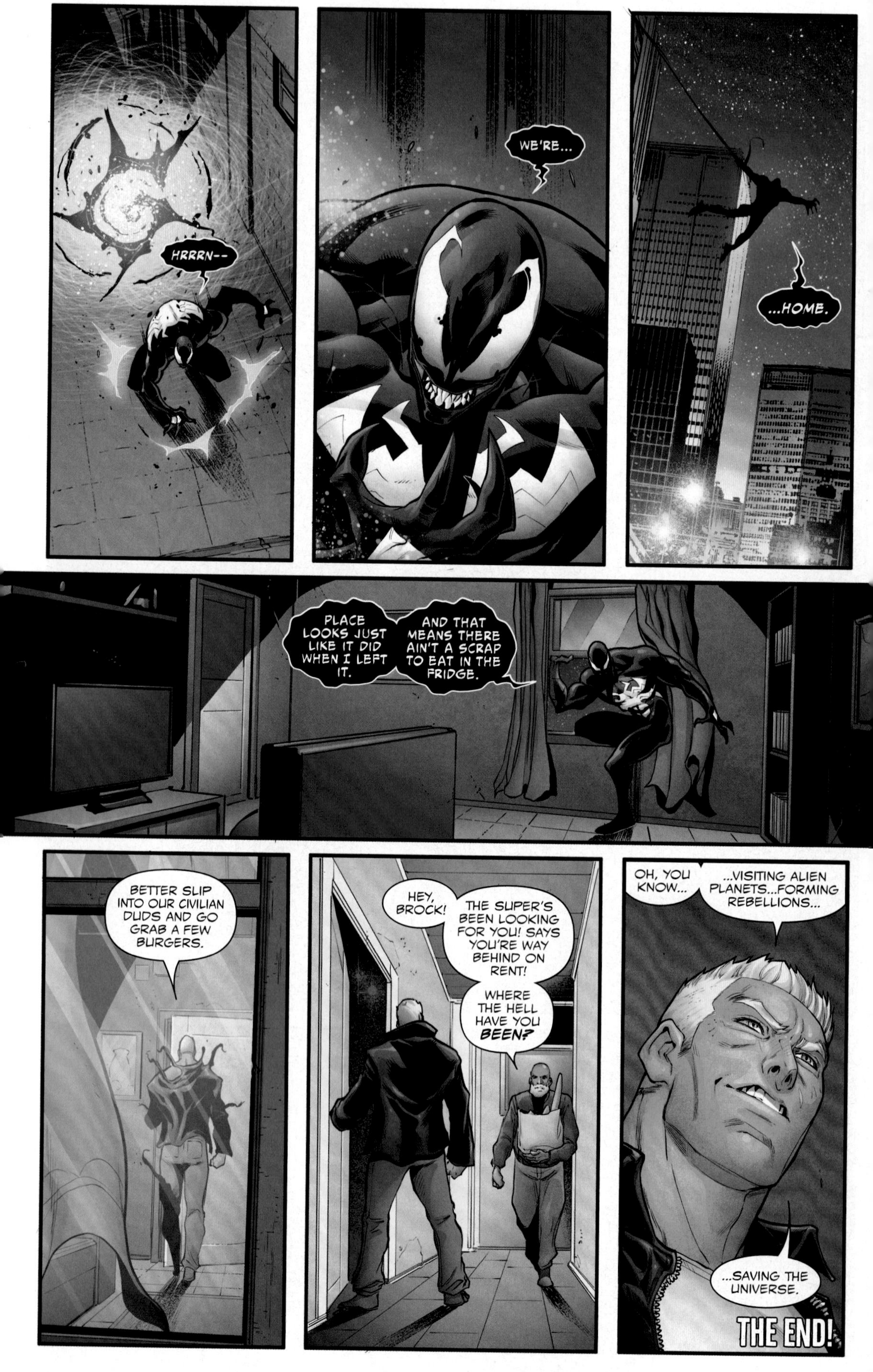
HRRRN--
WE'RE...
...HOME.
PLACE LOOKS JUST LIKE IT DID WHEN I LEFT IT.
AND THAT MEANS THERE AIN'T A SCRAP TO EAT IN THE FRIDGE.
BETTER SLIP INTO OUR CIVILIAN DUDS AND GO GRAB A FEW BURGERS.
HEY, BROCK!
THE SUPER'S BEEN LOOKING FOR YOU! SAYS YOU'RE WAY BEHIND ON RENT!
WHERE THE HELL HAVE YOU BEEN?
OH, YOU KNOW...
...VISITING ALIEN PLANETS...FORMING REBELLIONS...
...SAVING THE UNIVERSE.
THE END!

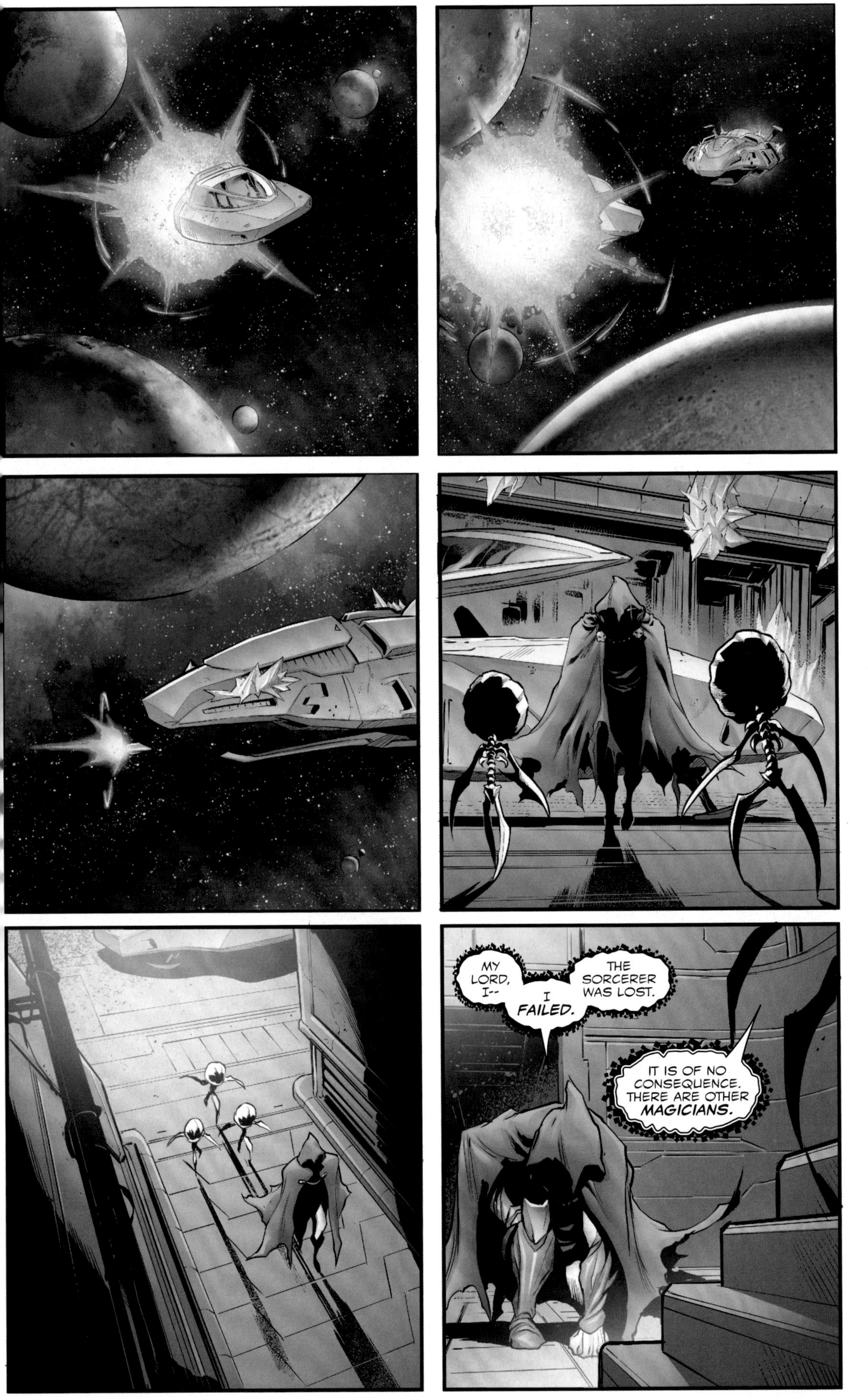
MY LORD, I--
I FAILED.
THE SORCERER WAS LOST.
IT IS OF NO CONSEQUENCE. THERE ARE OTHER MAGICIANS.

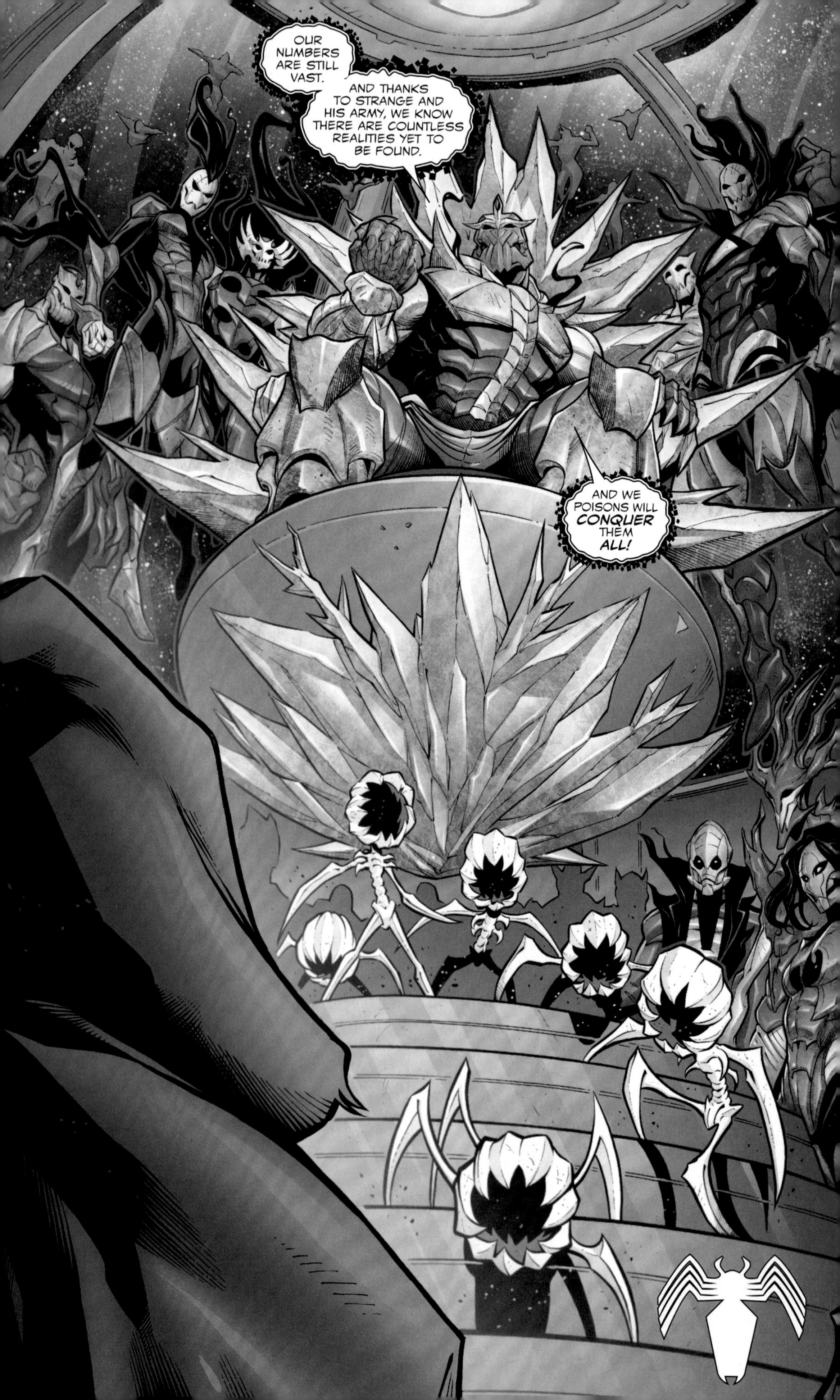
OUR NUMBERS ARE STILL VAST.
AND THANKS TO STRANGE AND HIS ARMY, WE KNOW THERE ARE COUNTLESS REALITIES YET TO BE FOUND.
AND WE POISONS WILL **CONQUER** THEM **ALL!**

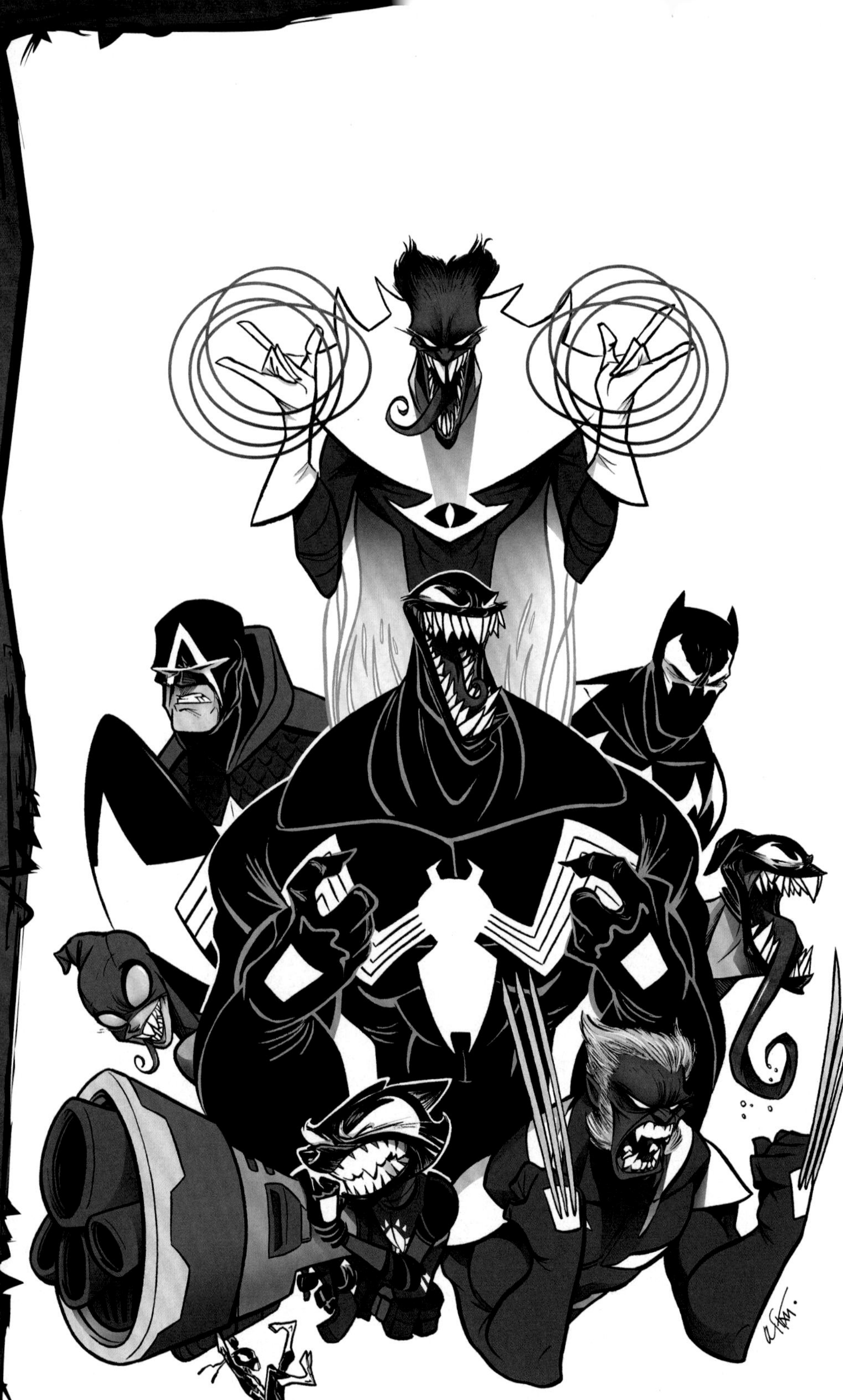

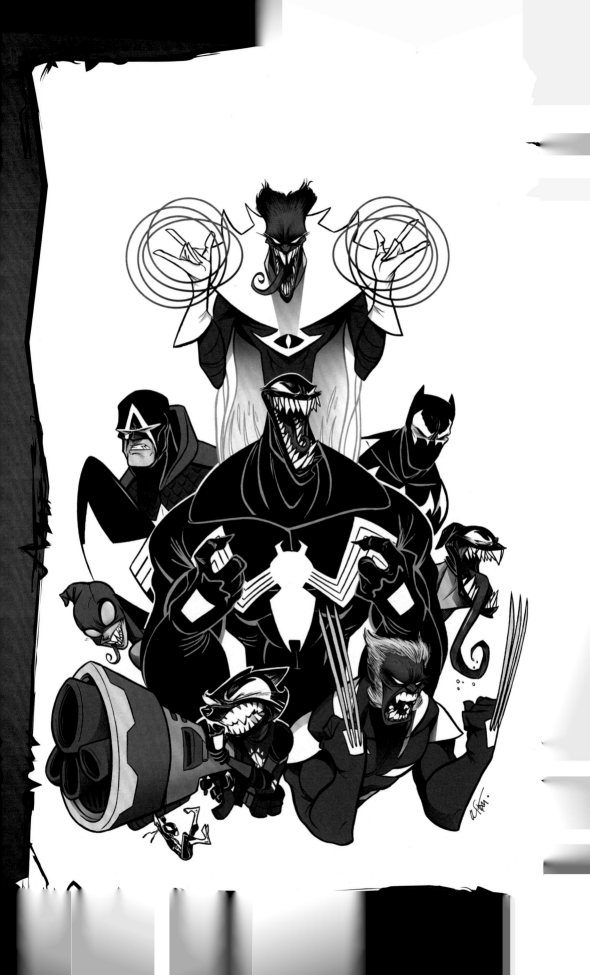

#1-5 CONNECTING VARIANTS BY **CLAYTON CRAIN**

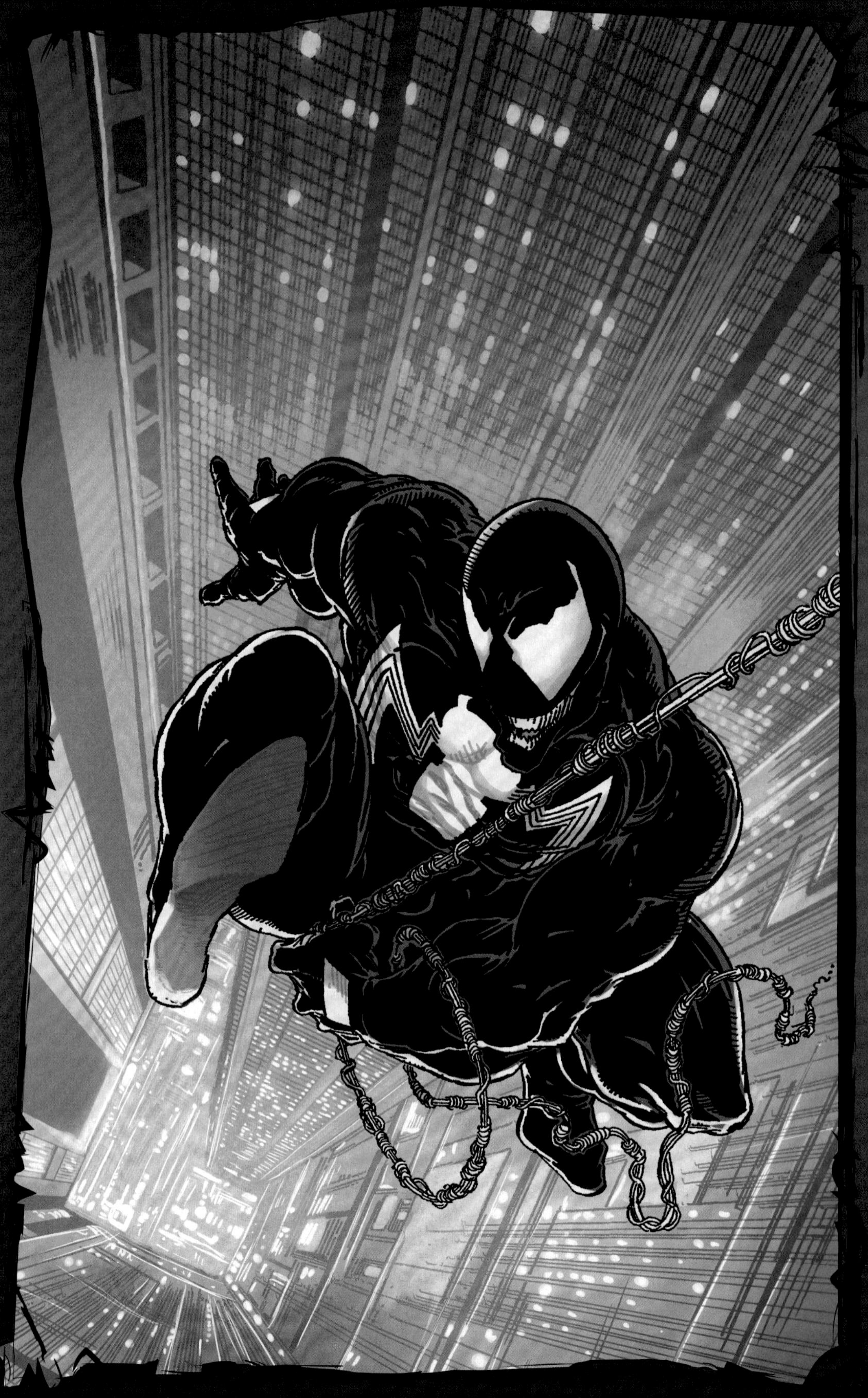

TODD McFARLANE & FRANK MARTIN WITH JOE FRONTIRRE

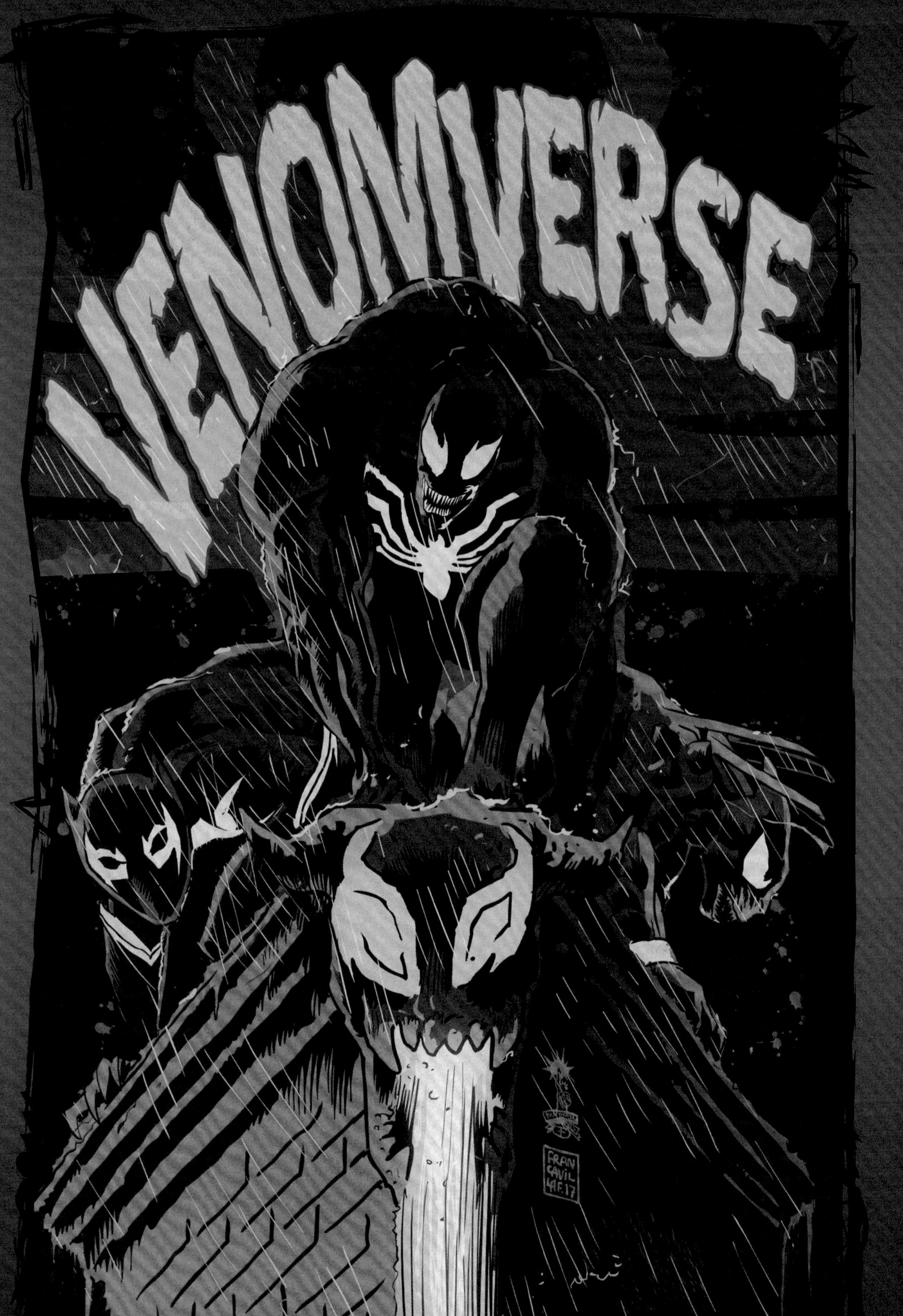
VENOMVERSE
FRAN
CAVIL
LA F.17

FRANCESCO FRANCAVILLA

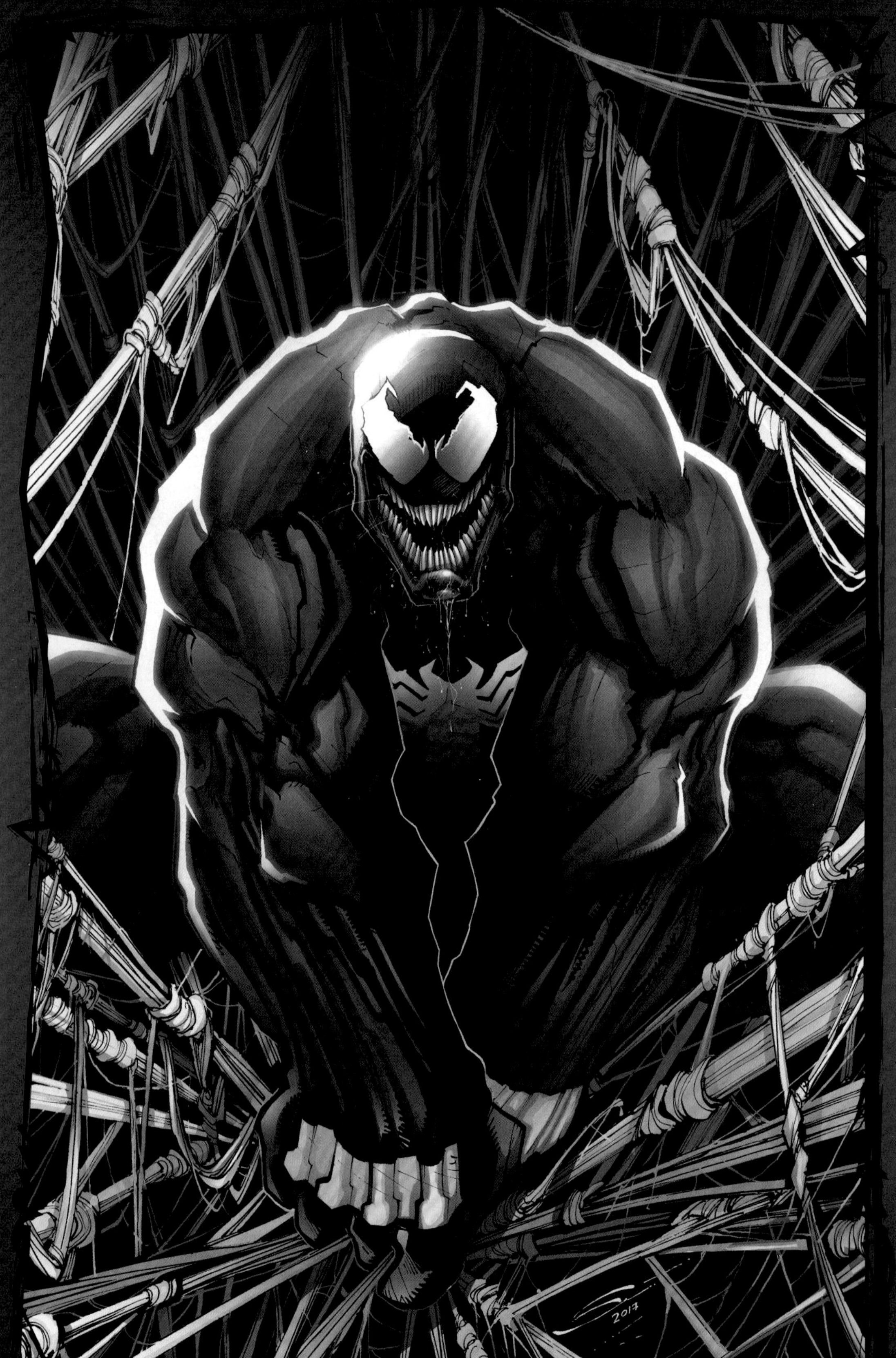

GERARDO SANDOVAL

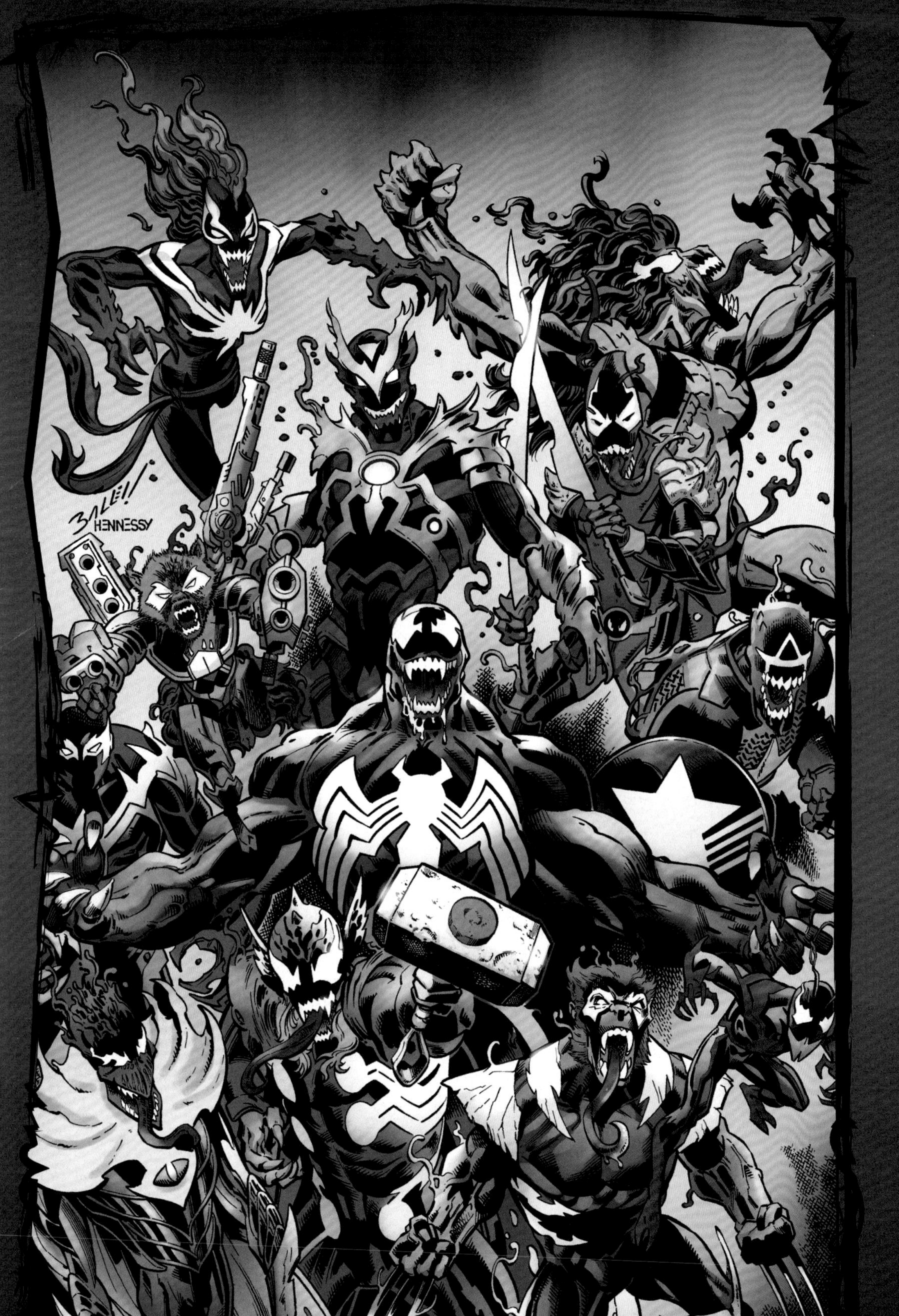
HENNESSY

MARK BAGLEY, ANDREW HENNESSY & JASON KEITH

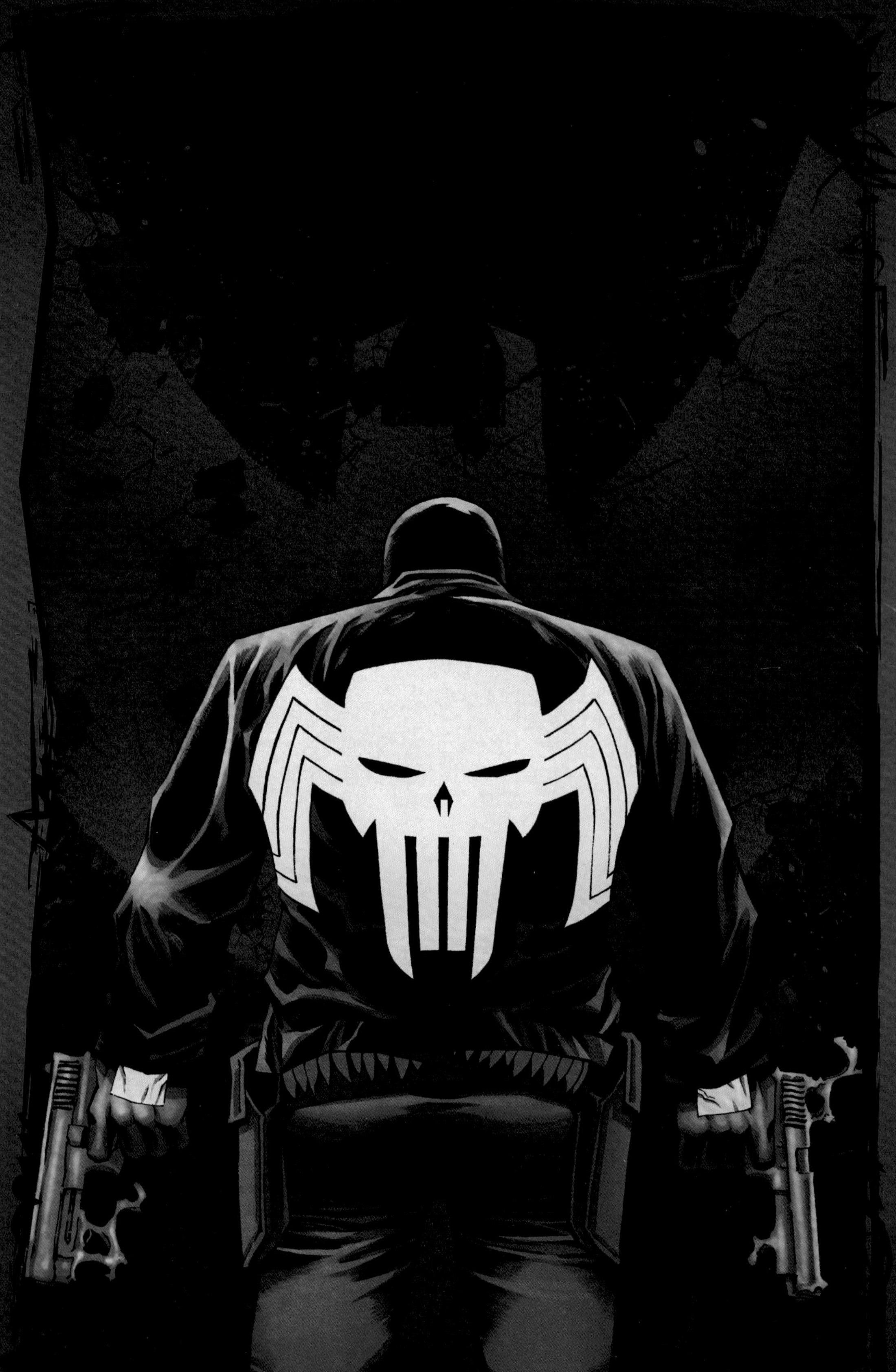

DECLAN SHALVEY & JORDIE BELLAIRE

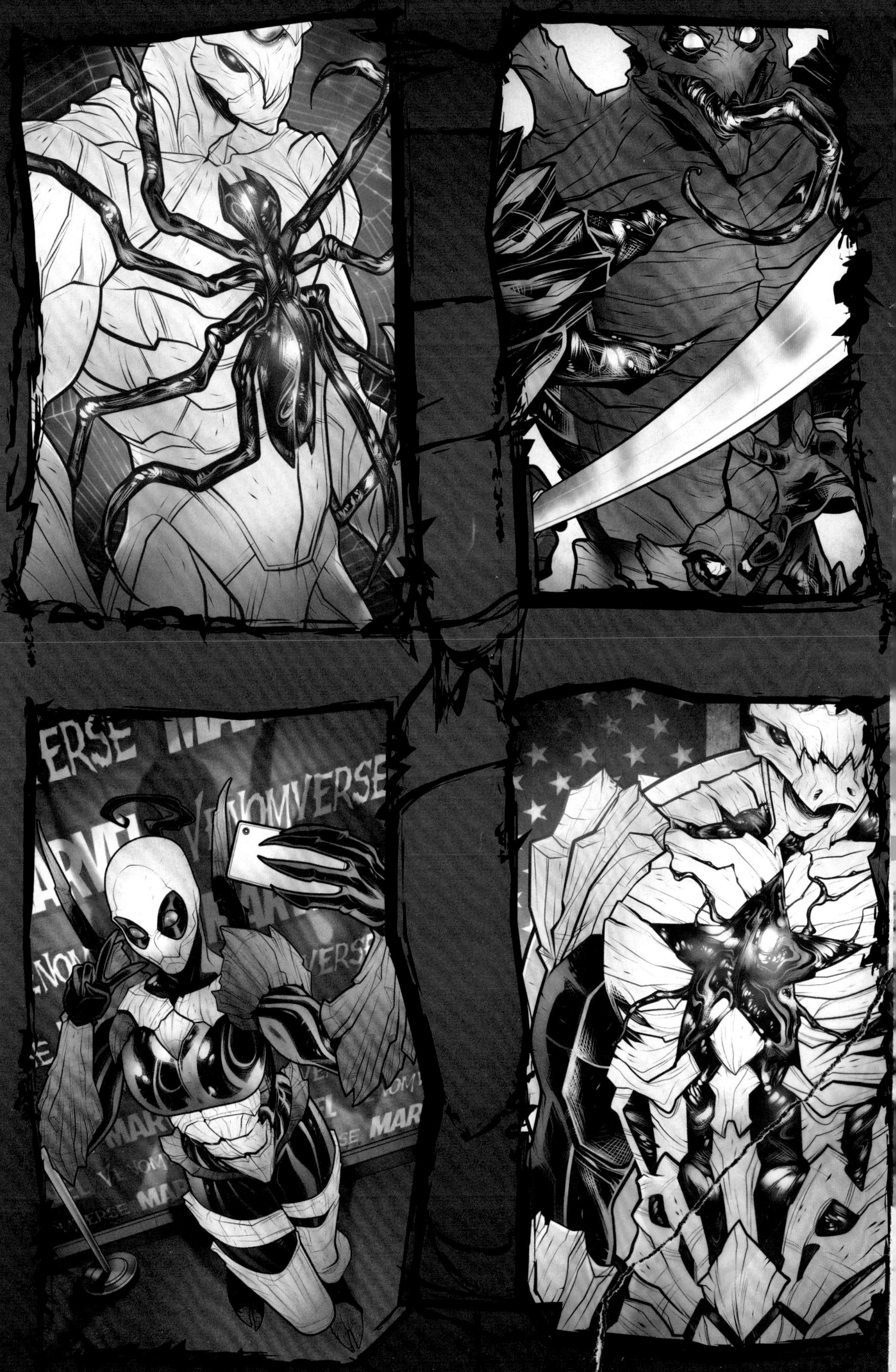
ERSE

ELIZABETH TORQUE

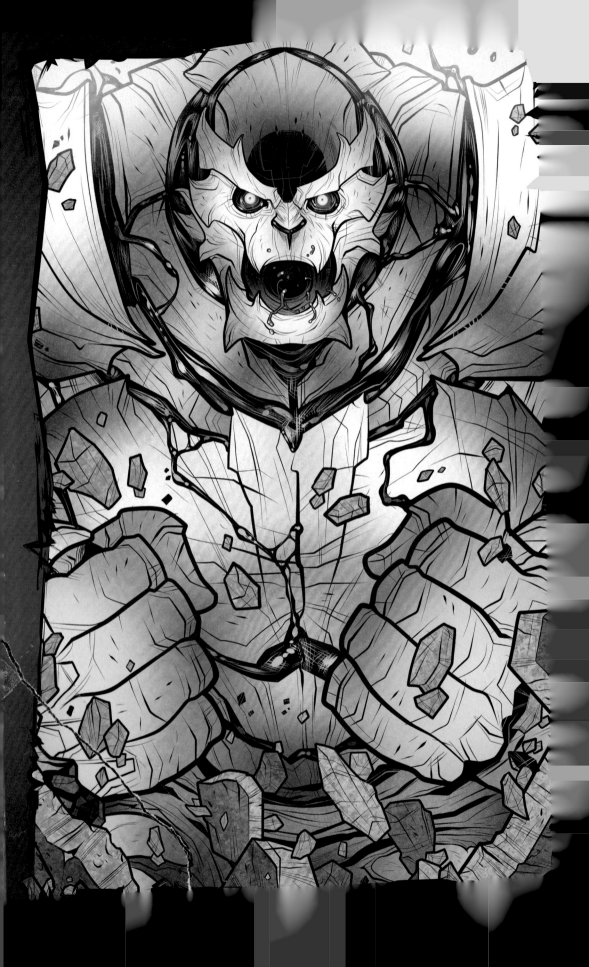